# Immaterial I

# Theory, Culture & Society

*Theory, Culture & Society* caters for the resurgence of interest in culture within contemporary social science and the humanities. Building on the heritage of classical social theory, the book series examines ways in which this tradition has been reshaped by a new generation of theorists. It also publishes theoretically informed analyses of everyday life, popular culture, and new intellectual movements.

EDITOR: Mike Featherstone, *Nottingham Trent University*

SERIES EDITORIAL BOARD
Roy Boyne, *University of Durham*
Nicholas Gane, *University of York*
Scott Lash, *Goldsmiths College, University of London*
Roland Robertson, *University of Aberdeen*
Couze Venn, *Nottingham Trent University*

THE TCS CENTRE
The *Theory, Culture & Society* book series, the journals *Theory, Culture & Society* and *Body & Society*, and related conference, seminar and postgraduate programmes operate from the TCS Centre at Nottingham Trent University. For further details of the TCS Centre's activities please contact:

The TCS Centre
School of Arts and Humanities
Nottingham Trent University
Clifton Lane, Nottingham, NG11 8NS, UK
e-mail: tcs@ntu.ac.uk
web: http://sagepub.net/tcs/

*Recent volumes include:*

**The Body and Social Theory 3e**
Chris Shilling

**French Post-War Social Theory**
Derek Robbins

**The Domestic Economy of The Soul**
John O'Neill

**Peer to Peer and The Music Industry**
Matthew David

# Immaterial Bodies

## Affect, Embodiment, Mediation

Lisa Blackman

Los Angeles | London | New Delhi
Singapore | Washington DC

Los Angeles | London | New Delhi
Singapore | Washington DC

SAGE Publications Ltd
1 Oliver's Yard
55 City Road
London EC1Y 1SP

SAGE Publications Inc.
2455 Teller Road
Thousand Oaks, California 91320

SAGE Publications India Pvt Ltd
B 1/I 1 Mohan Cooperative Industrial Area
Mathura Road
New Delhi 110 044

SAGE Publications Asia-Pacific Pte Ltd
3 Church Street
#10-04 Samsung Hub
Singapore 049483

Editor: Chris Rojek
Editorial assistant: Martine Jonsrud
Production editor: Katherine Haw
Copyeditor: Richard Leigh
Proofreader: Derek Markham
Marketing manager: Michael Ainsley
Cover design: Wendy Scott
Typeset by: C&M Digitals (P) Ltd
Printed in India at Replika Press Pvt Ltd

**Library of Congress Control Number: 2012931143**

**British Library Cataloguing in Publication data**

A catalogue record for this book is available from
the British Library

ISBN 978-1-84920-472-9
ISBN 978-1-4462-6685-4

# Contents

# About the Author

Lisa Blackman is a Reader in the Department of Media and Communications at Goldsmiths, University of London. She works at the intersection of body studies and media and cultural studies. She is the editor of the journal *Body & Society* and a co-editor of *Subjectivity*. Her previous books include: *Mass Hysteria: Critical Psychology and Media Studies* (Palgrave, 2001, with Valerie Walkerdine); *Hearing Voices: Embodiment and Experience* (Free Association Books, 2001); *The Body: The Key Concepts* (Berg, 2008). *Immaterial Bodies: Affect, Embodiment, Mediation* is her fourth book. She teaches courses which span critical media psychology, affect studies, embodiment and body studies, and experimentation in the context of art/science. She is particularly interested in phenomena which have puzzled scientists, artists, literary writers and the popular imagination for centuries, including automatic writing, voice hearing, suggestion, telepathy and automatism.

# Acknowledgements

The idea for this book started to take form in 2005 when I began reading the work of two key sociological figures of the twentieth century, Edward Ross and William McDougall, both considered foundational to the shaping of the discipline of social psychology. What preoccupied them and was part of the discursive field which circulated across the fields of psychology, sociology, philosophy, law, economics and literature was a focus on hypnotic suggestion and the potentialities and corresponding fears that accompanied this. This starting point reflects the exchanges that have been central to this book and without which it would never have been conceived. The inter-disciplinarity that was characteristic of the late nineteenth and early twentieth centuries is one that I carry through today such that my own disciplinary location is far from settled. However, I have found an intellectual home at Goldsmiths, University of London in the Department of Media and Communications since 1994 and I thank all of my friends and colleagues at Goldsmiths for accepting my quirkiness and allowing me to pursue my interest in phenomena such as voice hearing, suggestion, affect, embodiment and subjectivity. I particularly want to thank Sara Ahmed, Sarah Kember, Joanna Zylinska and Julian Henriques for sharing ideas. To Julian I might add that you are a great support, have a remarkable generosity of spirit and are one of the very best interlocutors I could possibly ask for. I would like to thank all of my colleagues in the Department for making academic life more bearable especially Natalie Fenton, Angela McRobbie, Pasi Valiaho, Damian Owen-Board, Jacob Love and Rachel Moore. A big thanks to all those on the Q Corridor that were left behind when the Department relocated to NAB, including Gavin Butt, Nicole Wolf, Lyn Turner and Irit Roggof. I also want to thank Janet Harbord, a former Goldsmiths colleague for stimulating conversations in the early part of the book and friendship thereafter. My conversations and on-going collaborations with Couze Venn and Mike Featherstone have enriched my intellectual life. Thank you for inviting me into the fold and for trusting me with the editing of *Body & Society*. Thanks also to all those in the academy I have met and been extended by along the way, including Patricia Clough, Beverley Skeggs, Lynette Goddard, Anna Gibbs, Monica Greco, Vikki Bell, and all those feminist academics past and present who allow one to breathe a bit. Thanks to all my students who have allowed me to make my preoccupations relevant to their worlds and to Celia Jameson and Louise Chambers for camaraderie whilst teaching some of this material. A big thanks to Valerie Walkerdine for the conversations we had in Lanzarote one hot sunny August in 2006 where I started to first write two of the chapters of the book gazing out of an Artist's studio onto a view of an awe inspiring volcano. Sadly such scenes of wonder have not accompanied the writing of the latter chapters but since that time I have been lucky to meet the most wonderful partner, Isabel Waidner and it is to her that my biggest thanks go. She has been my best and most enthusiastic reader and the work and my whole being is all the better for it. This book is dedicated to her.

# Preface

## Body and Affect Studies

Speed, movement, mobility, immateriality, fluidity, multiplicity and flows are all concepts that are profoundly reorganizing how the ontology of both subjectivity and corporeality are examined, understood and analysed within contemporary cultural theory. The solidity of the subject has dissolved into a concern with those processes, practices, sensations and affects that move through bodies in ways that are difficult to see, understand and investigate. The emphasis on immateriality over ideological and discursive processes is a call by some for an emancipatory politics of change. For others, this call for a paradigm shift across the humanities is undermining the capacity for ideological critique important for challenging inequities and oppressions. Cultural theory seems caught at a crossroads that is mirrored by the demands of advanced capitalism for rational subjects who are not swayed by social influences, at the same time as a suggestive realm is mobilized, created and orchestrated.

This set of circumstances is profoundly different from the concerns which inaugurated the 'sociology of the body' which took form during the 1980s and 1990s. The sociology of the body was characterized by a call for bodily matters to take up a central place within sociological theorizing. Since this 'turn to corporeality', there have been many revisions across the humanities of what the important elements of this orientation might be; this includes the foregrounding of difference, discipline, performativity, embodiment, movement, desire, kinaesthesia, the senses, and, increasingly within contemporary formulations, the posthuman, process, multiplicity, enactment, affect, life and immateriality. The latter concepts have played an important part in radically refiguring the body such that the idea that the body can be considered singular, natural or even distinctly human has been questioned in different ways. As I have argued in previous work, bodies are seen to always extend and connect to other bodies, human and non-human, to practices, techniques, technologies and objects which produce different kinds of bodies and different ways, arguably, of enacting what it means to be human (see Blackman, 2008a).

The body is not therefore a 'thing' to retreat to, a material basis to explain how social processes take hold. The body has been extended to include *species bodies, psychic bodies, machinic bodies, vitalist bodies* and *other-worldly bodies*. These bodies do not conform to our expectations of clearly defined boundaries between the psychological, social, biological, ideological, economic, and technical, for example. If there is one guiding principle towards which work on the body and embodiment has moved, it is the assumption that what defines bodies is their capacity to affect and be affected. The focus upon the affective capacities of bodies, human and non-human, is extending the terrain of body studies in new and exciting directions. Although it is arguable whether such a focus will achieve the paradigm shift associated with the turn to discourse and the subsequent turn to the body within the humanities, some are proclaiming the 'turn to affect' as extending some of the trends that we find within body studies, directly and indirectly, in innovative ways (see Blackman, 2008a, for further discussion).

The field of body studies has proliferated since the 1980s and 1990s, now existing as a transdisciplinary locus of inquiry. Non-dichotomous concepts for theorizing the body and embodiment have become central to theories and practices of art, architecture, science and technology, performance, medicine and so forth. Work on the body and embodiment has been recognized as increasingly important for the study of areas and practices which now recognize that sense-making cannot be confined to meaning, cognition or signification. Screen studies is an area where the analysis of embodied perception and sense-making is seen to be crucial to understanding how films 'work' (see Stacey and Suchman, 2012). Increasingly within television studies, the body's potential for mediation is foregrounded as an important aspect of understanding televisual consumption. This can be situated alongside the importance of embodiment for understanding our relationship to architecture, technology, performance, art and dance. When we add to this the importance of understanding issues perhaps seen as being more closely connected to corporeality, including our experience of medical technologies and practices such as transplantation or cosmetic surgery, and issues such as obesity and eating disorders which disclose the mediated nature of processes such as eating, studies of the body and embodiment provide an important link and focus across art, cultural and science studies.

The 'turn to affect' has become a focus for these debates to take form, particularly as they intersect with the question of how to understand the role of the body and embodiment within processes of subjectification. One focus of these debates, as many scholars have argued, is the limits of reason and rationality in understanding how power and ideological processes work. The view for some that power works 'autonomically', bypassing reason and criticality and seizing the body at the level of neural circuits, the nervous system, the endocrine system or other systems assumed to work independently of cognition, is an assumption that is already subject to critique. As I write this preface the historian of science Ruth Leys (2011a) has written a cogent account of some of the problems within affect studies and particularly with the view that affect is non-intentional. Affect relates to all those processes that are separate from meaning, belief or cognition and that occur at the level of autonomic, pre-conscious bodily reactions, responses and resonances. This separation is one that she argues produces a 'materialist theory' of the body and emotions and ignores the crucial question of how to theorize the body and embodiment in ways that do not set up a 'false dichotomy between mind and matter' (p. 457). This question is of course not new. The intersections and productive tensions that affect introduces to body studies and that already existing theories of the body and embodiment introduce to affect studies is one key focus of this book and will be examined in Chapter 1.

Leys (2011a) argues that what is needed to avoid the materialism of much of contemporary affect theory is what she terms a genealogy of anti-intentionalism. As we will see in Chapter 1, scholars within affect studies often link the emergence of humanities scholars' interest in affect to the publication of Eve Kosofsky Sedgwick and Adam Frank's (1995) collection on the work of the American psychologist Silvan Tomkins. Tomkins was writing mainly in the 1960s, in the context of debates within psychology on the nature of emotions and whether emotions should be considered cognitive or primarily physiological in nature. Tomkins argued against cognitive appraisal theory, found in the work of the American psychologists Schacter and Singer for example, and argued that emotions were primarily inbuilt, hard-wired neurological responses that were separate and prior to cognition. Leys writes that the success of the anti-intentionalist paradigm within psychology at the time, represented by the work of Tomkins and later by the evolutionary psychologist, Paul Ekman, has become one of the accepted views of emotion that has become imported into affect studies. Leys (2011a) focuses particularly on the seminal work of Brian Massumi (2002a), and argues that Tomkins and Massumi share a commitment, implicitly or explicitly to what she terms the 'Basic Emotions paradigm' (p. 439). Leys laments the lack of attention paid by affect scholars to the conditions of possibility which led this paradigm to become authorized within psychology, and is one which she argues has been taken up within affect studies uncritically as a model for thinking affective processes. She argues that the importance of genealogy to understanding affect is important as the success of the anti-intentionalist paradigm is one that is both subject to critique and also has a relatively recent history, within and outside the psychological sciences.

### A Genealogy of Anti-Intentionalism

This book will intervene within these debates by taking seriously this genealogical call to respond to the supposed anti-intentionalism of affect. As Leys (2011a) argues, affect theorists have turned to the work of contemporary psychologists and neuroscientists to validate this view, as well as to a different archive of psychologists and philosophers writing at the turn of the last century, including William James, Henri Bergson and Gabriel Tarde, for example. The genealogy of anti-intentionalism that this book will write will be located within this archive, one that I primarily characterize as a 'subliminal archive'. It is shaped by a diverse set of scientific and literary preoccupations with invisible animating forces. From the writings of James, Bergson and Tarde, the experiments in divided attention which took place at James's psychological laboratory at Harvard between a psychologist and the avant-garde literary writer Gertrude Stein, through to an interest in a seminal book written by the subliminal psychologist Frederic Myers (1903), *Human Personality and Its Survival of Bodily Death*, there is a fascination with the concept of prosopopoeia; that is, how the inanimate can be animated, and how, rather than talk about singular entities, the human, for example, we might instead talk about aggregates of human and non-human actors and agencies.

The book will return to these nineteenth- and early twentieth-century debates which primarily concerned the nature of perception, selfhood and embodiment. These debates, which involved the emergent disciplines of psychology, sociology and physiology, as well as debates within the medical sciences and those made by lawyers and economists, often focused and centred upon experiences such as voice hearing, hypnotic suggestion, telepathy and related experiences. These phenomena were all seen to breach the boundaries between the self and other, inside and outside, material and immaterial, human and non-human, and even dead and alive. These phenomena in the present are often viewed as irrational perceptions, or, in the case of hypnotic suggestion, as evidence that the person has lost their will and succumbed to the will of another. What all these experiences were seen to share was an ontology where the borders and boundaries between bodies, human and non-human, were considered porous and permeable, although this belief was often overlaid by a set of cultural fears and fantasies about being governed and controlled by imperceptible forces and agencies, which distribute agency between the self and other in asymmetrical ways (see Andriopoulos, 2008, for a discussion of this in relation to hypnotic suggestion).

Another interesting factor of the debates was their transdisciplinarity, with concepts, ideas and exchanges circulating across art, literature, medicine and science. One example of such exchange is found in the writings of the American psychologist and pragmatist philosopher, William James. The brother of the novelist Henry James, and son of Henry James Senior, William James originally trained as a medical doctor, before developing his interests in philosophy whilst being employed as a psychologist at Harvard University. James's interest in the humanities and sciences was not unusual; indeed, as we will see throughout the book, most influential scholars of the nineteenth century wrote on a range of eclectic subjects.

To take two examples pertinent to the book, Gabriel Tarde (1902, 1962), the French sociologist/psychologist, and Gustave Le Bon, the French loyalist and crowd psychologist, both wrote about a diverse range of subjects. This included treatises on areas as diverse as 'tobacco, Arabian civilization, photography, socialism, education, and military psychology..., geography, archaeology, futurology and poetry' (see Apfelbaum and McGuires, 1986: 33). This was partly because disciplinary boundaries were still very much in their infancy, but also, as I will argue throughout the book, because medical scientists, philosophers, novelists, physiologists, economists, artists and so on were all united in their interest in matters spiritual, psychic and psychopathological. That is, their understandings of embodiment, corporeality, perception, sensation, criminal responsibility, and allopathic medicine, to name some of the interests, were developed through terms and concepts that connected up studies of hypnotic trance, psychotic delusions and hallucinations with studies of mediumship, telepathy and related psychic phenomena. One of the key paradoxes of these debates that William James focused his attention on was what he termed 'the problem of personality'. I will spend some time in the next section outlining this problem as it will form a central genealogical focus of *Immaterial Bodies*.

## The Problem of Personality

William James is probably better known to contemporary readers for his poetic descriptions of consciousness as being akin to a stream – a flow of ideas, images, sensations and affects which are characterized primarily by movement. Hence the metaphor of the stream captures the fluidity and permeability of consciousness, which ripples, flows and ebbs rather than being housed by a singular unified bounded subject. The topology of subjectivity that James presents is one which views the human subject as being akin to a channel or conductor of thought, open and permeable to the other, invoking a sense of a shared collective consciousness, rather than one closed and located within atomized subjects. The 'problem of personality' in the nineteenth century was articulated as a particular problem of suggestive or affective communication. Interests in affective or suggestive communication were framed through a concern with how ideas, affects, beliefs, traditions and emotion could spread throughout populations with a rapidity that seemed to defy the action of logic or rationality. Philosophers such as Henri Bergson, the sociologist Gabriel Tarde, and William James all attempted to provide answers to this problem by arguing in different ways that what defined human sociality and subjectivity was the capacity of 'ordinary suggestion'. The human subject was not self-contained, individualized, clearly bounded and separate from others, but rather the borders and boundaries between self and other were considered porous and permeable.

The invocation of a version of 'immateriality' to understand human subjectivity was primarily drawn from the aforementioned scholars' interest in matters spiritual, psychic and psychopathological. They were all members of the Institute for Psychical Research and framed their understandings through terms and concepts that connected up studies of hypnotic trance, psychotic delusions and hallucinations with studies of mediumship, telepathy and related psychic phenomena. This trinity of scholars have also been resurrected by many contemporary cultural theorists who have refigured bodies as processes, defined by their capacity to affect and be affected (Despret, Massumi, Latour). As we have seen, the 'turn to affect' has been framed as a response to the problems of cultural inscription and discourse determinism which have been argued to show up the limits of work on text, language and discourse across the humanities. Discursive approaches are seen to have sidelined the body, emotion, affect and sensation in understanding communication processes. However, one key argument of *Immaterial Bodies* is that the paradox of personality that James identified is not resolved simply by moving to affect, unless we also engage with the parameters of the debates which concerned nineteenth- and early twentieth-century scholars. James, like many of his contemporaries, was also influenced by debates concerning the nature of will – how one could theorize and understand agency and self-determinism in the context of permeability and porousness between self and other. This paradox, which was captured by James's 'problem of personality', was far from resolved and entered into his musings on the nature of various concepts, such as habit and personality, and is one that I will argue resurfaces in an unacknowledged way in contemporary debates on affect and embodiment.

One way in which this paradox returns is in the thorny question of how to theorize the nature of the subject, or the complex ontologies of subjectivity that are being suggested by the renewed engagement across the humanities and social and natural sciences with affect, the non-representational and the immaterial. All of these concepts have been offered as terms which refer to registers of experience which are primarily trans-subjective (that is, they are not contained by bounded singularly human subjects), which introduce the non-cognitive into our theorizing of perception, knowing and sense-making, and which demand collaborations across disciplinary boundaries in order to reinvent new ways of being human, and develop new concepts for exploring embodiment and experience. The concept of embodiment is one central to body studies which is, as we have seen, a transdisciplinary area of study which grew from the sociology of the body, and now involves work across a diverse range of arts, humanities and science-based disciplines (see Chapter 1).

### Art, Science and Humanities Research

The potential links and collaborations across cultural and science studies have of course not had an entirely amicable relationship. Once the subject of the infamous 'science wars' (Sokal and Bricmont, 1998), it is often forgotten that transdisciplinary collaborations are more common than such divisions might imagine or suggest. In a recent book written by the Australian psychologist Philip Bell (2010), which harks back to these wars, body studies and cultural studies become the subject of vehement attack. That a psychologist might be threatened by scholars from the humanities offering a revision of psychological concepts such as perception, habit and affect is perhaps understandable, given the investment by psychology in retaining a truth value for the theories it produces. However, what is more surprising is the lack of attention given to the histories of transdisciplinary engagement across the humanities and sciences, which have become part of psychology's forgotten history of emergence. Indeed, this attack on the humanities becomes even more insidious in the context of the UK coalition government's attacks on and devaluation of arts and humanities research as having little economic impact or value. Indeed, the decision to remove or reduce funding for arts, humanities and social science research and teaching within the university sector assumes that there have always been clear divisions between the humanities and sciences. That through an act of 'cleansing' one can remove humanities research, reduced at best to the 'social aspects' of science, technology and medicine, and retain a purified notion of science as one that does not need the arts and humanities for its own development, innovation, creativity and success.

As many have argued, this rigid demarcation and division is one ideologically driven by marketization and privatization and shows an ignorance of how science and humanities research are informed and influence each other. Innovation and creativity do not come from the demands of the market; rather histories of scientific progress and creativity come as much from 'paradigm shifts' identified by Thomas Kuhn in the 1960s as the impact of cultural beliefs, ideas and concepts on the framing of scientific concerns and experimentation. One example of this in the context of the exchange between the psychological sciences and media cultures has been identified by Anna McCarthy (2009) in her examination of the exchanges which took place between the famous American experimental social psychologist, Stanley Milgram, and Allen Funt, the creator and producer of *Candid Camera*, one of the first reality TV programmes in the 1970s. *Candid Camera* employed hidden cameras and used simulation and deception in the form of 'staged pranks' for comedic value. The deception enacted on the unwitting participant would be revealed at the end of the prank by the invitation to 'Smile, you're on *Candid Camera*'. McCarthy shows how Stanley Milgram turned to Funt's work as a model for his own forms of social psychological experimentation into the nature of conformity and obedience.

What is important to signal in this preface is that histories of exchange and collaboration are integral to scientific forms of experimentality, not simply an adjunct that can be removed and isolated without damaging the very innovation, creativity and critical thinking that enable scientific thinking to develop. The subject of transdisciplinary exchange is one that is at the heart of this book, and I hope will act as a cautionary reminder to those who might think and act otherwise. Indeed, as Michel Foucault cogently taught us, histories of progress are never simply histories of the unfolding of some purist notion of scientific truth. Histories of the present are histories of how what we might be tempted to isolate as the 'internal' and external' conditions which allow understanding to emerge can never be demarcated in this way. There is no 'internal' that can be isolated from the 'external' and in that respect the distribution and circulation of concepts, ideas, beliefs, understandings and forms of action within and across science, art and culture are integral to the emergence of knowledge practices such as science, medicine and those that might be more easily dismissed by some as of lesser value, namely culture and the arts. An understanding of past collaborations across such demarcations is crucial to understanding where and how we might invent new concepts for understanding who and what we are and, indeed, might be allowed to become.

One context of transdisciplinary engagement important for this book is one that coalesced around the 'problem of affective transfer' and the importance of spiritualist and psychic research for understanding problems common to emerging humanities-based and scientific disciplines during the late nineteenth to mid twentieth centuries. That is, from discussions of media technologies, such as early cinema, the radio and the printing press, through to discussions of crime, perception, hypnotic suggestion, psychopathology, instinct, habit, electricity, and communication systems such as the wireless and telegraphy, what was shared across knowledge practices, such as philosophy, science and medicine, was an understanding that sense-making, whether conducted by animals, spirits, machines or humans, occurred in registers which extended across time and space. This sense-making was considered difficult to see and articulate, and as thoroughly collapsing the boundaries between self and other, animate and inanimate, inside and outside, and human and non-human.

This observation is of course not new; many arguments have already been made regarding the importance of nineteenth-century spiritualist research for understandings of cinema as a hypnotic medium (Andriopoulos, 2008; Crary, 1990), or television as an 'occult domestic phenomenon' (Andriopoulos, 2005: 622; Sconce, 2000). Possibly less well known are the centrality of spiritualist arguments for understandings of habit, instinct and perception as they were shaped and formed as concepts during the emergence of the psychological sciences at the turn of the last century. Charles Bingham Newland, a biologist by training who exerted a profound influence on Edward McDougall, considered one of the founding figures of

American social psychology, published a book in 1916, *What is Instinct? Some Thoughts on Telepathy and Subconsciousness in Animals* (Bingham Newland, 1916). He used the analogy of the Marconi wireless system to understand the basis of instinctual behaviour amongst non-human species. The Marconi wireless system was 'a material apparatus tuned to transmit and receive the intangible through space' (p. 1).The focus on immaterial processes of communication, which he argued had been reduced to instinctual forces within physiology (located within different species nervous systems), obscured the way that the 'seen and unseen are closely connected' (p. 6).

The unseen or immaterial equated for Bingham Newland to an instinctive subconscious mind which was shared by a group and provided the conditions for the rapid, automatic, group behaviour which could be observed in nesting, migration, herding activity, stampedes, homing instincts, swarming and so forth. Thus, the kinds of foresight and sensing that might be found amongst insects, moths, flies, birds and fish (all the subject of Bingham Newland's book) were all evidence of the basis of instinctual behaviour within telepathic processes such as teleaesthesia. Teleaesthesia was defined as 'perception at a distance or power of vision transcending time and space' (Bingham Newland, 1916: 189). In other words, instincts were not simply hard-wired biological drives, to be understood by physiology, but represented complex systems of communication or affective transfer, which were shared, transmitted and co-constituted between members of species. Thus, the idea of telepathic rapport, or action at a distance, was a common way to understand communication processes, whether the discussion was focused on machines, animals, insects, humans or technologies. The idea of telepathic transfer largely became discredited, overtaken by an increasing focus on what were billed as more rational communication processes. These were represented in the psychological sciences by concepts such as the attitude (see Rose, 1985). However, arguably the cultural fantasies conveyed by telepathic transfer have refused to go away.

### Affect

Within the contemporary context of cultural theory, the 'turn to affect' is one arena within which such fantasies have arguably resurfaced. The primacy of affect as an important yet under-researched process and mechanism of subject formation is one that has provided the kind of common ontology linking the human with the natural sciences, that links affect back to both spiritualist research in the nineteenth to mid-twentieth centuries, and to cybernetics research from the 1940s through to the 1970s (see Blackman, 2010a). Both spiritualist research and cybernetics provided occasions for the kind of interdisciplinarity that is forming around the subject of affect within the present. The Macy conferences held between 1946 and 1953 brought together physicists, mathematicians, electrical engineers, physiologists, neurologists, experimental psychologists, psychiatrists, sociologists and anthropologists to discuss a range of topics which were made intelligible through the development of the concept of information enshrined within information theory (Weiner, 1989).

Some hundred years previously, the subject of spiritualist research had also provided opportunities for cross-pollination and transdisciplinary collaboration in relation to the 'problem of communication'. This context brought together scientists, engineers, anthropologists, sociologists, psychologists, medical doctors, physicists, spiritualists and psychiatrists to discuss telepathy and its relevance for understanding communication processes. The problem of communication as it was presented by studies of telepathy was articulated through a concern with forms of communication that crossed borders and boundaries between the human and the non-human, the material and the ephemeral, the self and the not-self, and the living and the dead. The concept of telepathic rapport travelled across emergent disciplines, and also appeared within medical, legal and literary contexts which invoked communication as a largely intangible, immaterial process. These three contexts (spiritualism, cybernetics and contemporary media cultures) all provide important surfaces of emergence for examining corporeality in the present. Attending to this will extend our understandings of the subject of affect and embodiment, common to both contemporary research in the neurosciences and the humanities. This must do justice to what Stefan Andriopoulos (2005: 637) has termed the 'half-hidden borrowings' from spiritualist and psychic research that have largely been forgotten.

### Haunting(s)

Avery Gordon (2008) has invoked the concept of haunting as of important methodological significance for sociological theorizing. In the foreword to Gordon's book, *Ghostly Matters: Haunting and the Sociological Imagination*, Janice Radway concurs with Gordon's calls for a renewed attention in humanities research to how certain things, entities, processes or ideas have become 'marginalised, excluded or repressed' (Gordon, 2008: 4). Gordon shifts the focus on the 'visible and the concrete' characteristic of empiricist methodologies to those aspects of our 'complex personhood' (p. viii) that have been lost. In a reconfiguration of genealogical research shared by other feminist sociologists such as Vikki Bell (2007), Gordon makes an argument that disrupts the usual focus in Foucauldian genealogical study on historical discontinuities, arguing that what is missed in such methodological framings are those aspects of historical continuity that are passed and transmitted through silences, gaps, omissions, echoes and murmurs.

Vikki Bell uses the concept of lineage or intergenerationality to point towards what tends to be left out by genealogical analysis. She suggests that although we might uncover historical discontinuities between different epistemes, this approach wilfully denies, through its historical method, the way in which affects, trauma, forms of shame and so forth are communicated intergenerationally. Turning to critical race studies and Gilroy's illuminating work on diaspora, she re-establishes the importance in this context of exploring how this background of felt dispositions is commemorated and routed (Gilroy, 1993). She describes these as 'those relations that are neither simply of identification nor of alterity, that is, those of genealogical connection' (Bell, 2007: 33). This is about 'generational carnal connection' (Bell, 2007: 37), relationships and dispositions which are transmitted by mediums and practices other than the speaking subject: this might include film, television, photographs, fiction and less inscribed, more embodied practices of remembering (Connerton, 1989).

This focus on 'hauntings' and the concept of intergenerational transmission is important in two ways for this book. In a focus on the hauntings which pervade the shaping and emergence of the psychological sciences, I am interested in how specific concepts and phenomena such as habit, suggestion, voice hearing, instinct, will and affect became shaped and formed in specific ways. This shaping, as we will see throughout the book, took place in a context where spiritualist and psychic research was prominent, and although psychology was largely to reject such immaterial matters, it is haunted by the disavowals and refusals that have characterized its project. The genealogy at the heart of this book then shares with other genealogies of subjects that attempt to revise and offer what we might term a post-psychological reinvention of what psychology claims as its subject matter. This includes the important genealogical work of the Belgian anthropologist Vincianne Despret (2004a, 2004b) on affect and emotion, and of Ruth Leys (2000, 2007, 2010a, 2011a), the historian of science who has taken psychological matters such as trauma and, in a more contemporary context, affect and emotion as her focus.

This work is set alongside genealogical studies and cultural histories that take perception (Crary, 1990), will and inhibition (Smith, 1992), distraction (Swanson, 2007), autonomy (Rose, 1999), the double brain (Harrington, 1987), the bicameral mind (Jaynes, 1976; McGilchrist, 2009), habit (Camic, 1986), and suggestion (Chertok and Stengers, 1992; Orr, 2006) as their focus. This transdisciplinary work, coming from disciplines as diverse as art history, anthropology, sociology, the neurosciences, philosophy and cultural studies, has also offered human-ities scholars productive and inventive ways of theorizing and analysing embodiment. This work has contributed to an exchange and circulation of ideas that I hope my own work can extend, specifically in the con-text of contemporary debates in relation to affect and embodiment.

### Voices

In previous work, I undertook a genealogy of voice hearing (Blackman, 2001, 2007a), taking a phenomenon that has largely been specified, understood and acted upon within the psychological and psychiatric disciplines and approached largely as a sign of irra-tional perception. My own work in this area, in collaboration with the Hearing Voices Network, has helped problematize the view that voice hearing is merely a meaningless epiphenomenon of a disease process. The Hearing Voices Network, in conjunction with service users, professionals who are willing to listen, as well as scientists will-ing to concede that there is more to voice hearing than mapping the brain through imaging technologies and brain scans, have impacted upon the practice of psychiatry itself. It is now more common to find voice-hearing groups as part of outpatient psychiatric services, encouraging voice hearers to focus on their voices, listen to them and share them with other group members.

When I started my research on the phenomenon of voice hearing in the early 1990s in the UK, the view held by psychiatric profes-sionals, which seemed absolutely intractable at the time, was that voices were simply signs of disease and that if you talk to the voice hearer about their voices you will simply be reinforcing their dis-eased and troubled reality (see Blackman, 2001, 2007a). I am glad to say that this view is no longer the predominant view of many psy-chiatric professionals, some of whom, led by the pioneering work of the Dutch psychiatrists Marius Romme and Sandra Escher, are now more open to exploring voices as communications. This has been consolidated in a co-edited book, *Living with Voices: 50 Stories of Recovery* (Romme et al., 2009), which brings together the views and practice of Romme and Escher with the accounts of service users, including Jacqui Dillon (the current Chair of the Hearing Voices

Network), and other psychological practitioners willing to listen to voice hearers. The arguments made in the book will be the subject of Chapter 6 – set alongside contemporary neuropsychological work, and that coming from more marginal areas of the psychological sciences. These are areas which are all challenging some of the dominant paradigms of brain research, which still approach voice hearing as a brain deficit to be mapped by brain-imaging techniques and scans (see Chapter 7).

The work I will explore reconfigures voice hearing as a different way of knowing; a form of communication that perhaps connects the voice hearer to alterity. This presumption has been inspirational for projects such as Grace Cho's (2008) beautiful and aptly haunting account of her own experience of the intergenerational transmission of memory. This project was undertaken within the discipline of cultural studies, and is situated within contemporary debates on affect that are taking form across the neurosciences and humanities. Cho takes the concept of voice hearing as a modality of knowing that cannot be reduced to irrationality or disease. Rather, such a modality of communication, she suggests, discloses our fundamental connectedness to each other; to our pasts, and even to past histories that cannot be known. These might be histories that are never or barely articulated, but importantly are communicated, albeit non-representationally, through silence and secrecy.

Cho's study is a way of linking up what Davoine and Guadilliere (2004) term histories beyond trauma. That is, connecting up those histories that have never be told, authorized or documented within official histories, such as the forgotten Korean War, with micro-histories of trauma and shame. Davoine and Guadilliere are analysts who have worked for over three decades with psychosis. Many analysts are reluctant to work with hallucinatory phenomena, preferring instead to work within the confines of language and ideation. Davoine and Guadilliere have pioneered work within studies of the intergenerational transmission of trauma, particularly approaching psychosis as an attempt to bring into existence a social trauma that has been foreclosed. This is an attempt to explore precisely those carnal generational connections that exist genealogically but which cannot be articulated. For Davoine and Guadilliere the subject is always a subject of history, even though those histories may have been cut out of what they call 'the sanctioned social narrative' (p. xii).

Cho's study will also form one of the bases of Chapter 6, and is an example of the second way in which the concept of 'haunting' is integral to the approach developed within this book. Haunting is both a methodological and analytic tool, as evidenced in the preceding discussion, but also refers in this book more explicitly to the phenomena which will form the subject of the book: suggestion, voice hearing and telepathy, as well as other experiences, such as the bicameral mind (Jaynes, 1976) which suggest some kind of transport, under particular conditions, between the self and other, inside and outside, and material and immaterial. The self is literally haunted by another; indeed, if the phenomena I examine are examples of haunting, this may be the normative ontology of the subject. These phenomena and the scientific and humanities-based research I will examine suggest a very different paradigm for understanding some of the ontologies of subjectivity being introduced by affect studies; this might include Karan Barad's relational ontology and Patricia Clough's quantum ontology, for example.

### The Double

In the afterword to the relaunch special issue of the journal *Body & Society* on affect, Clough (2010a) says that relational ontologies are problematic, and argues instead that quantum ontologies are more useful for imagining affective processes. Quantum ontologies are seen to 'enact intra-actions that are not in the world, but are of the world' (Parisi, 2004). This statement by Parisi is intended to show the focus of quantum ontologies on novelty based on singular events that can never be repeated again. What we have here is a reification of movement as the defining feature of becoming, whereas relational ontologies are seen to be too fixated on individuation – on the one rather than the many. This is akin to William James's focus on consciousness as a stream; what Parisi terms the 'specious present' acknowledging James's work. However, as I have argued throughout this preface, this focus on one aspect of James's theorizing obscures his simultaneous focus on the 'problem of personality'; on how individuals live singularity in the face of multiplicity, or what I am also going to term, throughout the book, the problem of being 'one yet many' (see also Blackman, 2008b). This question has been framed in the present as the question of how we can be 'more than one and less than many', or how we can 'hang together' in light of the multiple possibilities of becoming that exist. The paradoxes and puzzles that this creates in offering a relational and processual account of corporeality and subjectivity are one of the focuses of this book.

This problem moves critique in a different direction to that which has perhaps become instantiated by Deleuzian perspectives – that is, particularly as they have been taken up by corporeal feminists such as Elizabeth Grosz and Rosi Braidotti in their calls for developing non-dualistic language and thought. The paradigm that will form the subject of this book is one that is very influenced by neuroscientific work on the double brain and bicameral mind. These are concepts linking work on the phenomena of suggestion, voice hearing and telepathy in the present (see Chapter 7). This work suggests that rather than reify either movement or individuation, we need to attend to that fact that we can be both one yet many, depending upon the different milieux that produce the possibility of experience. This more ecological approach to subjectivity recognizes the brain's capacity for both individuation and multiplicity, and is starting to challenge many of the assumptions that are entrenched across psychology, biology and the neurosciences. Work on the double brain has not been given much attention by humanities scholars, despite calls for more collaboration across the humanities and neurosciences.

This book will explore the importance of the paradigm of the double, rather than neuroscientific work on the double brain *per se*, for extending contemporary understandings of embodiment and affect. The paradigm of the double will take as its focus a number of key sites and surfaces of emergence for discussion. These are sites which are all marked by a transport or traffic between the self and other, material and immaterial, science and culture, and inside and outside. These sites include the crowd (Chapter 2), the séance and telepathy, particularly in the context of debates about emerging media technologies (Chapter 3), the clinical and therapeutic encounter (Chapters 4 and 5) and live performance and theatre (Chapter 5). What is important, the book will argue, is a re-engagement with what has been obscured, silenced and occluded in conceptions of immateriality that reduce the psychic to the body through understandings that privilege the brain or neurobiological body (see Cromby et al., 2011). This is a developing orthodoxy across cultural theory where the neurosciences and biological sciences have become authorized knowledge practices for validating the shift to affective bodies. The problems with this will be engaged through a genealogical analysis that will take this shift to affect as the subject of its inquiry (see Chapter 1).

There are many articles and a growing number of books engaging with this shift. These include a focus on the emancipatory potential and possible limits of affect, and calls for transdisciplinary work that creates a dialogue or conversation between the humanities and the sciences (particularly the life, neurological and psychological sciences).

This is the subject of *Immaterial Bodies* that it is hoped will offer a different way through these debates. I will ask what is being forgotten, silenced, erased and occluded in the contemporary turn to affect. It has become fairly commonplace for humanities scholars to draw on particular psychological concepts to theorize communication and cultural transmission, including perception, habit, memory, the senses and so forth. This book will explore what attending to experiences which always already open the subject to the other – suggestion, voice hearing and telepathy – might offer in the way of theorizing the thorny question of how we might understand the body's potential for mediation. This is set within the context of increasing evidence that suggests that bodies cannot be reduced to materiality and that the body's potential for psychic or psychological attunement – what I am terming 'immateriality' – is one that the turn to affect must adequately theorize.

# 1

## The Subject of Affect: Bodies, Process, Becoming

In a recent book bringing together work on affect across the humanities, affect is viewed as

> integral to a body's perceptual *becoming* (always becoming otherwise, however subtly, than what it already is), pulled beyond its seeming surface-boundedness by way of its relation to, indeed its composition through, the forces of encounter. With affect, a body is as much outside itself as in itself – webbed in its relations – until ultimately such firm distinctions cease to matter. (Seigworth and Gregg, 2010: 3)

This quote encapsulates one of the key problematics that will be the subject of this book and that characterizes the entry of affect into body studies as a distinctive and important area of concern and study. As the quote suggests, bodies are not considered stable things or entities, but rather are processes which extend into and are immersed in worlds. That is, rather than talk of bodies, we might instead talk of brain–body–world entanglements, and where, how and whether we should attempt to draw boundaries between the human and non-human, self and other, and material and immaterial. The quote suggests that bodies are open, defined perhaps by their capacities to affect and be affected, and that this register of bodily affectivity is that which introduces a vitality into bodily matters that demands attention and concern.

As this chapter will explore, the focus on affect also moves away from a distinctive focus on the human body to bodies as assemblages of human and non-human processes. The human body is potentially displaced, extending our concern with corporeality to species bodies, psychic bodies, machinic bodies and other-worldly bodies, for example. These bodies may not conform to our expectations of clearly defined boundaries between the psychological, social, biological, ideological, economic and technical, and may not even resemble the molar body in any shape or form.

This new trend of body theory, with its focus on affective energies and creative motion, characterizes bodies in two ways: by movement and process. Rather than considering bodies as closed physiological and biological systems, bodies are open, participating in the flow or passage of affect, characterized more by reciprocity and co-participation than boundary and constraint (Seigworth and Gregg, 2010). If talk of the natural body was displaced within the sociology of the body in the 1980s, then talk of the distinctly human, singular body is displaced within affect theory with its resounding focus on multiplicity and movement (see Manning, 2007, 2010). The problem that affect theory raises, and with which this book will engage, is how we live singularity in the face of multiplicity. The 'we' in the 'how we live' of course implicates a human subject, which at first glance flies in the face of the reconfiguration of the body as singular and distinctly human that affect theory challenges. However, without refusing this important shift I do want to suggest that our theorizations of affect require attending to the models of subjectivity that we implicitly and sometimes explicitly invoke in our reinventions of the human, the body, politics and life.

## The Sociology of the Body

The current conjuncture within which this book has been written is very different from the concerns which guided humanities scholars in the 1980s and which led to the delineation of a distinct subdiscipline of sociology known as the 'sociology of the body'. Since then the focus on the body and embodiment across the humanities has grown into a diverse transdisciplinary field of study. Body studies stretch from art to architecture, from biotechnology to medicine, from biomediation to health and illness, from science and technology studies to film, and from digital media to the neurosciences, to name just some of its travels. Studies of the body are no longer confined to the more social dimensions of what were taken to be a body's ongoing immersion in the world, characterized by all the areas within sociology which have shown the always already mediated nature of what we might take the natural or the biological to be. These areas include the sociology of health and illness and the sociology of medicine, which have contributed much to displacing the view that a body can be studied in isolation, abstracted from its very real conditions of existence and living. What was distinctive about this work was the focus on a 'human body', and introducing what were taken to be the dimensions of embodied experience neglected or obscured by biomedicine. This includes the review essay written by the sociologist Arthur Frank published in the journal

*Theory, Culture & Society* in 1990. This seminal essay developed his reflections upon his own experience of a heart attack and cancer diagnosis and the reconfigured sense of embodiment or 'morphological imagination' which followed this (see also Frank, 2010; Sobchack, 2010). These reflections were an important factor in the conditions which led to the inauguration of the journal *Body & Society* co-edited by Mike Featherstone and Bryan Turner in 1995. This was set up as a companion journal to *Theory, Culture & Society* and has published some of the leading work in this exciting and innovative field of study.

The sociology of the body, as it came to be known, was pioneered by a number of British sociologists who argued that understandings of and analysis of the body and embodiment should not be confined to what might be understood as the more obvious aspects of embodiment; such as research which took medicine or health and illness as its subject. Mike Featherstone (1990/2007) pioneered analysis and understandings of embodiment which linked work on consumer culture with attention to ageing, seeing the body as much more than surface and appearance. Bryan Turner (1996) painstakingly showed how some of the sociologists who have shaped the sociological imagination were making implicit assumptions about bodies in their analyses of how social processes worked and took hold. Characterizing sociology's engagement with the body and embodiment as an 'absent present', he showed how an explicit rendering of the implicit assumptions made about bodily matters within the discipline (within the work of Durkheim, for example), might be a crucial way forward in analyses of key sociological concepts, such as power, ideology, agency, technology and discourse (see Blackman, 2008a, for further development). Chris Shilling (2003) and Nick Crossley (2001) have both made an important contribution to the further seriousness given to bodily matters, moving discussions to the myriad processes, practices, techniques and habits through which bodies are enacted and brought into being as particular kinds of entity. The concept of body technique is an established method for analysing embodiment within this work, recasting the body as process rather than fixed entity, whilst retaining a focus on the more lived or phenomenal dimensions of experience.

The sociology of the body is now an established subdiscipline of sociology, recognized by international sociological regulatory bodies as an important part of the sociological enterprise. This important tradition has brought corporeality into debates about identity and culture, communication, power and regulation, subjectivity, technologies, performance, representation and discussions of race, class, ageing, disability, gender and sexuality. It connects with work in feminism, queer and post-colonial studies identifying normalization as being central to the body cultures which exist and circulate within neoliberal forms of governmentality. The body is now no longer peripheral to humanities study, and as we will see within contemporary work, further links and reconfigures how we might approach the human, life, technology and governance (see Blackman, 2008a, for an overview of the contemporary field of body studies).

Whilst this book departs from this tradition, it also builds upon the important work which has shaped this field of study. One of the distinctive shifts which characterizes contemporary body studies and which is reflected in the focus of this book is the subject of affect. Whether the focus on affect across the humanities becomes a shift or a turn remains to be seen, but it is clear that the intensification of work on affect across media and cultural studies, anthropology, sociology, science and technology studies, geography, philosophy, politics and related disciplines such as architecture, design and art is building at an exponential rate. This arguably discloses the humanities' contemporary 'absent present' – that is, a making explicit of those registers of experience that are at work in objects, artefacts and practices, for example, but which have been largely absent in theorizing. This is because, as many affect theorists have argued, for the last three decades the humanities have tended to privilege representation, discourse, signification and ideological processes as being the key to understanding subjectification.

Affect refers to those registers of experience which cannot be easily seen and which might variously be described as non-cognitive, trans-subjective, non-conscious, non-representational, incorporeal and immaterial (see Blackman and Venn, 2010). Seigworth and Gregg (2010: 9) extend this further where affect might figure across different perspectives as 'excess, as autonomous, as impersonal, as the ineffable, as the ongoingness of process, as pedagogico-aesthetic, as virtual, as shareable (mimetic), as sticky, as collective, as contingency, as threshold or conversion point, as immanence of potential (futurity), as the open'. Affect is not a thing but rather refers to processes of life and vitality which circulate and pass between bodies and which are difficult to capture or study in any conventional methodological sense. As Seigworth and Gregg (2010) show, although studies of affect have been marginal to humanities concerns, the reference to those dispositions, largely immaterial and incorporeal, which circulate and bind communities, can be found in the early work of Raymond Williams's (1977) and his reference to 'structures of feeling'. Affect is not a new process or phenomenon, but it is now taking form within the interstices of a number of disciplines and approaches which take the subject of affect as their concern.

## Body Studies and Affect Theory

Affect theory presents a number of challenges to body studies, whilst equally body studies present a number of challenges to theorizations of affect. Affect theory enacts and brings together a number of approaches to affect which differ in the place they accord the 'human' within their analyses. This differentiation is often made explicitly in relation to the kind of body or view of bodily matter presumed within different approaches to affect. I want to start by outlining in some detail a seminal approach to affect which has been brought into the humanities primarily by Patricia Clough (2007, 2008, 2010a), Erin Manning (2010), and Brian Massumi (2002a). This approach brings together the work of Deleuze and Guattari, Spinoza, Whitehead and Bergson and puts these thinkers into dialogue with work in the contemporary sciences, particularly computational science, quantum physics, cybernetics, evolutionary science and the neurosciences. This perspective refigures our conceptions of bodies, life, technology and the human in its argument that takes discussions of affect beyond the body-as-organism. The body-as-organism is a concept used to characterize distinctly human bodies (however technically mediated they might be seen to be), from those which introduce a 'post-biological threshold' into our theorizing. The 'post-biological threshold' refers to a view of bodily matter which displaces the distinction between the organic and inorganic, material and immaterial, and living and non-living where, rather than talk of bodies, we might talk of human/machine assemblages (Thacker, 2004, 2005, 2010).

Clough uses the concept of the biomediated body, in preference to the body-as-organism, in order to refer to the way affect participates at every level and scale of matter, from the subatomic to the cultural, such that matter itself is affective; what she terms the 'affectivity of matter' (2010a: 210). The concept of the biomediated body resonates with Spinoza's conception of an *individuum*, which 'is a composition of differential relations between bodies/things, and it can refer to human and non-human forms alike' (Williams, 2010: 249). The biomediated body is never distinctly human and thus affect is tied to non-intentional, pre-personal forces that reveal the 'imperceptible dynamism of matter' (Clough, 2010a). The distinction between the body-as-organism and the biomediated body is further distinguished according to the concept of *autopoiesis* and its limits. It is worth spending some time outlining this distinction as it is crucial to the approach to affect being developed within this challenging perspective.

## Autopoiesis

Autopoiesis is a term within cybernetics used to study thermal dynamics and the assumption that bodies strive to achieve equilibrium and homeostasis. The limits of autopoiesis revolve around the extent to which the body can be thought of as either a closed or open system. Clough draws from recent engagements by Deleuzian philosophers such as Ansell-Pearson (1999) with concepts of evolution, arguing that change and genetic diversity are difficult to comprehend within a model which is seen to emphasize continuity and stability over movement and transformation. Ansell-Pearson has turned to work within evolutionary science by Lynn Margulis and Dorian Sagan (1986) whose writings on 'machinic evolution' and endosymbiosis offer a crucial qualification on the limits of autopoiesis (see also Parisi, 2004). In short, bodies are not closed and might be thought of more as 'symbionts all the way down' (Hird, 2010: 37). Although Clough does not explicitly consider Hird's work, there are interesting parallels between Margulis and Sagan and her approach to co-evolution. That is, if we take what Hird terms micro-ontologies of the body, particularly bacteria, viruses, parasites and fungi, what we see are bodies understood more as communities than as individual closed entities (see also Cohen, 2009). Hird takes Donna Haraway's (2007) figuration of companion species and applies the concept of co-evolution and co-enactment to those relations that are less difficult to see. Where Haraway focuses on dog–human relations, Hird (2010) as well as Margulis and Sagan (1986) focus on 'not-species', such as bacteria, which reveal how bodies at a cellular level, in terms of both genetics and morphology, should be thought of in terms of intra-action (Barad, 2007), rather than in terms of interaction, which presumes the ideal maintenance of self–other boundaries and distinctions.

Ed Cohen (2009) also makes this point in his recent genealogy of the concept of immunity-as-defence. Immunity-as-defence relates to the assumption that self–other boundaries are enacted at an immunological level and that problems in cellular defence explain immunological disorders. However, auto-immune diseases and phenomena such as microchimerism (see Martin, 2010) remain inexplicable from this view of the immune system which is primarily seen to be involved in boundary-making and defence. The concept of the fortress defended self that is enacted through immunity-as-defence is a form of biopolitical individualization (Cohen, 2009). Cohen traces this concept back to the legal specification of personhood which became enacted within the Habeas Corpus Act of 1679. Within this Act the human organism was reconceived as a form of property imagining bodies as having distinct insides and outsides, for example. The work referred to so far, from immunology, molecular biology, quantum physics, mathematics, cybernetics and neuroscience, all either confounds this distinction or offers views of bodily matter which are primarily informational and which present bodily matter as inherently 'lively' (Clough, 2010a).

This reconfiguration of matter, including biological matter as *informational*, comes as much from molecular biology as it does from some of the new and novel technical framings of the body to be found across the sciences. Increasingly through the use of digital and 3D virtual technologies the human body is being reimaged within molecular biology, for example, as digital information. This often forms the basis of quite fantastical projects to image and imagine what bodies might become. This includes their enhancement, alteration and transformation at the molecular level (at the level of codes, enzyme activities, neurotransmitters and transport genes, for example). Nikolas Rose argues in his book, *The Politics of Life Itself: Biomedicine, Power and Subjectivity in the 21st Century* (2007), that increasingly within biomedicine itself, the singular, bounded, carbon-based body is being replaced by the proliferation and emergence of technologies and practices which enable the enhancement, alteration and even invention of new bodies. Even within medicine, the body-as-organism is itself being challenged by new medical technologies and imaging devices, which introduce movement into our conceptions of the body. These technologies enable the body to travel beyond the boundary of the skin recast as mobile information to be altered, engineered, and transformed within laboratory and computational settings. Rose calls this a delocalized and mobile conception of life that is not housed or contained by conceptions of the body as a closed, functional living system; the body-as-organism, for example.

Clough (2010a) uses the term 'post-biological' to describe the common ontologies which are linking some of the work that she discusses within the sciences with approaches to affect within the humanities.

This term is useful as it refigures biology as dynamic and open such that boundaries between the self and other, inside and outside, living and non-living, and material and immaterial are seen as porous and permeable; as commune rather than immune systems, for example (Cohen, 2009). One other important element to Clough's approach is that matter is always subject to a fundamental technicity. The focus on technology within Clough's approach to affect is one that is shared across studies of digital and new media (Hansen, 2006; Stiegler, 1998) where the body is seen to always already be subject to technological mediation. However, one of the key differences for both Massumi (2002a) and Clough (2010a) is in relation to the extent to which studies of technological mediation trouble or disrupt the body-as-organism. As I have already outlined, this is framed by Clough in relation to the concept of autopoiesis – that is, relationality (which we might find in the work of Haraway, for example), with its concept of intra-action, does not go far enough in displacing the human and the living in our understandings of affect. Clough (2010b) is explicit about the problems she suggests are inherent to relational ontologies in an afterword to the journal *Body & Society*'s special issue on affect (Blackman and Venn, 2010). This claim deserves some attention as it is an important differentiation and one that is crucial to understanding the view of bodily affectivity being proposed.

Clough explicitly relates the problems with relational ontologies to the concept of autopoiesis. She argues that work on relationality does not go far enough in displacing the human, because often the 'autopoietic organism-milieu' is presumed (2010b: 226). Although relational perspectives recognize that entities do not pre-exist their relating and that indeed relation is the generative principle of becoming, what are often also given attention within relational perspectives are the 'psychic dynamics of subjectivity and sociality' (Clough, 2010b: 226; see Walkerdine, 2010, for example). These psychic dynamics, for Clough, are often seen to revolve around the establishment of maintenance and boundary, and therefore are seen to reproduce stability and fixity. The focus on the maintenance of boundary is equated to the limits and problems with autopoiesis.

I will deal with this problematic in the book by shifting the discussion away from autopoiesis to what I am going to term, following the work of Anna Gibbs, the problem of mimetic communication (2010, 2008). Mimetic communication is equated in Gibbs's (2010: 186) formulation to 'corporeally based forms of imitation, both voluntary and involuntary'. The formulation that I am going to develop links mimetic communication to nineteenth-century conceptions of affective transfer, linked to telepathy, hypnotic suggestion and phenomena such as delusions and hallucinations, rather than to work in infant research and animal studies that primarily locates mimesis within the brain and nervous system (see Gibbs, 2010). Before I turn to this in more detail, I want to remain with debates about technicity and autopoiesis, which are central to differentiating some of the diverse approaches to affect that we find across the humanities.

## Bodies, Affect, Technicity

In this section I want to turn to the vexed question of technicity and how we can think of mediation in the context of bodily affectivity. As Clough has argued, mediation or the technical framing of bodily matters differs in the extent to which approaches are able or willing to conceive of the limits of the body-as-organism. Although approaches to affect are diverse and far from forming a coherent affect theory, one explanatory principle might be to differentiate according to the distinctions made between the biomediated body and the body-as-organism. Gregg and Seigworth's (2010) *Affect Theory Reader* provides a useful overview of some of the different traditions and orientations to affect that can be found across the humanities, and they draw on this distinction in their meta-commentary on the status and place of the human within theorizations of affect.

The first approach that they differentiate refers to a field central to body studies which is characterized by work on bodily integrity (see Blackman, 2010b). Body studies has a rich tradition of phenomenological and post-phenomenological work which explores the dynamic, kinaesthetic processes that enable bodies to respond to changes in both morphological structure and environment. Bodily integrity is the term coined by researchers interested in the incorporations and extensions that enable bodies to live and respond to changing conditions and that challenge any notion of bodies as being fixed or stable, for example. The term 'body' is usually replaced by the concept of body-subject within these traditions, which displaces a mind–body dualism but does not reduce bodies to material (physiological, neurological, biological) processes. The incorporations enacted by a body-subject include technical, material extensions which articulate the body in new ways (a prosthetic limb, for example), but do not occlude the complex psychic incorporations that enable new bodily configurations to be brought into being.

Vivian Sobchack (2010) uses the term 'morphological imagination' to refer to the more *affective* dimensions which characterize these incorporations. Within these perspectives bodies are considered psychically or psychologically attuned, where the potential for psychological action is distributed throughout bodies – to nerves, senses, the gastric and perceptual systems, for example (see also Wilson, 2006). In other words, the concept of body-image, with its ocularcentrism and inherent cognitivism, is replaced with a more kinaesthetic, non-visual sense of incorporation which is derived from work in psychoanalysis and phenomenology. I will spend some time later in the chapter qualifying how I am going to use the terms 'psychic' and 'psychological', but my argument from the outset is that these terms are still important as they identify something about the status of the human (however contingent and historical the human is taken to be) that is crucial to understanding affective processes. In discussions of bodily integrity psychic incorporations are not simply reduced to autopoiesis, nor to a pre-existent perceiving subject experiencing the world through consciousness.

As we will see in Chapter 7, the very concept of consciousness, aligned to a perceiving subject, is one that is challenged by work on bicameral consciousness and the double brain. In Chapter 7 we will turn to work on the double brain within neuroscience which, when read alongside work on bicameral consciousness (Jaynes, 1976; McGilchrist, 2009), points towards a more distributed embodiment than that which attempts to house the brain and consciousness within a bounded, unified individual. This work suggests that 'consciousness' and brain function might be said in some cases to be shared, or at least to point towards the fundamental connectedness of the self to the other – human and non-human. Post-phenomenological work on bodily integrity also challenges the idea that incorporations are about re-establishing fixed, stable bodily schemas or morphological imaginations, which are tied to a perceiving subject experiencing the world through consciousness. Some examples taken from a special issue of *Body & Society* might be instructive in this respect as they draw out some of the challenges for thinking about bodies, technicity and affectivity that this work introduces.

## Bodily Integrity

Within work on bodily integrity the capacity for psychological action does not remain with a singular human subject. This is not a closed psychological subject, but includes a more trans-subjective sense of the psychic or psychological as a shared, collective encounter or event. Slatman and Widdershoven (2010) discuss the case of Clint Hallam, who was one of the first recipients of a hand transplant in 1998. Although functionally the hand enabled Hallam to perform everyday actions, such as brushing his teeth, some three years later he asked for the hand to be removed. The medical decision to remove the hand was forced by Hallam who stopped taking the immuno-suppressant drugs that prevented his immune system from rejecting the donor body-part. Bodily integrity is an issue for bioethics, as the extent to which a donated organ or body-part can be successfully incorporated is not just a cellular or immunological matter.

Organ donation has become an accepted practice, made possible by the cocktails of drugs that enable donor organ and host to acceptably co-exist. However, transplant of a visible body-part, such as a hand or even face, makes the issue of co-existence much more an intersubjective and intercorporeal event. Although many accounts of kidney, heart and liver transplantation draw attention to the reconfiguration of bodily integrity as being about twoness, being able to accept a donor organ which is often experienced as foreign, and in some cases reconfiguring one's morphological imagination as being singular-plural (Nancy, 2000), a visible body-part locates this process of incorporation much more in relation to the other. Hallam's rejection of his transplanted hand was about its *feel*, and how it literally did not feel right despite its functional performance in relation to particular acts and practices. Hallam literally experienced his hand as monstrous and this monstrosity was also felt by his intimate others. The touch of Hallam's donated hand always incorporated the touch of the host, a malign presence that could not be eradicated from the exchange.

Slatman and Widdershoven (2010) draw attention to the euphemisms surrounding this case and a medical team who were very aware of the possibility for what they termed the 'Frankenstein syndrome' (p. 73). As they argue, as 'a transplantation patient, you have to live with the thought that a piece of a dead person's matter is now part of you – and imagine that this strange part may take over control' (p. 73). The idea of the double and possession was popularized by cinema, literature and science in the late nineteenth and early twentieth centuries in relation to hypnotic crime and the dangers of hypnotic trance and suggestion (Andriopoulos, 2008). These cultural fantasies were about an 'imperceptible being with a will and agency of its own' (Andriopoulos, 2008: 3) and a set of fears and anxieties generated about being governed by 'foreign powers' (see also Hustvedt, 2010). Andriopoulos (2008) argues that these cultural fantasies have not gone away and, in a fascinating analysis of law, science and art in the late nineteenth and early twentieth centuries, cogently shows how the theme of possession is central to the cultural history of modernity. We might therefore not be surprised by the inability of Hallam and his intimate others to incorporate the transplanted donor body-part, where, as we will see throughout the book, the fear and dangers of possession exist in close proximity to arguments which suggest that bodily integrity can never be grafted onto the singular, atomized individual.

As Andriopoulos cogently argues, the history of possession as an integral part of cultural histories of modernity opens up certain paradoxes in our understandings of the body. Possession discloses the porous and permeable nature of embodiment and the coupling of the human with the non-human, including machinic, species and other-worldly entanglements such that distinctions between the natural and unnatural are destabilized. However, these couplings are also fraught with anxieties and cultural fears and fantasies which perhaps introduce caution into our considerations of how we live singularity in the face of multiplicity.

Slatman and Widdershoven (2010) use the case of hand transplantation and particularly the success of Hallam's graft at a cellular and immunological level, in contrast to its failure at an intersubjective and intercorporeal level, to comment on our understandings of bodily integrity. Although the limits of body-image as a concept for understanding bodily integrity have a long history within phenomenological and post-phenomenological work (see Ferguson, 1997), Slatman and Widdershoven are keen to retain the importance of the visual and appearance for understanding the strangeness of Hallam's grafted hand. However, they also recognize that images, in this case the image of a foreign hand grafted to one's body, also work *affectively*. Slatman and Widdershoven emphasize the affective, haptic dimension of the visual in their engagement with the concept of body-schema (Gallagher, 2005).

Haptic, or affective, communication draws attention to what passes between bodies, which can be felt but perhaps not easily articulated. The more non-visual, haptic dimensions of the lived body distribute the idea of the lived body beyond the singular psychological subject to a more intersubjective and intercorporeal sense of embodiment (see also Csordas, 2008). This is embodiment as intercorporeality (see also Weiss, 1999). As Weiss (1999: 5) argues, to describe embodiment as intercorporeal 'is to emphasise that the experience of being embodied is never a private affair, but is always already mediated by our continual interactions with other human and non-human bodies'. The concept of body-schema, which is central to Weiss's engagement and reconfiguration of practices such as anorexia, is one that draws attention to the limits of the concept of body-image for analysing the lived body.

## From Body-Image to Body-without-an-Image

As many people have argued, we do not live our bodies photographically (see Coleman, 2008). That is, that although the mirror and the visual are emphasized, particularly within makeover and consumer culture, based perhaps on popular physiognomic assumptions (Wegenstein and Ruck, 2011), this closes down our understanding of bodies to static, two-dimensional things or entities. Massumi (2002a) terms this 'mirror vision', where, as the term suggests, what is emphasized is the look or appearance of the body, where bodies might be looked at as if they are static images. The concept of body-schema introduces a non-visual or non-representational sense of the body, what is often referred to as haptic communication. This is not just about how a body looks either to oneself or others, but rather about how a body *feels*, where that feeling does not simply emanate from within (in relation to a psychological measure such as self-esteem, for example), but is rather an intensity generated between bodies. Massumi (2002a) uses the concept of movement vision to capture the energies, sensations, forces and intensities which are always in movement between bodies, such that bodies are always in transport. Indeed, Maxine Sheets-Johnstone (2009, 2011) argues that movement, or what she terms 'animation', is the foundation of living or life (see also Manning, 2007, 2010; Stacey and Suchman, 2012).

The areas of body-image and bodily integrity are interesting for affect studies as they offer a convergence between phenomenological and post-phenomenological work, based on the lived (human) body, with theorizations of affect, which as we have seen in the work of Massumi (2002a) and Clough (2007, 2008, 2010a) emphasize the workings of affect within conceptions of the body which are never distinctly human or singular. So although Massumi's concept of movement vision draws attention to the registers of affect, feeling and intensity and their fundamental trans-subjective and intercorporeal nature (the more affective, haptic dimensions of images, for example), the biomediated body is both organic and inorganic, living and non-living, material and immaterial. It is not just that the human body is technologically mediated but that affect does not require a distinctly human body in order to pass and register.

Mike Featherstone (2010) has developed aspects of this work to understand the relationship between body, image and affect, particularly within consumer culture. It is worth spending some time with his argument as it gives us another opportunity to consider the complexities of the relationship between bodies, affect and technicity. He argues that 'the relationship between body image and self-image may not work in such a simple way as the visual rationality of mirror-vision implies' (p. 196). Featherstone's (2010) development of Massumi's concepts of movement vision and his corresponding reconfiguration of body-image to body-without-an-image provides an interesting way of reframing the makeover and body-transformation projects within consumer culture. Featherstone's critique of body-image discourse focuses upon those forces which are generated and pass between bodies that are more difficult to see – what he terms the 'affective image' and the 'affective body'. He argues that these forces or intensities are part of body-image discourse, and stylists and makeover experts are very aware that the makeover is much more than simply changing appearance and the visual register of bodies.

The reformation of bodies, within the context of the ubiquitous before and after transformation so beloved of the makeover, is one that is also about im/material processes – those that increase the body's capacity to affect others. This affective charge is aligned to the development of a 'look', which is as much about generating charisma, presence, atmosphere and what Thrift (2010) terms 'allure'. Thrift argues that glamour and beauty practices, which are part and parcel of celebrity culture, are characterized by particular technologies that work affectively to generate allure. As Featherstone (2010: 196) similarly argues

> the transformation demands not just the reforming of the body surface and volume through fitness regimes and cosmetic surgery, but a complete transformation also requires something akin to a course in method acting, to learn to play the part of the new person one has elected to become. To have a body and face that has the capacity to stop people in their tracks and make them take a second look, to make them want to verify, note and even record the persona which has instigated the shock of beauty.

Both Featherstone (2010) and Thrift (2010) draw attention to the mediated nature of those processes and practices that generate such allure. Featherstone examines how the concept of body-image or mirror vision is very reliant on photographic technologies which produce the body as a static, two-dimensional, bounded image captured most tellingly by the portrait. However, the portrait itself is more than just image. As Featherstone argues, following the work of Annette Kuhn (1985), the image is also imago; the look perhaps which is generated beyond the image as a 'prosthetic for imaginative work' (Featherstone, 2010: 198; see also Coleman, 2008; Lury, 1995). Thus, to look or think photographically also requires an attunement to the affective work of images; to their suggestive capacities of captivation and enchantment. This might be described as the more ineffable quality of presence or style often used to describe some Hollywood studio photographs of film stars in the inter-war years (Featherstone, 2010). This ineffable quality is also represented by the proliferation of photographs of streetstyle that circulate on blogs and in books, such as *The Sartorialist* (Schuman, 2009), which are said to capture the cultivation of presence.

Featherstone equates the affective image/body to Massumi's concept of 'movement vision', aligned to a body in process, and focuses on how developments in media and digital technologies now allow or even create 'new possibilities for the visualization of affect' (Featherstone, 2010: 194). Featherstone turns to the work of Mark Hansen (2006) and his discussion of video artists such as Bill Viola who have used digital recordings to slow down images so that what is normally imperceptible can be registered on the screen. This allows those intensities which are felt rather than seen to be registered, mediated and visualized via digital technologies. This is a view of the image as informational which requires both body and image to take form (Featherstone, 2010). Bodily affectivity for Hansen relates to the way in which images must be embodied in order to be actualized, and do not exist as static, preformed images.

The shift from body-image to body-without-an-image is important for refocusing our attention on bodies as processes, but, as we have seen within this work, the question of how affect is mediated is one that tends to oscillate around the status of the body within different perspectives. Although Featherstone acknowledges the assumptions embedded within the concept of the biomediated body, most of his discussion is very much centred on the human body, albeit a human body that is always subject to mediation. As he argues, what we need to take account of rather is how people move between different registers, between body-image and body-without-an-image, between 'the mirror-image and the movement-image, between affect and emotion, between the subject-object and the

15

sensation of visceral and proprioceptive intensities' (2010: 213). This suggests a certain 'doubling' (see also Chapter 7 of this book), rather than the move from either a closed to an open body, or from a distinctly human body to one that troubles any such distinction. The question of how we might approach this 'doubling', where the subject can be both 'one yet many' (see Blackman, 2008b) or 'more than one and less than many' will be explored in Chapter 7 by focusing on recent interdisciplinary engagements with the 'double brain' (see McGilchrist, 2009). This work, which spans art, philosophy, neuroscience, sociology and literature, opens up the question of the *milieu* and technicity in the context of affective processes (see also Venn, 2010). The question considered in Chapter 7 is precisely how we can analyse different brain–body–world couplings that might enact being both singularity and plurality in complex ways.

I want to approach this 'doubling' by considering a related debate within affect studies over the extent to which affect can be considered non-intentional (see also Leys, 2011a). This debate returns us to the question of whether affect requires a (human) subject in order to register or materialize. Some people have explicitly related the idea of 'affect without a subject' to the influence of Spinoza's philosophy on Deleuzian ideas (Williams, 2010). As Williams argues (p. 246), affect

> is also de-subjectifying in an important respect as for Spinoza it is also a kind of force or power that courses through and beyond subjects. Thus, it cannot easily be inscribed within the borders of subjectivity. For Spinoza, affects are forms of encounter; they circulate – sometimes ambivalently but always productively – between and within bodies (of all kinds), telling us something important about the power of affect to unravel subjectivity and modify the political body.

It is for this reason that affect is considered autonomous, prepersonal, non-intentional and a force that exceeds the psychological subject (Massumi, 2002a). Affect within this perspective does not require an anthropocentric or psychological subject to understand or register its workings. Affect relates to 'processes without a subject' (Williams, 2010: 247).

## Affect and Science

In order to consider the status of affect as non-intentional and the related question of the extent to which the human body should be granted equivalence to non-human forms, I want to turn to the work of Ruth Leys, the historian of science. Her most recent work has focused on the problems with constituting affect as non-intentional (see Leys, 2011a). Leys (2010b, 2011a) argues that one of the beliefs driving affect theorists within the humanities is that affect is non-cognitive – separate from cognition, meaning and interpretation. This separation often grants the non-cognitive primacy, where the focus often becomes the material body, and the bioneurological mechanisms through which affect might register and pass. As other writers such as Claire Hemmings (2005) have argued, there is a danger with this view that there might become a disconnection between *ideology* and the body and meaning and affect. This might produce, as one of its consequences, 'a relative indifference to the role of ideas and beliefs in politics in favour of an "ontological" concern with people's corporeal-affective experiences of the political images and representations that surround them' (Leys, 2010b: 668).

Leys (2007, 2011a) illustrates one possible consequence of this ontological commitment in her engagement with an approach to affect within the humanities informed by the work of the American psychologist, Silvan Tomkins. As she illustrates, this work is contested within the psychological sciences and the context and parameters of such contestation are obscured in current work on affect. Tomkins's theories of affect were introduced into the humanities by the late queer theorist Eve Kosofsky Sedgwick (2003). In 1995 Sedgwick and Frank wrote an introduction to a reader on Tomkins's work which, as Leys (2007) argues, hailed Tomkins's 'neurocultural' approach to affect as being important for humanities scholars. It was seen to offer a critique of constructionism and psychoanalysis, replacing anxiety and arousal with what was taken to be a more complex system of affective states and forces (see Gibbs, 2010). Constructionist approaches for a long time had struggled with how to understand investment within normalizing processes, turning to a combination of Lacanian psychoanalysis and Foucauldian approaches to discourse to provide a theory of subjectivity (see Butler, 1993; Henriques et al., 1984, for example). However, the non-materialist approach to investment, which for many revolved around the discursive production of fantasy and desire, was seen to problematically produce the body as inert dumb matter (see Blackman, 2008a).

Tomkins's work was seen to be exciting as it offered an account of motivation which bypassed meaning and interpretation in favour of a more materially grounded approach to investment which foregrounded the 'biological' as having an inherent dynamism or liveliness. Human subjects were *not* seen to be driven by complex psychic dynamics of subjectivity and sociality, but rather by discrete affects which were innate states hard-wired into the brain. These states were seen to produce an energetic dimension to behaviour which operated outside of interpretive systems of meaning and cognition. In other words, Tomkins's work represents an anti-intentionalist approach to affect, where affects are produced as 'automatic, reflex-like corporeal' responses (Leys, 2007: 125). The question is whether the separation between the intentional and non-intentional can be mapped onto a distinction between the psychological and the biological or between the immaterial and the material. I am particularly interested in whether the immaterial can also be modelled materially without making such a split, hence my preference for the hybrid term 'im/material'.

Leys (2010b, 2011a) echoes an anxiety about making such a distinction and argues that the ontological commitment to non-intentionality as materiality enacted by some affect theorists within this tradition ignores or obscures the shaky empirical ground Tomkins's work rests upon. I am sympathetic to Leys's challenge and the crux of her argument, which as a historian of science is oriented towards the importance of genealogical study for analysing the context and contestation surrounding Tomkins's work within the psychological sciences. This raises the question of how, as humanities scholars, we engage with the psychological, life, biological and neurosciences in our engagements with affect, and what are some of the problems and possibilities generated by a closer alliance to the sciences. Gibbs (2010), an Australian cultural theorist, has extended Tomkins's work in the context of her approach to mimetic communication – that is, to those processes, such as the phenomenon of emotional contagion, which are seen to be more corporeally based and which circulate and pass between bodies. She argues that the mimetic capacity in humans is innate in order to explore the more immediate, visceral, non-intentional ways in which bodies are conscripted by media technologies. This might be through the use of particular devices such as the close-up shot of the face, for example. This approach to biomediation is one which theorizes the body and embodiment, rather than meaning and signification, as being central to how media technologies are seen to work and take hold (see also Blackman, 2012).

Gibbs (2010) is, however, very aware of the dangers of providing an empirical grounding for her approach to mimetic communication. Although she does assume that mimesis is a fundamentally innate capacity (drawing primarily from animal and infant research), she also refocuses our attention away from the potential positivism of this statement towards the question '*what if* one conceived the world in this way?' (p. 189). This is similar to Massumi's (2002a) approach to the sciences which he terms 'creative contagion' (see Chapter 4 for an extended engagement with Massumi's work). This approach brings into the humanities what might often be seen as rather positivist empirical research in the psychological, cognitive and neurosciences (see Chapter 7). The reductionism of this strategy is potentially destabilized through putting it into dialogue with quantum physics, Spinoza, Bergson and Deleuze. However, although I am sympathetic to this work and what it opens up, I am also aware of the importance of more genealogical approaches to both science and affect, which allow one to consider the wider contexts of complex and often contested circuits of debate, legitimacy and authorization within scientific theories and research. This is often overlooked in the humanities' engagements with science, which is becoming much more characteristic of work within affect studies (see Thrift, 2004).

Callard and Papoulias (2010: 31) consider the inherent positivism that is sometimes invoked in the sizeable shifts that are being made in the humanities' reappraisal of the sciences. This is also a concern for Leys (2010a, 2011a), who argues that the lack of historical engagement with the complexity of debates within the sciences often leads to a kind of cherry picking. This often obscures or ignores the contestation and complexity of the assertions of a particular theory or author. As Callard and Papoulias (2010) argue, science is often used to 'ground the *content* of theorists' claims (about what affect is and does, that is)'. That is, empirical studies are used as evidence to ground or authorize a particular definition of affect – that it is a non-intentional force, for example. This is a concern for Leys (2010a, 2011a) who in a series of articles offers a genealogy of the work of Tomkins, particularly as it has been taken up by the contemporary American psychologist, Paul Ekman (2006).[1]

This engagement with the histories of contestation over Ekman's approach to the emotions and facial expression, Leys argues, are occluded by the recent engagement with Tomkins by affect theorists across the humanities. Leys considers why Tomkins's work was seen to offer a radical overhaul of constructionism, given his alignment with evolutionary science and particularly the work of Charles Darwin. The production of the 'naturalistic body paradigm', associated with Darwin's evolutionary account of human behaviour and development (Shilling, 2003), is one that for years has been refuted in the humanities for its essentialism and its alignment with the production and reproduction of social inequalities and inequities. The more cautious and circumspect approach to the sciences that I will develop in my engagements with science does not refute the common ontologies that are emerging across the sciences and humanities. This is where in many theories within both science and the humanities 'social' and 'natural' phenomenon are now viewed as more complex, indeterminate, relational and constantly open to effects from contiguous processes (see Blackman and Venn, 2010). It is, however, important to open up the debate as to how we use, read and deploy practices of experimentation within the sciences. We need to consider what we might be ignoring in our own engagements with affect when we turn to and engage mainstream positivist empirical research and theory to analyse affective processes.

One of the focuses of this book will be on more marginal work in the sciences which engages with phenomena, such as voice hearing, suggestion, rhythm and work on the double brain. I will argue that these phenomena are important because they always already imply relationality and operate as 'threshold phenomena'. That is, these phenomena already suggest some kind of transport between the self and other, inside and outside, and material and immaterial. This transport cannot be understood by the concept of social influence with its presumption of pre-existing entities interacting. However, an important focus of the phenomena I analyse throughout the book is that they also tend to be viewed as signs of irrational perception within the psychological sciences and neurosciences; this is particularly so when we consider suggestion and voice hearing. As I outline in the preface to this book, I approach these phenomena as modalities of communication, rather than irrational forms of perception, that disclose our fundamental connectedness to each other, to our pasts, and even to past histories that cannot be known (see Cho, 2008; Davoine and Guadilliere, 2004).

My focus in relation to these phenomena will be genealogical, considering how detailed historical engagement is important for engaging science in the context of contemporary work on affect (see also Blackman, 2010a). In Chapter 6, I will consider practices of experimentation in the context of voice hearing, framing my engagement with affect through developing work on diasporic vision (Cho, 2008), embodied remembering and transgenerational haunting (Davoine and Guadilliere, 2004). This tradition of work on affect retains the importance of the psyche or the psychological, seeing bodies as more than material substrates of affective transfer. However, the psyche that is invoked is trans-subjective, material and immaterial, living and non-living, and organic and inorganic. This work rejects from the outset the kind of psychological subject that is often brought in through the back door in work on affect. This is the assumption, as we have seen, that affect does not require a subject – that affect relates to processes without a subject. I will show in the next section that although this represents a view of affect held by many affect theorists, this often does not hold up when we consider a genealogy of such a statement as it is enacted in different theories. I will argue that some kind of capacity for mediation aligned either to the brain, nervous system or more general theory of subjectivity is often required in order to make such a statement. These concerns reflect some of my own training within the psychological sciences, and my subsequent excursion through critical and discursive psychology, and latterly within the disciplines of media, cultural and body studies.

## Affect and the Psychological Subject

The 'turn to affect' is often positioned as a counter to the psychological subject, and more specifically as a rejection of the need for theories of subjectivity (see Hemmings, 2005; Massumi, 2002a). This relates to the assumption, particularly within the shift from the body-as-organism to the biomediated body, that affective processes do not require a subject. Affect within these perspectives often becomes constituted as immaterial forces or incorporeal sensations understood through the concept of (virtual) flow or movement. The potential of affect once registered by a human subject is often closed down or arrested in some way, reflected in the assumption that once affect is experienced as emotion or feeling, for example, its virtual potential is thwarted (see Massumi, 2002a). As Clough (2010: 209) suggests, following Massumi, if conscious perception equates to a narration of affect, there is always 'a never-to-be-conscious autonomic remainder'. This assumption is often made by separating affect from cognition and presuming that affect bypasses cognition and is registered prior to its translation into emotion or feeling. The registering of affect is often aligned to the action of the central or autonomic nervous system, for example, or to concepts such as the mirror neuron, which are seen to grant affect its potential autonomy from meaning and interpretation. This is often equated to the half-second delay between affect and cognition (see Thrift, 2004). This statement is often authorized through borrowing from psychology and the neurosciences and using theories on the affective, social and emotional brain, or on image reception in psychology in order to grant immediacy to affect.

This work is very important for undermining the autonomous rational subject of psychology and for opening up discussions of subjectification to processes which pass between subjects and which problematize the interiorized self (see also Seigworth and Gregg, 2010). Clough (2010a) suggests that theories of affect thus challenge nineteenth-century models of the body which, she argues, were assumed to be informationally closed to the environment. Affect thus opens up analyses of subjectification to the realm of potential, 'as tendencies or incipient acts, indeterminant and emergent' (p. 209). Although affect is pre-individual or trans-subjective in this sense, this does not mean that affect cannot be materialized or mediated. Indeed, one of the focuses of work on the biomediated body is precisely to explore how affect can be captured through strategies of biopolitical governance. Clough argues that although affect within such approaches is always seen to produce 'the chance for something else, unexpected, new', capitalism has developed more strategies and techniques for modulating and augmenting affect in ways that might close down hope and extend biopolitical racisms (see Berlant, 2010; Clough and Wilse, 2011; Massumi, 2010). This is one of the ambivalent dualities that work on affect makes visible.

Although affect is primarily considered pre-individual, it is always subject to mediation, or what Clough calls 'technical framing'. Affect is materialized in ways which reveal both the potential for change and hope, as well as the more insidious ways in which populations might be governed beyond normalization (see also Hauptmann and Neidich, 2010). The important point when considering subjectivity within these perspectives is that investment or the capture of affect does not require a human subject governed by psychic dynamics of subjectivity or sociality, but a nervous attunement or synchronizing of body with technology. Thus the psyche is often foreclosed and replaced by a lively nervous system or bodily materiality that is viewed as dynamic, responsive and autonomous from intentionality and cognition. Indeed, a range of mechanisms for registering affect have been proffered which all replace psyche with a more lively biology or neurophysiological or psychological body. This might include mechanisms aligned to the brain, endocrine system, nervous system, olfactory system and so forth.

In Chapter 7 we will consider the grounding of sociality within the brain or neurosciences, which is a distinctive feature of affect studies. Although this work is interesting and important, I want to contend that the displacement or foreclosure of the psyche is neither entirely achieved nor accomplished within this work. There are a number of aspects to my contention that will be discussed throughout the book. I hope I will contribute to discussions of affect and the body by modelling embodiment not only as expressing a lively materiality but also as psychologically or psychically attuned. The conception of psychological or psychic attunement I seek to develop is one which does not separate mind from body, self from other, or even human from non-human and material from immaterial. My approach to the psychic or psychological will start with a more subliminal subject that can be found in nineteenth-century models of personhood which were not assumed to be informationally closed to the environment. These models which are often referred to as vitalist (see Cohen, 2009; Fraser et al., 2005), revolved around the concept of affective transfer that can be found in discussions of telepathy, suggestion, mediumship and so-called psychotic phenomena such as voice hearing or delusions (see Blackman, 2010a). The psychic was presumed to be a threshold experience produced at the interface or intersection of the self and other, material and immaterial, human and non-human, and inside and outside such that processes which might be designated psychological were always trans-subjective, shared, collective, mediated and always extending bodies beyond themselves.

The key focus of much of the reflection in relation to these phenomena was not so much whether bodies were open or closed, singular or multiple, but rather how subjects lived singularity in the face of multiplicity. This is what William James referred to as the 'problem of personality' (see Chapter 2), and I will contend that this problem has not gone away, but has rather resurfaced in contemporary discussions of affect. If the subject is neither entirely open nor closed, then we need some way of theorizing and conceptualizing the threshold conditions, what I am going to term the conditions of 'psycho/mediation', through which affect flows and circulates, in ways that do not reduce either to the idea of intensive forces or to movement understood as flow (see Henriques, 2010, 2011). If my contention persuades, then equally the positing of some generic mechanism of affective transmission or transfer, whether the autonomic nervous system, endocrine system or brain, which is seen to produce synchrony between body and technology, also seems too general and causal. I will argue that too much work on affect presumes that affect flows through synchrony and alignment, where mechanisms of affective exchange are seen to augment or diminish such flow (seen as the body's capacity to act and be acted upon). Rather I want to explore different conceptions of affective exchange which do not presume flow (see Chapter 5), and which do not reduce the complexity of relationality to a neurophysiological body (see Chapters 6 and 7).

The approach I develop throughout the book suggests that the definition of affect as the body's capacity to affect and be affected is too broad. It could also be interpreted as some 'thing' that bodies have: a quality, a vital element – a capacity existing independently of relationality, that is expressed through affect, or is a substratum for it (see Blackman and Venn, 2010). This is even so in approaches which posit affect as processes without a subject, and can be found, for example, in the positing of imagination 'as an anonymous conductor of affects within and between individuals' (Williams, 2010: 248). This allowed Spinoza to conceive of affect as a generative force which flows through and between bodies. Williams's (2010) genealogical engagement with aspects of Spinoza which have been left out of Deleuze's work suggests that in order to construct affective processes in this way, Spinoza required a general theory of imagination which takes his work much closer to psychoanalysis than might be presumed. In other words, the non-subjective nature of affect requires, however minimally, a theory of subjectivity, and these mechanisms are still very much the subject of debate and contestation. I say this as one of the aims of this book is to open up discussions of the psyche and psychology within the spirit of the trans-subjective, in ways which are in keeping with the destabilizing of the distinctly human, and singular psychological subject that affect promises.

My approach is not an attempt to *psychologize* affect, but rather to open up the psychological to post-psychological work that allows the complexity of brain–body–world couplings and entanglements to be analysed. This requires a decoupling of memory, perception, the senses and the psyche from a bounded, singular and distinctly human body, and the development of an analytic that can engage with the intergenerational and intercorporeal transmission of affect, the status of the non-knowing or non-conscious in our theorizations, and the importance of attending to experiences and practices which challenge the foundational model of autonomous subjectivity at the heart of the psychological sciences. This is a processual approach to both the materiality and *im*materiality of the body, something that is perhaps lost if we frame affect as a 'processually oriented *materialism*' (Seigworth and Gregg, 2010: 14, my emphasis). Throughout the book I will engage with work at the margins of the neurosciences and psychological sciences which deal with forms of knowing that exceed rational, conscious experience. This will include work that is often subsumed within the 'psychology of anomalous experience', such as the placebo effect, voice hearing and practices of suggestion, as they might be enacted within particular brain–body–technology couplings. This is a post-psychological project that takes experiences that offer a 'puzzling challenge' to the psychological sciences, and relocates them within the complex brain–body–world entanglements that produce particular kinds of 'psychological' effects and affects.

## Conclusion

The approach I will develop throughout the book is transdisciplinary, drawing from work across the neurosciences, physiology, study of narrative and discourse, media and cultural studies, body studies, art, performance, psychology and psychoanalysis. This approach not only entails a dialogue across science and the humanities, but also suggests that the circulation of concepts across such boundaries is one that has been crucial to science-in-the-making, and which continues to be despite the current attack on the humanities (in its funding in terms of research and teaching) by many neoliberal governments.

This chapter suggests that a genealogy of affect must recognize affect's long history that pre-exists Sedgwick and Frank's (1995) validation of Tomkins's work in the humanities, and Massumi's (2002a) publication of *Parables for the Virtual* (see also Leys, 2011a). Although, as Seigworth and Gregg (2010) suggest, both books present a watershed moment for affect's emergence within the humanities, by placing affect as the subject of genealogical inquiry I hope to show its much longer history of emergence, verification, oscillation, formation and circulation. This is a deeply political project given the current status of the humanities *vis-à-vis* the sciences, and is one which I hope will interest humanities scholars as well as those working in the sciences who know, intuitively or otherwise, that the work of the humanities is important for the invention of new ways of being human, and new concepts for exploring such processes of self and subject-making.

## Note

1  Leys (2011a) argues that this paradigm, which she refers to as the Basic Emotions Paradigm, is 'seriously flawed' (p. 439). She goes on to suggest that it is striking how compatible 'Deleuzian-inspired ideas about affect as a non-linguistic, bodily "intensity" turn out to be with the Tomkins-Ekman paradigm' (p. 442). And that what 'fundamentally binds together the new affect theorists with the neuroscientists is their *shared anti-intentionalism*' (p. 443).

## 2
_____

# The Crowd and The Problem of Personality

## The Problem of the One and the Many: Crowd Psychology

In the summer of 2011 the United Kingdom experienced a contagious spate of rioting and looting which spread throughout London and then to other major cities, including Manchester and Birmingham. The commentary emerging from these events took form around a vocabulary which brings into play concepts of crowd or collective psychology. From mass hysteria to people power, images of burning buildings and young people looting were counterposed by images of people coming together with brooms and cups of tea. The latter images have come to symbolize the efforts of local people to 'clean up' the mess and destruction, and in so doing to constitute themselves as part of a concerned community. What we witness again and again, from the riots of the Paris Communes which concerned nineteenth and early twentieth century writers and regulators, to contemporary formations of the collective and the crowd, are both the dangers and possibilities of contagion and viral forms of communication. The dangers exist alongside the potential of new forms of subjectivity and collectivity made possible by people coming together as part of a crowd or public. The uprisings in countries such as Libya and Egypt are a case in point.

In the nineteenth and early twentieth centuries the paradox that contagious communication presented was posed in a particular way. This was primarily framed as the problem of the 'one and many': how social unity is achieved in the face of contagion, suggestion, mental touch and so forth. One distinction that is often made in the present, between earlier forms of crowd psychology and those we might find in contemporary representations, is that in the nineteenth and early twentieth centuries these were imagined in the more static image of the crowd. The crowd was primarily represented by bodily proximity and a particular spatial location. What we witness in the twenty-first century is the transformation of the crowd into a series of more flexible, adaptable and mobile entities. These improvised crowds are imagined in the iconic image of social networks such as Facebook and

Twitter, and communication practices such as Blackberry Messenger, allowing a temporary and transient public to be formed on- and sometimes off-line.

Not wishing to add to the commentary in relation to these contemporary instances of contagious communication, I do want to use the opposed images of mass hysteria and people power (which of course, depending on your position, can be used interchangeably to refer to both constituencies) to reflect on some of the questions, themes and issues opened up by the genealogy of affect constituted throughout this book. One of the central focuses of the book returns to a historical question posed by William James which, following his formulation, I have termed 'the problem of personality'. This problem took form within the context of particular surfaces of emergence, such as the crowd, the séance, and the development of communication technologies such as film, the printing press and radio during the late nineteenth to early twentieth centuries. These sites were seen to be linked via communication which was seen to act 'at a distance'. That is, communication was seen to defy fixed boundaries between the self and other, material and immaterial and even the dead and alive, and to operate in registers which were 'invisible' and not easy to see, register, measure or verify. The observation of such processes was felt affectively, where communication was seen to move or propel action, thought, emotion and feeling in ways which could not be contained by rational explanation.

One of the questions raised about such processes was whether modes of individuation made possible by the crowd or the séance were simply recording such processes, verifying non-rational registers which were all around, or whether these sites were actually producing or creating psychic realities. To take the crowd as a case in point, was the crowd an instance of a specific milieu capable of inducing people to act in certain ways, or do crowds allow for the flow of destructive energies or forces which are latent or located within specific people prior to the crowd formation? The latency of crowds has often been aligned to the action of instincts seen to be the expression of animality and primitivism. In this formulation identifying possible susceptibilities *within* people to crowd psychology becomes an issue of government and regulation. During the nineteenth and early twentieth centuries, discussions of the crowd and crowd psychology as a particular mode of individuation were also closely related to concepts of mental touch, more aligned to telepathic modalities of communication. Telepathy was associated more explicitly with the séance and emergent communication technologies of the time (Chapters 3, 4 and 5). These sites were not characterized necessarily by bodily proximity or a static image of the crowd, with some commentators preferring the term 'public' to capture the dispersion of affects across both space and time. Thus processes of communication 'at a distance', encapsulated by the concept of mental touch, always implicated processes of mediation in creating or constituting a public or public opinion. These processes are not so dissimilar to those we witness in the present in relation to the capacity of social media to create publics, temporary or otherwise.

The continuities between the twentieth and twenty-first centuries are not so far apart as they might at first seem. As well as the susceptibility of crowds to carry out actions they might not enact in other contexts or situations, there is also an acknowledgement that mediation works in non-rational registers that are still little understood. The oscillation between suggestion as an ordinary phenomenon produced within practices, and an exceptional and abnormal *susceptibility* found in certain places and people continues to this day. The role of suggestion within histories of modernity, and its neglected status, has been the subject of important work by humanities scholars who are revitalizing suggestion as an important process and practice of mediation. One angle of such work is a commitment to rescuing suggestion from its association with the lack of a particular psychological capacity, usually understood through the concept of will, and to recasting suggestive processes as important in understanding practices of governance (see Blackman, 2007b; Borch, 2005; Orr, 2006; Thrift, 2007). This includes the recent engagement across the humanities with the nineteenth-century philosopher and scientist, Gabrial Tarde, and the importance he credited to suggestion in understanding the workings of governmental processes (see Blackman, 2007b; Candea, 2010).

## The Unruly and Dangerous Crowd

This chapter will focus on one of the key surfaces of emergence through which ideas of suggestion and contagious communication took form at the end of the nineteenth and early twentieth centuries. The crowd was primarily to become viewed as a mode of individuation which would allow for the flow of destructive energies. This was captured by the reflections of the crowd psychologist Moscovici (1985: 4), who argued that the crowd was ultimately figured as a 'social animal which has broken its leash'. The crowd was one of the sites which were seen to reveal the close relationship of the human to the animal, the rational to the irrational, and the instinctual to the emotional. The crowd focused debate amongst scientists, philosophers, literary writers and regulators about the nature of the human, the animal and the psyche. Crowd behaviour was seen to reveal the subject's openness to the other, human and non-human, and the cultural fears, fantasies and desires which regulated this openness. The paradoxes that this discloses are important in any revitalization of suggestion in the present, particularly when we turn to the subject of affect.

The discussion of suggestion as a particular way of framing affect has become an important part of work on affect. This chapter will link these debates to nineteenth-century writings on the problem of contagious communication, or what Ruth Leys has framed as the problem of imitation or mimetic desire. The problem of imitation was conceived through concepts and explanatory structures translated from studies of hypnotic suggestion and took centre-stage in nineteenth-century discussions of movement or change. A newly emerging science of association, linked to the work of key figures, such as Tarde, Le Bon and Freud, grappled with explaining and understanding apparent sites of individual and social metamorphosis condensed into the image of the crowd or the public. The problem of the crowd, or what later became framed as a problem of mass psychology (Moscovici, 1985), provided a way of connecting up a range of different sites, contexts and metaphysical questions about the nature of consciousness, the psyche, humanness and animism. The ontological assumptions made in relation to suggestion emerged from trying to understand modes of individuation which were located within sites including the crowd, the séance, the scientific laboratory, and within the new kinds of public created within emerging media technologies. The key paradox which linked these sites is one that I am going to term, following William James, 'the problem of personality' (see Blackman, 2008a).

This problem articulated the possibilities as well as the fears surrounding the subject's openness to the other – human and non-human. The problem was set up by William James in the foreword to a much cited text written by the psychologist Boris Sidis (1898), titled *The Psychology of Suggestion: A Research into the Subconscious Nature of Man and Society*. The problem of personality was not to be confused with any idea of fixed or stable personality traits or characteristics, but rather with a reworking of consciousness derived from observations of the hypnotic state. What was often termed the subliminal self was seen to be revealed through 'fixed ideas, hysteric attacks, insane delusions and mediumistic phenomenon' (James in Sidis, 1898: v). Thus the séance and practices such as automatic writing and thought transference were seen to be key sites for the disclosure of psychic realities which were seen to reveal the multiplicity of the subject. Thus 'abnormal life', as a description of what were considered marginal states or experiences, was not considered as irrational perception but rather as an important modality of communication. The problem was formulated particularly in relation to James's poetic descriptions of consciousness as being akin to a stream; a flow of ideas, images, sensations and affects which are characterized primarily by movement. Hence the metaphor of the stream captures the fluidity and permeability of consciousness which ripples, flows and ebbs rather than being housed by a singular unified bounded subject.

The topology of subjectivity that James presents is one which views the human subject as being akin to a channel or conductor of thought, open and permeable to the other, invoking a sense of a shared collective consciousness, rather than one closed and located within atomized subjects. The 'problem of personality' in the nineteenth century was articulated as a particular problem of suggestive or affective communication. Interests in affective or suggestive communication were often framed through ideas of telepathic transfer – that is, that ideas could spread though a kind of dematerialized communication. This issue became condensed into the image of the dangerous crowd, which brought together particular conceptions of affective openness with discussions of the regulation and conduct of 'impulsive energies'. Philosophers such as Henri Bergson, the sociologist Gabriel Tarde, and William James all attempted to provide answers to this problem by arguing in different ways that what defined human sociality and subjectivity was the capacity of 'ordinary suggestion'. The human subject was not self-contained, individualized, clearly bounded and separate from others, but rather the borders and boundaries between self and other were considered porous and permeable. However, as we can see in the following quote, even at the level of consciousness, the process of synthesis or unity was also a puzzling challenge for scientists and philosophers:

'What are the limits of the consciousness of a human being? Is 'self' consciousness only a part of the whole consciousness? Are there many 'selves' dissociated from one another? What is the medium of synthesis in a group of associated ideas?' (James in Sidis, 1989: v)

This became formulated as the problem of 'the one and the many' (see also Blackman, 2008a) which circulated across discussions of law, economics, psychology, philosophy, literature and so forth at the turn of the nineteenth century. An edited collection by the Faculty of Political Science at Columbia University in 1909 framed the problem as the problem of 'the many and the one'. As they asked: 'How do many minds act as one, many brains as one brain?' (p. 51). The resolution of this problematic was seen to potentially be of huge social and political import. Sidis argued that hypnotic suggestion might provide solutions to many problems, including within schooling, the legal system, and the therapeutic relationship:

> A knowledge of the laws of the subconscious is of momentous import in education, in the reformation of juvenile criminals and offenders, and one can hardly realize the great benefit that suffering humanity will derive from a properly methodical use of the subconscious within the province of therapeutics.

The crowd became one site within which hypnotic suggestibility took form as a particular problem of personality *susceptibility*. This was to be understood through explanatory concepts, such as will, habit, inhibition and instinct, which travelled across science, culture, literature and the legal system (see Andriopoulos, 2008). We will explore this circulation and translation by particularly focusing on the way in which concepts such as will, inhibition, suggestion and habit took shape within the emerging psychological sciences. This is not an exhaustive account but identifies some of the key debates, concepts and modes of problematization which were central to the way suggestion took form. This was primarily as an abnormal phenomenon associated with collective psychology. This was viewed as the expression of a 'mob mentality' associated with animality and primitivism.

One of the arguments made about suggestion in contemporary work on affect is that scarcely perceptible influences, operating below the threshold of conscious awareness, are central communicative modalities through which information, emotion, feelings, ideas and beliefs circulate, register and even take hold. These modalities are not simply aligned to subjection, but open up the possibility of 'unsuspected possibilities for new ways of thinking, being and acting' (Gibbs, 2010: 187). For some, suggestive processes are 'the fundamental communicative principle', which explain these processes of transmission (p. 187). In this vein Gibbs aligns suggestion to mimetic communication, which she characterizes as 'corporeally based forms of imitation, both voluntary and involuntary' (p. 186). These processes and their mediation are seen to reveal how bodies, human and non-human, become synchronized. As we explored in Chapter 1, the registering of such communicative processes in much work on affect is aligned to the human autonomic system. Affect does not require a psychological subject to register; but rather a subject governed by a lively materiality; a nervous system which is attuned to processes which bypass conscious rationality. Thus as Gibbs argues, mimesis discloses the 'bioneurological means by which particular affects are transmitted from body to body' (p. 191). There is no need for a psyche in this work as bodily materiality itself is now seen to speak and communicate with the other without any conscious awareness of such communication. This is what Clough (2010a: 210) terms the 'affectivity of matter' (see Chapter 1).

Nigel Thrift (2008) also gives suggestion a central importance in understanding people's motivation to act. The issue of what might compel somebody to action is linked to the 'human capacity for mimesis' (p. 238). Action is not the result of calculative rationality or conscious processing, but rather the subject is reconfigured as a 'subject of *automatism*' (p. 239). The invoking of automatism is seen to refer to processes which cannot be contained by the concept of will (see Chapter 6). As we will see throughout this chapter, the concept of will became central to the way in which the psychological sciences and particularly social psychology attempted to resolve the problem of personality. Thrift uses the concept of automatism to refer to capacities which entrain subjects and attune subjects to the other, aligning affect to 'imitation-suggestion' (p. 252). However, as well as pointing towards the fundamental relationality seen to govern the subject, he also points towards the 'corporeal vulnerability' seen to characterize the subject's affective openness (p. 242). This is the paradox of suggestion, or what I am also terming the ambivalent duality which characterizes the phenomena that are of interest in this book. Thrift develops the paradoxes of suggestion by exploring affective openness in the context of politics and regulation, as well as those strategies subjects might engage in 'order to produce affectively controllable worlds' (p. 239). Suggestion can be aligned with fixity and stasis as well as opening the subject to creative potential and reinvention. This ambivalent duality is cogently summed up by Crary (1999: 230), who suggests that 'the volatility of hypnosis as a cultural and scientific object was due to its dual status as a potential technique of control and a set of enigmatic phenomena that resisted intellectual mastery and dualist conceptualizations'.

## Suggestion as a Primitive Modality of Communication

In order to understand the paradox of suggestion, or contagious forms of communication more generally, it is necessary to explore how suggestion was to take form within the newly emerging psychological sciences. Increasingly the subject able to exercise and maintain clear and steadfast boundaries between self and other became naturalized and normalized. This subject was considered able to regulate feelings which were located within the realm of the automatic and involuntary. It is important to examine the amplification of these terms through distinctions made between the primitive and the civilized, the inferior and the superior, the lower and the higher, and the instinctual and the acquired. Such distinctions were specifically made in relation to the crowd which was considered highly suggestible and as 'irrational, impulsive, uncivilized, bloodthirsty and dangerous' (Barrows, 1981: 46). The image of the crowd served as a barometer and description of particular psychosocial types – the insane, the poor, the female and the alcoholic (p. 46) – through which suggestion was increasingly located and refigured. It is the creation of this particular conception of otherness, characterized as biosocial inferiority or degeneracy, which identified certain groups as possible and actual threats to invention and progress. This was framed through their apparent suggestibility to particular kinds of 'psychical influence'.

Previous genealogical inquiry has shown that the terms and classifications of otherness were an important extension and authorization of a classed and colonial project, which continued its evolution within the emerging human and particularly psychological sciences (Blackman and Walkerdine, 2001; Henriques et al., 1984; Rose, 1985). In this chapter I will return to this historical moment and explore the emergence and sedimentation of a particular model of personhood, understood through the concepts of inhibition and will. This led suggestion to be considered an exceptional, abnormal phenomenon, rather than an ordinary capacity of sociality. The particular form of psychological control which established social influence as a force or threat to the boundaries of the atomized individual became what Smith (1992: 114) identifies as a 'nodal position'. This was to become a common discourse about the nature of humanness. It was this mode of continuity and its repeatability and iterability which linked a diverse range of sites, including neurophysiology, general physiology, neurology, psychiatry, experimental psychology and philosophy (Smith, 1992).

## The Importance of Control

> Wherever one turned at the beginning of the nineteenth century, there was a sense that the mind's grasp over the body was tenuous but imperative. (Smith 1992: 1)

The nineteenth and early twentieth centuries were marked by a fascination with the concept of hypnotic suggestion (see Andriopoulos, 2008). Within philosophy and science key writers were drawn to and interested in studying psychic, spiritual and religious phenomena, as well as the phenomena of hypnotic suggestion, voice hearing and delusions (see also Blackman, 2010a). This included philosophers who have become important within contemporary debates on affect, including Henry Bergson and William James; those who were later to become part of the debate establishing the boundaries of social psychology and sociology, including Gabriel Tarde; and Sigmund Freud, who translated notions of hypnotic suggestibility through the concept of transference (Chertok and Stengers, 1992). The studies of consciousness which ensued took notions of psychic energy and more incorporeal understandings of matter as a means of raising questions about the nature, limits and boundaries of humanness. Mesmerism, hypnotism, trance, and studies of psychic phenomenon such as telepathy, telaesthesia, telekinesis, rapping, séances and mediumistic practices, were all vehicles for exploring what were taken to be apparent breaches of bodily and mental functions (Peters, 1999; Smith, 1992). The very divisions which have become so central to psychological knowledge, and appear and reappear in a myriad of sites of self-production, were far from settled. Distinctions between the inner and the outer, the self and other, the private and the public, and the human and the ethereal were sites of perplexity and undecidability, with respected and eminent figures of philosophy and science making studies of psychical research an important string to their bow.

What I want to establish in this chapter is how the very separations which were achieved within the making of social psychology hinged around the acceptance and making 'true' of a particular hierarchy of order over disorder, will over feeling, and the human over both the animal and the ethereal. The self-enclosed, bounded individual was the interference point in the blind spread of particular kinds of imitative processes, and embodied the longings and hope for science of establishing how regulation and patterning could be achieved over possible anarchy and disorder. Gabriel Tarde was a proponent of the importance of the leader; of one who could invent and facilitate the imitation of ideas, practices and beliefs which would hinder or thwart the proliferation of socialism, revolution and terrorism. This involved the recognition that suggestibility was the crucial mechanism through which ideas and beliefs could become part of a collective state of desire and action (see Blackman, 2007b). In other words, the very idea of metamorphosis was akin to a hypnotic state. Collective states were viewed as the expression of psychic modifications and changes which were analogous to states of hypnotic trance and stupor. Barrows (1981: 139) also shows how important hypnoticism was 'as a foundation of the social sciences' through the central role accorded to imitation across the social and political sciences. Thus Moscovici (1985: 2) links the centrality of imitative processes to a recognition of the importance of discussions of the 'power of the leader' to science and philosophy at the turn of the last century, and for what he argues to be the important work of social science in the twentieth century and beyond.[1] The following quote from Gabriel Tarde (1962: 25, cited in Moscovici, 1985: 38) shows the proximity of his writing to Gustave Le Bon,[2] and also shows the concern with the possible discontinuity between invention and leadership if suggestibility was not utilized to popularize a liberal, middle class tradition: 'The truth is that for most men there is an irresistible sweetness inherent in obedience, creduality and almost lover-like servility towards the admired master'.

Le Bon's (1896) book *The Crowd: A Study of the Popular Mind* reworked concepts of hypnotic suggestibility in relation to the problem of group or crowd psychology. It was hugely popular, being translated into many languages, and became one of the stated bases of the emergence of social psychology. It was also one of the conditions of possibility for Freud's (1922) work on the psychopathology of groups, as well as the emerging discipline of media studies (Blackman and Walkerdine, 2001). It is recognized that Le Bon's writings were a concatenation of ideas of hypnotic suggestibility refigured through particular kinds of racial and classed hierarchies of intelligence (see Blackman and Walkerdine, 2001). Le Bon was a French Royalist who was concerned with 'how it is that an individual can, under certain conditions, come under the influence of a crowd and commit acts he is normally not capable of committing' (Jones and Gerard, 1967: 331). Le Bon turned to studies of hypnosis in order to frame the problem of crowd psychology. Like many of his contemporaries he was impressed by the writings and practices of the French neurologist Jean-Martin Charcot. Freud had gone to study with Charcot in 1885 at the famous La Salpêtrière hospital in France in order to refine his own practice and study of the alterations in thought, feeling and behaviour made possible by hypnotic trance. He later diverged from Charcot in his own interpretation of hysteria as a psychological rather than a neurological condition (see Chertok and Stengers, 1992; Ellenberger, 1970). Le Bon mobilized the idea that hypnotic trance was a particular induced somatic mode of awareness and used this to understand crowd psychology. He was particularly concerned with how to understand the revolts and uprisings of the Paris Communes and understood suggestion as a mode of communication which forged powerful social bonds. He framed this through the action of instincts that were given free reign in crowd situations where people were seen to lose their rationality and become more suggestible. Le Bon therefore refigured suggestion as an abnormal phenomenon that was aligned with an instinctual economy. This connected up a notion of inherited biological predispositions with behaviour, thought and feeling considered automatic and involuntary (Foucault, 2003). This voluntary–involuntary axis was mapped onto a distinction between the primitive and civilized central to evolutionary theories of degeneracy prominent at the turn of the twentieth century (Darwin, 1909).

The person swayed by the crowd was to become a prototypical being who embodied the attributes which connected the human with the animal. This concatenation between the mysterious workings of the unconscious and the identification of the primitive within the civilized acted as a potent unifying strategy. The working classes, colonial subjects, women and children became the bearers of this fear of the primitive and its potential irruption into the smooth running of the social order. Contact between persons, groups, leaders and demagogues was fraught with the potential for certain people to be 'reduced to a primitive state and [to be] swayed not by logic but by emotionally charged words' (Jones and Gerard 1967: 331). As Orr (2006: 42) suggests, the apparent psychopathology of crowd behaviour that Le Bon mobilized in his writings aligned the crowd with 'an array of pathologized "others" – neurotic, feminine, "primitive" and racialized "others", the mass of working classes and the poor'. The view of the psychological subject that was to take root within the psychological sciences was one where the normal subject was seen to exercise certain psychological capacities, such as will and inhibition, fortifying them against social influence processes (Smith, 1992). Smith suggests that inhibition as a concept connected up a number of contrasts between the higher and the lower, reason and emotion, mind and body, and the elite and the masses, which were co-ordinated in relation to 'an individualistic sense of self' (p. 5). Inhibition was viewed as a form of psychological control that would enable the domination of the instincts and the action of the mind over the body. As Smith (p. 5) argues:

> The act of inhibition is dynamic and implies conflict, perhaps between powers within the individual, perhaps between the individual and outside forces. The relation may refer simply to one force controlling another, or it may imply the suppression of some spontaneous or natural energy. The language often suggests that control, expressed as inhibition, whether internalized or coming from without, is a fundamental condition of social life.

In relation to understandings of panic that governed social psychological inquiry during the Second World War and the subsequent Cold War in the USA, Orr (2006: 128) argues that the concepts of suggestion and 'emotional contagion' were replaced by 'an emphasis on the normative, reasonable, even adaptive features of crowd behavior'. Quoting the social psychologists Lindesmith and Strauss (1956: 456), she argues that 'much of what is called suggestibility actually involves judgment and reasoning and may represent a quite realistic adaptation' (Orr, 2006: 129). This shift between suggestion, as a form of contagious communication, and sympathy, understood as a form of conscious judgment and deliberation, became part of suggestion's ambivalent duality that social psychology enacted in different ways. In an interesting commentary on how this duality was co-ordinated, Orr draws attention to the role that social psychology increasingly played in communications research that aimed to explain collective behaviour, as well as providing techniques and strategies to the military, industry and the mass media to induce suggestive commitment amongst the 'masses' to certain beliefs, ideas and practices. Although *will* had become the psychological capacity that defined the normative human subject (Smith, 1992), what remained was an understanding that feeling, affect and emotion were important in communication processes, and that the so-called masses must be 'moved' beyond a logic of reason and rationality in order to induce subjective commitment.

Social psychology increasingly was to play a role in US panic pre-vention and production (in relation to the fears generated by the Cold War) and enacted suggestion in this context as a mode of communica-tion that could be manipulated in order to regulate and manage psy-chic life. This included the understanding, for example, that radio was a technique that could induce mass-mediated suggestion or what was also understood as 'contagion without contact' (Orr, 2006: 48). This mobilization of suggestion as a form of contagious communication that could *create* psychic realities represented, for Orr, 'the curious theoretical vertigo in which social suggestion becomes reasonable just as reason starts to experiment with its oh-so-suggestive symbolic pow-ers' (p. 132). The relationships between *suggestion* and *sympathy* were articulated through a number of contrasts and dualisms that produced suggestion as an object aligned with the body, emotion and primitive-ness. This bipolar logic aligned sympathy with the mind, reason and civilized thought, feeling and conduct, with suggestion produced as a primitive modality of (bodily) communication.

### Gabriel Tarde and the Politics of the Imagination

Gabriel Tarde (1962) was also a key figure who became cited as one of the stated bases of the emergence of Anglo-American social psy-chology (see Blackman, 2007b). Tarde is more known to the contem-porary sociological community through the work of Latour (2004) and Deleuze (1994) and is viewed by some as the founding figure or forefather of actor network theory (Latour, 2002; Toews, 2003). There is now a sizeable scholarship on the importance of Tarde's thinking for contemporary social theory, and his work is synonymous now with the subject of affect (Alliez, 2001; Borch, 2005; Candea, 2010; Gibbs, 2008; Thrift, 2007, 2008). Tarde's work is important because it did not simply subscribe to understandings of crowd psy-chology. Rather, he argued that what defined the subject was their capacity for ordinary suggestion. However, his thinking was also very much a product of its time, and the oscillations and ambivalent dual-ity surrounding the status of suggestion entered into his own formu-lations. I have shown in previous writing how Tarde engaged with and reworked concepts from evolutionary biology (Blackman, 2007b; see Barrows, 1981, for a more detailed discussion). He estab-lished a set of contrasts between the higher and the lower, the civi-lized and the animal, and the leader and the follower, in his discussions of the importance of understanding social influence processes conceived as a form of hypnotic suggestibility. The key

sentiment and political bent of Tarde's work was one which reso-
nated with many writers of the time and imported a particular
knowledge of crowd psychology as providing the means to better
equip bona-fide leaders to govern them (see Chapter 4 for an extended
discussion of Tarde's work).

What is interesting for latter-day discussions of the importance of
affect for social theory is the very particular kind of *feeling* body
which was an integral part of the way in which imitative processes
were seen to reproduce themselves between actors within a field of
complex social processes. Appeals to reason and rationality, didactic
command and instruction, and staged forms of persuasion would miss
the mark, and even make followers more resistant to change and
transformation. What was needed were appeals to the heart, to feeling, to passion, to the imagination, to a realm of affect which was
co-present with the psychic and emotional rather than the intellect
and reasoning. As Moscovici (1985: 104) proclaims, 'the age of the
crowd was the age of the imagination, and he who rules there rules
by imagination'. Moscovici (p. 139) characterizes these appeals as
creating an 'illusion of love' through the use of a range of techniques,
affective, bodily and psychological, designed to maximize and facilitate processes of suggestion and imitation. These might include the
use of symbols, flags, images, singing, music, affirmations, phrases,
speeches and slogans. These would be delivered through the hypno-
tizing use of repetition, rather than didactic command and instruction. Individuals would be touched in ways which might be
non-conscious or create the feeling that they are the originator of the
thought, belief or action, rather than simply mechanically reproducing the beliefs of a charismatic other. There would be a resonance or
tuning where suggestion was viewed as a particular form of psychical
influence which could be produced within specific forms of exchange.

As we can see from Moscovici's discussion of the technical production of suggestion within this context, the body's potential for
mediation was not simply aligned to the nervous system. The concept of the imagination was also viewed as an important process
integral to suggestion's fundamental technicity. Suggestion was
viewed more as a potentiality or affordance which allowed for the
co-constitution of ideomotor-psychic processes within a particular
setting or milieu. One of the key concepts which drew together the
particular ways in which the imagination was structured within this
milieu is the idea of *impression*. Connor (2003: 100) links the idea of
the skin as having active powers to register and express feelings and
states between people, what he terms 'the translation of otherwise

inchoate states and feelings into epidermal terms', to theories of maternal impressions in the nineteenth century. These theories were based on the idea that there was an intimate and symbiotic relationship between the mother and her foetus, such that the boundaries between self and (m)other were porous and permeable (see Wilson, 2010, for a discussion of the phenomenon of micro-chimerism which enacts a similar kind of boundary unmaking within the present). This folding and infolding between mother and foetus was achieved through a kind of 'sympathetic impression' (Connor, 2003: 118), where both could touch and be touched through processes of 'psychic imprinting' (Connor, 2003: 103). A feminized space of *relationality* provided a way of thinking about social influence, which did not instate the figure of the clearly bounded individual exerting their will and exercising rationality as the means to set them apart from others. The metaphor of psychic or 'mental touch' which produced this non-logocentric way of thinking about relationality was one which depended on 'the idea that the skin is not simply a boundary or interface ... the skin begins to wake and wonder, an actively unfolding and self-forming organism rather than merely passive stuff' (Connor, 2003: 118).

Of course the idea of the skin having the means to covert the psychic into the somatic is central to psychoanalytic thought, usually conceived as a process of somatization (see La France, 2009) However, the idea of 'mental touch' that Connor (2003) develops is more than simply seeing the skin as a thinking, feeling organ (Anzieu, 1989). 'Mental touch' presented a breach to the self-enclosed subject, which revolved around the concept of sympathy or sympathetic action. The notion of sympathy which appeared in many discussions of the psychological and the action of the imagination was central to the writings of Daniel Hack Tuke (1872, 1892). This treatise, the *Dictionary of Psychological Medicine*, published in two volumes, was one in which the distinctions between the voluntary and the involuntary, the inside and the outside, the physical and the psychic, were redistributed in ways which did not separate the individual from milieu (see Blackman, 2001, for further discussion of Tuke's writing). What we see here is not the establishment of clearly defined boundaries or separations between objects, but the distribution of contrasts between the inner and the outer, the physical and the ethereal, the corporeal and the psychic, and the voluntary and involuntary, such that social influence was not simply about force or threat to the boundaries of the individual. Connor (2003) identifies many of the metaphors, particularly surrounding the skin, indicative of the connections between the human and the non-human which produced a very different way of knowing bodies, and particularly *feeling* bodies. Social influence was not about brute power or force, but conceived more as a lightness of touch, where 'everything is at once inside and outside everything else' (p. 281). These processes were such that they would touch and produce *affects* 'almost without touching' (p. 282). Tarde (1962: 2) equated this notion of touch to being seduced or hypnotized by a single point of light. The idea being that metamorphosis or conversion is incorporeal, immaterial and is brought about by speed and lightness. It appeals to a sentient body which is not dominated by reasoning and rationality.

The relationship of the passage and connection between the idea of 'mental touch' and notions of consciousness derived from studies of hypnotic trance and mediumistic phenomena will be studied in more detail in the next chapter. What it is important to highlight for the discussion in this chapter is how 'mental touch' co-existed along-side the imperative of separation or boundary, of holding apart and holding onto. It was this hierarchical view of humanity which was beginning to take shape within the social sciences, and particularly within social psychology. The concept of will or inhibition, and the explanatory structures which produced the meaning of these terms, radically restructured the field within which the very idea of social influence was to become conventionalized, regularized and to con-nect up a range of different sites and contexts. Smith (1992: 9) high-lights how the Latin root of inhibit – *habere* – means to 'hold in' and is oriented to processes which arrest, hinder and repress. This view of control, as being hinged on the capacity to hold in, to hold at bay, to hold apart and so forth, was one which was to tie particular notions of psychological control, to work being developed within physiology and neurophysiology.

As Smith (1992) cogently illustrates, a language and hierarchy of higher and lower functions, and of the control of the mind over the body and the brain over the nervous system, was to translate and connect up a range of diverse theories and ethical sites, including moral philosophy, pragmatic philosophy, psychical and hypnotic studies, and materialism, in relation to a very specific conception of the psychological subject. This normative conception of personhood was articulated through the relations between will–inhibition–instinct–habit and suggestion. The distinction between higher and lower was increasingly deployed to differentiate those who were considered more susceptible to social influence from those who were seen to exercise capacities which made them leaders rather than followers. The lines could be redrawn and refigured through the cultivation of *habit*. The social psychologist William McDougall (1910) argued that habit was one of the means to strengthen and modify the instincts, which were located within the realm of the automatic and instinctual, but could, through attention and volition, acquire secondary characteristics. These were considered forms of imitative action which produce and reproduce particular patternings and regularities. Repetition was an important element and technique of habit formation and would weave together the inherited and acquired within a complex system of combination, association and substitution. Thus what McDougall (1910: 253) called the 'sentiment for self-control' was considered one of the highest acquisitions of so-called civilized practices and was the soil or ground from which patterns of invention and imitation took shape or form (see Blackman, forthcoming).

Some took habit as an allegory for the optimism of self-transformation. This hope was combined with religious concepts of prudence, duty, self-denial, discipline and work enacted within techniques of repetition, combination and association. These had as their object and target the modification of the aspirations and habits of working-class men (Blackman, 2008c; Holyoake, 1906; Smiles, 1864). Inhibition or will became a major focus of attention and analysis across a range of different contexts, in which it 'returned in endless variations' (Smith, 1992: 69). In psychiatric contexts, the moral and physical were woven together in ways in which will or inhibition was seen to have been removed or destroyed, or simply to have little existed in the first instance. Notions of a moral insanity, one in which forms of insanity were considered more amenable to cure and transformation, particularly by what we might now understand as being more psychological or psychotherapeutic means, were increasingly contested and refigured (see Blackman, 2001). Drunkenness, insanity and hypnotic trance were connected up in novel ways where notions of suggestibility were translated and refigured through understandings which viewed all three states as being forms of 'mesmeric automatism' (Smith, 1992: 43) or ideomotor action. In other words, the will or inhibition was seen to have been removed, either through disease, the action of an intoxicating agent or the will of another. This reduced the actions of the person to a form of automatism. Thus sites of disorder, such as 'emotional outbursts, childish behaviour, drunkenness and dreams' (Smith, 1992: 41) were all linked through a concept of insanity which revolved around the suspension of will. What we can clearly see was the emergence and increasing unification of forms of 'social disorder' framed through a very particular ontology of personhood.

The habit–will–suggestion–instinct axis which shaped this ontology of personhood was one which conventionalized, regularized and institutionalized the concept of 'social influence'. Suggestibility was reconceived as social influence aligned to the suspension of will. The capacity to exercise control in the face of imitative processes was aligned with the will, volition, the brain and reason, with the spine, emotion, automatism and the involuntary providing the limits of the person's capacity to invent rather than imitate. This was the beginning of an attempt to differentate intentionalism from non-intentionalism. Thus a field of complex processes where distinctions between the inner and the outer, the corporeal and the incorporeal, the physical and the social, and the voluntary and the involuntary were considered undecidable and a source of wonder and perplexity were redistributed through a common nodal point. This allowed the demarcation of specializations and localizations to be accomplished. These differentiations were woven together in different ways across the social and physical sciences, where 'the term inhibition gave a physical appearance to the psychological will' (Smith, 1992: 168).

Smith's genealogy of the term 'inhibition' is connected more generally to a more Foucauldian-inspired history of 'what it has been to be human' (1992: 6). He explores through a detailed investigation and analysis of neurophysiology, neuroscience, experimental psychology and physiology the ways in which inhibition and will became increasingly integrated and linked through a developing science of control and communication, established in the neurosciences, in the twentieth century. This research and its connections across disciplinary specializations particularly focused upon what was known as the 'reflex model'. Mechanisms known to regulate the reflexes were viewed as analogous to those physical mechanisms seen to provide the basis of psychological or voluntary control. Habits were those acquired patterns of associations which could limit the scope of reflex actions (the automatic), and therefore initiate movement through particular patterns of reflection, association and habit. This was often equated with the building and cultivation of corresponding reflexes. This concern with the inhibitory action of the reflexes and the will was the focus of the experimental psychologist Wilhelm Wundt, who attempted to identify the localized centres through which the higher and lower functions were integrated and balanced – what he termed 'apperception'. However, for many authors the distinction between the simple and the complex was used as a means to differentiate so-called 'lower human types' from those who were seen to be able to develop complex associative patterns to regulate the reflexes. Thus sensation or feeling would not meet much antagonism or interference in certain 'types' of people, and would therefore become the basis of immediate, unmediated action. This achieves the kind of hierarchization of humanity which we meet head on in the work of Tarde, Le Bon and McDougall, through their engagement with evolutionary biology and psychology (see Blackman, 2007b).

### Slowing up of the Flow

The subtitle for this section is taken from a quote by the psychiatrist Eugen Bleuler (1923), who in the early twentieth century, along with Emil Kraepelin (1919), took the concept of inhibition as a central classificatory device in drawing up a nosology of mental disease and disorder. Although inhibition was viewed as imperative, and linked to the ordering of psychological and social processes, fixity and rigidity could also become a by-product of these active, reflective processes. Inhibition was linked to movement with one's ability to enact and move through a complex field of social processes, without being subject to immediate (and therefore past) sensations and feelings. However, inhibition could itself come to designate a state of stupor where the person would become 'too inhibited' and therefore unable to react anew each time to connections and associations between ideas. Smith (1992: 175) illustrates how these states of stupor were used to infer depressive illness, which was viewed as the opposite to the flight or movement characteristic of the normative psychological subject. Sedgwick (1994: 133) argues that in the twentieth century 'the assertion of will itself has come to appear addictive'. She charts a historical process within which the concept of will has become an explanation of many so-called addictive behaviours. This might include workaholism, shopaholism, and indeed any potential behaviour which results in habit formation. Within this process of co-constitution the relationships between will and habit are refigured such that 'too much free will' might result in forms of compulsion and addiction.

The foundational concept of social influence became distributed, regularized and actualized across the social and physical sciences. This concept attempted to weave together the paradox between movement and fixity, between flight and becoming arrested, and between the automatic and the habitual. This was accomplished through the combination, association and substitution of concepts from evolution-ary biology, neurophysiology, neuroscience and psychology, with con-cepts derived from studies of consciousness. As many have argued, this created the dualism between the individual and society, which has become antithetical in the claims of psychology to develop a convinc-ing theory of subjectivity (see Henriques et al., 1984). It is also one of the foundational dualisms that affect theorists are attempting to displace. The more relational ontologies emerging from this work are challenging the separations between nature and culture, the mind and the body, the corporeal and the textual, and the higher and the lower, which are naturalized within the concept of social influence. Although this work will be considered in more depth later in the book, I want to engage with related arguments which deal specifically with the discipline of psychology. Some strands of affect theory return to some of the concepts which circulated in the nineteenth century and which were largely negated or disqualified by the concept of 'social influ-ence'. The Belgian anthropologist Vincianne Despret (2004a, 2004b), who challenges the concept of 'social influence' in her work on affect and embodiment, terms this the excess, or remainder – what she calls the 'background versions' – which psychology reconfigured in its establishment of social influence as the object and subject matter of social psychology.

## The Problem of Personality: Personality and Social Psychology

When we turn to contemporary personality and social psychology we can see how the concept of social influence, which took form in the nineteenth and early twentieth centuries, has now become natural-ized and normalized. Indeed, it is presented as the object and subject matter of experimental social psychology's investigations and theori-zations. The concepts integral to social psychology also travel back and forth between personality psychology and other subdisciplines such as physiology and neuroscience. This is what Massumi (2002a) describes as a modulation or infolding which characterizes concepts as they move and are translated across specializations. For example, personality psychology, which has an established place in any under-graduate psychology canon, shares many affinities with social psy-chology (cf. Blackman, 2005). Although subject to deconstruction within critical and discursive psychology (Gough and McFadden, 2001; Potter and Wetherell, 1986), the problem of personality is framed through the identification, calculation and measurement of what are considered clearly defined, fixed traits or characteristics which are integral to a person's unique individuality. These traits are considered to be amenable to isolation and therefore to exist in some kind of pre-social and 'pure' form. They set the boundaries of the 'inner' self as distinct from the outer, usually conceived of as particular kinds of social influence processes. These assumed stable and consistent traits are measured through psychometric devices, and often associated with particular biological or genetic explanations.

We might refer to this essentialist way of approaching the problem of personality as individualistic, but also as characterizing a particular psychological version of selfhood (as distinct from a more sociological version). Indeed, Gough and McFadden (2001) use this distinction to delineate the practices of a *critical* social psychology, which would share a lineage and continuity with more sociological versions of selfhood. This is a self which 'is distributed across different social arenas rather than limited to a space within the person and is connected to multiple roles rather than one central core' (p. 79). The self has been decentred and distributed, destabilized, disrupted, fragmented and aligned with process, rather than the localization and organization of inner structural determinants. This is an attempt to move beyond the individual/social dualism, which within social psychology is usually characterized as the self-contained individual, distinct from a range of (social) influences, usually condensed into the role or action of 'the presence of others' (p. 100). Social influence conceived in this way is a negative force which arrests, thwarts, modifies or disturbs the action of the individual. I want to explore the oscillation between *psychological* and *sociological* versions of selfhood by exploring some of the arguments of sociologists who have engaged with the psychosocial significance of contemporary consumer culture. We will then track the ways in which the paradoxes and contradictions that their meeting produces are brought to the foreground when reflecting on how to understand and analyse more affective modalities of communication.

## The Problem of Personality: Personality and Consumer Culture

The problem of personality is not one which exclusively concerns the machinations and practices of social psychologists. Featherstone (1990) cogently shows how a new personality type, emerging in the course of the twentieth century, was directly aligned to the growth and expansion of consumer culture (Lasch, 1979; Susman, 1979, 1985). He suggests that it is one which solidifies the distinction between the inner and the outer body. Once this distinction is produced a number of competing ways of understanding personality and subject-formation take form. One example of this comes from contemporary makeover culture. Cressida Heyes (2007) has explored how the televisual make-over produces the outer body as ideally that which should reflect what is taken to be inside (see also Wegenstein and Ruck, 2011). She terms this a discourse of authenticity where what is important is that we subject ourselves in order to become *oneself*. Any transformation on the outer surface of the body must be read as revealing or disclosing the self that already existed prior to the makeover. This is one of the paradoxes of the makeover, and of the normalization processes that the fiction of autonomous selfhood creates; as she argues, 'the makeover must be authentically motivated' (Heyes, 2007: 24).

The decision to participate in the makeover must be experienced as a form of empowerment, a way of taking control of one's life, an act of agency or resistance to the cruel hand of fate, for example. As Heyes (2007: 25) goes on to argue:

> The claim that normalization is something done 'for oneself' is not entirely deceptive – especially in cultures where women's psychologi-cal suffering is trivialized, and where taking real risks to change is often viewed with fear and suspicion. Paradoxically, these ambivalences ('Will others approve?' 'Is this really who I am?' 'Shouldn't I just "put up with it"?'), when overcome, lend support to the claim that the prac-tices themselves are entirely self-motivated and primarily a matter of individual choice.

So although one might recognize the potential economic or career gains of changing one's appearance, (having a facelift for an older woman, for example, in the context of a work situation that might confront the woman with ageism), the choice or decision to undergo cosmetic surgery must be represented as one that is an expression of her own desire to be proactive, determined and courageous. Heyes presents a Foucauldian analysis of the televisual makeover and argues that this regime of normalization is associated with neoliber-alism. She suggests it fetishizes choice, control, autonomy and self-determination and downplays the influences that might impinge on a woman's decisions that might be more associated with norms of beauty, personhood and femininity, for example. It is more difficult to see the regulative aspects of neoliberalism because of the way our participation in social norms is constituted as the actions of freely choosing subjects.

However, this discourse of personality also co-exists with a com-peting discourse, one where what kind of personality one might con-ceivably be said to own (the body as propriety), or have, is displaced by a focus on how one can direct one's impressions, in order to 'compel people to like you' (Featherstone, 1990: 187). Individuals are also asked within consumer culture to 'become role players and self-consciously monitor their own performance. Appearance, gesture and bodily demeanour become taken as expressions of self, with bodily imperfections and lack of attention carrying penalties in everyday interactions' (Featherstone, 1990: 189). The self-conscious performance and staging of the self is one which would be aligned with a more sociological version of personality (as a set of roles or enacted performances). Erving Goffman (1959), for example, identified these distinctive communication processes as a mode of sympathetic action which doubles back on the individual, creating their sense of their own aliveness. Thus to be self-consciously aware of the impressions one is managing is not simply viewed as a measure of fakery or duplicity. Rather, it is a measure of the person's readiness to use their body as a vehicle for expressive information which sends additional information above and beyond the semantics of one's words.

The self-conscious will to manage one's impressions is countered by the ways in which one's 'bodily hexis' (Bourdieu, 1984) – one's ways of speaking, walking, eating, feeling, thinking and so forth – are acquired to the extent that they become non-conscious. Bourdieu suggests that they flow from the operation of a 'practical sense' enacted and embodied in motor co-ordinations and corporeal automatisms. We have here a distinction between a view of the self as performative marked by appearance and surface, and a view which explores the more engrained and durable ways in which the body is marked by habit. Habits are such that they mark the substance of the body and produce a sense of continuity or resistance to the capacity of subjects to be attentive and alert to the dynamics of self-management and impression formation. This distinction between surface and depth, appearance and personality or character is central to the formation of the kind of *self* or *personality type* which sociologists have tied to the advent of neoliberalism.

Cronin (2000) cogently shows how these distinctions are not resolved or settled, but rather frame the contradictions and ambiguities which face the consuming subject. This subject is obliged to choose (Rose, 1990) – what Cronin (2000: 279) terms 'compulsory individuality' – but simultaneously beset by the contradictions which govern this compulsion. She characterizes this as a dilemma between expressing one's *real* or *authentic* self, and the injunction to cast the self as a future project of becoming. Thus, 'the self that is' has to be managed alongside the 'self to be', which fuses what Cronin (2000: 277) terms 'seemingly contradictory temporalities'. Rather than opt for either of one or other of these versions of self-hood, she explores how people are differentially positioned in relation to these two dialogic discourses. What is interesting about her account is her argument that women are urged to resolve this tension through the exercising of their capacity for will or inhibition: 'doublings of images as the sites of both voluntarism and compulsion, and women as both agents and passive ciphers which emphasise will-power as the primary transformative force in an individual's life' (Cronin, 2000: 284).

We have encountered the formation of will as a particular nodal position for discussing the normative subject across the social and political sciences at the turn of the last century (Smith, 1992). The resolving of tensions and contradictions through the exercise of will or self-control is one which has a long lineage, but also is a concept which traversed and marked the bodies of those who were considered socially inferior. Cronin shows how the contrast between the 'self that is' and the 'self to be' travels across the circuits of consumer culture, and is condensed into the logos marketed by particular corporate industries to brand their products. Thus the Nike swoosh, with its concomitant invitation to 'just do it', conflates a number of ideals which mark the self that is and its future possibility. She shows how the will, as a space of pure voluntary (Sedgwick, 1994), produces 'discourses of anxiety' cross-cut by gendered dynamics of self-constitution.

I have also shown in previous work on magazine culture, that the kinds of dilemmas, tensions and contradictions which mark intimate relationships are shaped and channelled differentially through markedly different resolutions for heterosexual men and women. Thus for women, self-help, as a particular politics of self-transformation, emerges as a resolution which sits uneasily alongside the invitation to men to acquire knowledge about women's bodies, through particular practices of mastery or will, in order to bring about desired change in what is usually framed as sexual rather than emotional intimacy (Blackman, 2004, 2006, 2009). What is clear from both Cronin's discussion of 'compulsory individuality', and my own work on magazine culture, is that the distinctions between surface and depth and appearance and personality exist in dialogic relationships marked by tensions, dilemmas and contradictions. They are simply not either/or versions, but exist and circulate in complex ways which are reproduced and lived in particular social and psychic spaces.

However, there is also an excess which exists in the background of both of these concepts of personality. Susman (1979, 1985) describes how the idea of somebody having a 'good personality' is often linked to ideas of magnetism or charm – a kind of incorporeal aura which is co-present but not in any direct or obvious way. I will foreground this excess with a few examples which might resonate with readers on a more personal level. You might have had the experience of encountering somebody you either feel immediately repelled by or drawn to in ways you can't vocalize or recognize. You have a sense or feeling about them; you might describe this as being a particular 'vibe' or energy, a sense which is more incorporeal or even ethereal. This force might be likened to an intense erotic attraction if you feel moved towards them, or as being akin to an electric shock which would produce retreat, a movement away from. In either case there is something marking the encounter which with hindsight might be reorganized within a scrutiny of their and even your own bodily markers and non-verbal communication. You might assume these codes were not conscious, but through processes of reflection one can describe and identify them and achieve some kind of recognition.

The idea of charm or aura that Susman (1979, 1985) refers to when discussing some of the ways in which personality increasingly became framed in the twentieth century captures some of the excess or remainder I am pointing towards. Asendorf (1993: 158) refers to these formulations as based on an 'energy model' – a form of immaterial communication which might be better articulated by terms such as resonance, tuning and conducting. These all point towards and designate some kind of force which flows between human and non-human actors. These kinds of ideas about personality are those that are re-emerging within contemporary discussions of affect, disclosing perhaps an affective body or body-without-an-image (see Featherstone, 2010). These ideas were the central subject matter of sociology at the turn of the last century. Asendorf (1993: 168) reproduces a quote from the German sociologist, Georg Simmel, written in 1923, which designates this 'much more than' when thinking about the limits and boundaries of the human and consciousness.

> that the human individual does not, so to speak, come to an end where our senses of sight and touch define his boundaries; that is much more the case that there is a sphere beyond this, whether one conceives it as substantial or as a kind of radiance, whose extension exceeds all hypothetical effort and which belongs to his person like the visible and palpable to his

body ... the antipathies and sympathies between people not at all subject to rationalization, the frequent feeling of being captivated to a certain extent by the mere existence of a person, and much more.

Simmel was not alone in his musings on the immaterial and ethereal, and shared a fascination with matters psychic and spiritual with many other philosophers and sociologists. These include Henry Bergson, William James and Gabriel Tarde, who were all members of the Institute of Psychical Research in Paris, established in 1900. Bergson (1920) published a series of lectures in a book translated into English with the title *Mind-Energy*. The French title is *L'Energie Spirituelle* – 'spiritual energy'. The lecture published as Chapter 3 in the book, 'Phantasms of the Living and Psychical Research', was given as a presidential address by Bergson to the Society for Psychical Research in London on 28 May 1913. In it the problem of personality was framed at this milieu through concepts derived from spiritualism, psychic phenomena and studies of hypnotic trance. The more suggestive approach to communication that underpins 'aura' or charm is linked to nineteenth-century concepts of 'mental touch', which we will explore in the next chapter. 'Mental touch' was conceived as a kind of psychic energy which flowed through and between bodies where bodies acted much like lightening conductors or rods. They might resonate, attune or repel, depending on the forces of intensity and sensation. It opens up the problem of personality precisely to the importance of developing what Despret (2004a: 125) terms a 'theory of affected and affecting bodies'.

Despret (2004a) argues, along with Bruno Latour (2004), that William James was a philosopher of consciousness, who provides a theory of the capacity to affect and be affected (what Despret terms 'being-with'), which refuses any idea of pre-existing entities that somehow influence each other. This is a direct critique of the foundational concept of social influence as it took form within the psychological sciences. The concept of being-with emphasizes a relationality based upon practices of co-existence which are better described through concepts such as resonance, attunement and association. Despret's focus is social psychological forms of experimentation and the limits of science's capacity to reformulate propositions which might allow 'social influence' to be requalified. The work she advocates opens up the staging of experimentation to elements of perplexity and wonder. It also brings to light the limits of science's capacity to reformulate propositions which might allow this space of ambiguity to emerge and be qualified. Her key focus is on experiments, such as those of Hans the horse (see Blackman, 2008a; Despret, 2004a), which present a puzzling challenge for psychological models of emotion and influence. She argues that what enjoins human to non-human, human to human and so forth, is a realm of affect, which refigures and articulates suggestibility in new and interesting ways. The concept of articulation is not about reduction or simplification, but rather is a strategy which attempts to multiply possible versions through the development of propositions which are 'risky' (see Stengers, 1997). These are questions or statements that induce modifications, which engender 'more interesting, more complex, [and] more wordy' relations of co-existence and relationality (Despret, 2004b: 26). The focus is shifted to experimentation and how to invent new forms of experimentation that enable suggestion to emerge and become enacted as a more interesting phenomena (see Chapter 6).

## Conclusion

The revitalization of suggestion and its ambivalent duality is one that directs our attention to the importance of experimentation, technicity and milieu in understanding what suggestion could be and has been allowed to become. Suggestion is taken to refer to a diverse range of actions registered and transmitted between bodies that cross the divide between the somatic and the psychological. These might include feelings, instincts, memories, the senses, and motor automatisms, for example. As Evans (1995) points out, in *Group Psychoanalysis and the Analysis of the Ego*, Freud (1922: 90) made the following remarks concerning the importance of considering suggestion technically:

> the word is acquiring a more and more extended use and a looser and looser meaning, and will soon come to designate any sort of influence whatever, just as it does in English, where 'to suggest' and 'suggestion' correspond to our *nahelegen* and *Anregung*.

Although Freud was later to abandon suggestion in his understandings of the topology of the unconscious, the contradictions and hesitations regarding the status of suggestion can be found throughout his writings (see Campbell, 2009; Evans, 1995). These have been developed in the writings of Francis Roustang (1980) who has convincingly revisited suggestion in his own practice and theories of unconscious processes. He has repositioned suggestion as a potentiality rather than a fixed psychological capacity, which we might understand as a personality characteristic, for example. The latter echoes one of the predominant ways in which suggestion has been recast within contemporary psychology, as a measure or index of a particular person's susceptibility to hypnotic induction, rather than as a potentiality distributed across a range of actors and agencies, human and non-human (see Blackman, 2010a). I hope that the complex place of the psychological sciences within contemporary discussions of affect makes visible how the problem of personality, with all the contradictions and ambivalences that this engenders, is not simply over. This will be the subject of the next chapter and will be revisited throughout the book.

## Notes

1 Moscovici (1985) claims that the emergence and establishment of mass psychology in the nineteenth century addressed a reality which other sciences have failed to register or ignored, despite what he sees as the overwhelming evidence of social influence processes producing the kinds of 'total control' seen in the dictatorships of Castro, Mussolini and Mao, and through the workings of media technologies such as television, newspapers and radio which promulgate thoughts and feelings through a kind of 'mental touch'.

2 Many authors have pointed to the apparent similarities between the concepts that Tarde developed in his theories of mass communication and those popularized by Le Bon (Apfelbaum and McGuires, 1986; Barrows, 1981; Moscovici, 1985). Although as Barrows (1981: 182) highlights, 'Tarde and Le Bon disagreed over the increasing salience and significance of the crowd with Tarde re-figuring the crowd as a series of publics in light of new communication technologies such as the newspaper, telegraph, railroad etc.'.

# 3

## Mental Touch: Media Technologies and the Problem of Telepathy

There is now an expanding literature within the humanities which has begun to re-examine concepts of 'mental touch', which originated within nineteenth- and twentieth-century psychic research. Some of this work has been developed in the context of work on the senses (Howes, 2009), media technologies (Andriopoulos, 2005, 2008; Kittler, 1990; Sconce, 2000), and debates on affect and subjectivity (Blackman, 2010a; Campbell and Pile, 2010; Gibbs, 2008). This work recognizes that the management of attention, perception and sensation is important to understand our relationships to consumer culture, screen and televisual culture, digital technologies and so forth. Some of this work has begun to revitalize the idea of a 'sixth sense' (Howes, 2009) and to consider its usefulness in inventing and imagining our conjoining with the other, human and non-human. This work opens up considerations of affect and embodiment to technical mediation and how to conceive of the body's potential for mediation. This chapter's focus on 'mental touch' retains a focus on the psyche, or on concepts of the psychical which open up consideration of trans-subjective processes of mediation. These processes cannot be mapped onto a Freudian unconscious, nor contained by a human psychological subject (see also Chapter 6).

This chapter will consider how this work might contribute to the subject of affect, particularly in relation to arguments that suggest that affect does not need a subject to register. We will explore the implications of situating the ontologies of the subject enacted within some of this work within the historical antecedents and conditions which make them possible. This will entail an engagement with the kinds of fantasies enacted by particular understandings of mental touch in the nineteenth and early twentieth centuries, and their revitalization in contemporary understandings of affect. What these reflections will reveal is an unresolved paradox or dilemma at the heart of how we communicate.

Many authors have pointed towards the importance of nineteenth-century understandings of spiritualism for exploring any such dilemmas or paradoxes. In a consideration of the value of John Durham Peters's (1999) important book, *Speaking into the Air*, Bill Schwarz (2006) draws attention to two very different models of communication which have shaped contemporary media and cultural studies. Perhaps the term 'models' is rather misleading, however, as these are not simply differing conceptual positions, but rather radically different ways of specifying the links and boundaries between individuals, groups, technologies and so forth. These see communication either as an internal, solipsistic activity (bounded by failure), or as an activity that thoroughly collapses the boundaries between individuals. Schwarz (2006: 27) ties these responses, following the genealogical work of Peters, to the historical emergence and relatedness of two terms, solipsism and telepathy. Telepathy and related ideas of mental touch will be the subject of this chapter.

One variant of work which took seriously the idea of telepathic connections between people, characterized by notions of mental touch and the spiritual telegraph, was mass psychology. This specialization was intimately concerned with the problem of communication, and particularly with what Ruth Leys (2000) has termed the 'problem of mimetic desire'. Peters (1999) suggests that this more mimetic conception of communication assumed that affects, feelings, beliefs and so forth would spread through a kind of bodily affectivity. Contagious approaches to communication emphasized the ability of individuals to influence each other through 'sympathetic transmission' (p. 78). This notion of sympathy was derived from a more energetic mode of relating, which was not cognitive, semiotic or performative, but rather enacted through the mechanism of vibrational energy. One key aspect of this mode of relating was its deep disrespect for the separation of the individual from nature and society, and for the notion of strict boundaries between the 'me' and the 'not-me'. As I have already stated, this conception of communication also derived in part from studies of hypnotic trance, where key turn-of-the-century philosophers and social scientists, including William James and Gabriel Tarde (see Blackman, 2008b), foregrounded studies of ordinary suggestibility as a key foundation for studying sociality itself (Blackman, 2007b; Borch, 2005, 2006; Orr, 2006; Tarde, 1962). Although suggestibility and ideas of sympathetic (energetic) transmission were to be radically reconfigured, their haunting legacy lingers on. As Peters (1999: 94) argues in relation to the emergence and framing of early media studies and its borrowing from nineteenth-century mass psychology:

> Mesmerism's afterlife helped shape the understanding of mass media in the twentieth century as agents of mass control and persuasion that

somehow, via their repetition, ubiquity, and subliminally iniquitous techniques, bypassed the vigilant conscience of citizens and directly accessed the archaic phobias (or ignorance and sloth) of the beast within.

This is echoed by William Connolly's (2002) reframing of brain–body–culture relationships. He foregrounds the role of non-conscious perception and affect, which he argues is 'organized and deployed collectively' within media technologies and practices of everyday life (p. 20). He contrasts this with what is considered the object of much cultural theory – the normativity of deliberation or the interpretive resources of audiences. What has entered media and cultural theory, then, is a notion of suggestion as abnormal suggestibility, likening those who succumb to media or cultural influence as dumb, stupid or over-sensitive (cf. Blackman and Walkerdine, 2001): 'Many of them treat subliminal influences as if they were reducible to modes of manipulation or behavioural management to be overcome in a rational or deliberative society' (Connolly, 2002: 17).

Leys (2000) suggests that this is what was historically viewed as most threatening about mimesis: its insistence that the idea of the individual as having strict, unified boundaries, maintained through the act of will or habit, is undermined by the profound and ubiquitous action of non-conscious perception and bodily affectivity (cf. Connolly, 2002). The lack of fixed boundaries, and the inherent plasticity ascribed to the human subject, increasingly became a source of danger, threat and fear, and as Leys (1993: 281) argues, 'at a certain stage in the development of the social sciences there arose a fundamental methodological requirement to substitute for a self defined as continually permeable to the influence of others a self conceived as having fixed boundaries and a stable centre'.

### The One and the Many

I have argued throughout this book so far that what became known as the 'problem of personality' is associated with some of the paradoxes and contradictions which emerged within this context. The processual accounts of perception and attention developed within the writings of William James, for example, were part of these circuits of debate and contestation. Like his contemporaries, James was interested in events within populations that foregrounded the question of transmission or contagion. How is it that certain fashions, fads and trends seemed to spread throughout populations with a rapidity that seems to defy the action of logic or rationality? How do certain fears and forms of hysteria, mania and emotion spread such that they appear to bypass rationality and reason? What causes individuals in groups to behave in ways that might perplex, bemuse or undermine their sense of themselves as subjects in other contexts? What enables certain individuals to command the obedience, compliance, love and adoration of others, such that they would be exalted and revered as charismatic leaders? All of these questions provided the backdrop to the shaping of the various responses that began to emerge across and between the disciplines of social psychology, psychology, media studies and sociology at their inception.

What lay in the background to these concerns, and the concepts that guided their explanations, was both a fascination *with* and attempt to *know* and *understand* experiences that were ephemeral, 'invisible' and marked by a dissolution of the boundaries between self and other, inside and outside, and human and non-human. Psychologists, philosophers and sociologists were all drawn to phenomena that were little understood, but that seemed to contain within their mysterious workings possible answers to the riddle of what makes us both 'one and many'. Studies of hypnotic trance, psychical research, spiritualism, psychotic delusions and hallucinations, and even studies of insect societies such as wasps and hornets, were all seen to contain possible clues that would reveal the enigma of how to specify the basis of (human) communication.

As we saw in the last chapter, James's formulations were indebted to the work of the subliminal psychologist Boris Sidis (1898). The formulations of suggestion and suggestibility which Sidis developed were based on a subliminal view of consciousness, or what is also often described as 'double consciousness' (see Chapter 7). The self was seen to be made up of a primary and secondary self which were in constant passage or transit. Different practices, such as hypnotic trance, sleep, psychic practices such as crystal-gazing, shell hearing, automatic writing, telepathy and mediumship, could mediate this passage in different ways, making visible the imperceptible forces seen to compel people to certain actions and behaviour. The capacity of an idea or object to become part of a stream of consciousness, beyond the threshold of conscious awareness, was, for Sidis (1898: 16), something that 'never leaves us; it is always present in us'. 'Not sociality, not rationality, but suggestibility is what characterizes the average specimen of humanity, for *man* [*sic*] *is a suggestible animal*' (p. 17; emphasis in original).

James was also interested in homeopathy, automatic writing, mediumship and altered states of consciousness. Eugene Taylor (2002) considers some of James's diverse interests in the introduction to

James's book, *Varieties of Religious Experience,* first published in 1902. James's home life had a close proximity to the very experiences and phenomena that formed the subject matter of his later psychological reflections. His Father, Henry James, was interested in Swedenborg spirituality and one of his neighbours was Clement John Wilkinson, who translated Swedenborg's scientific and medical writings. Taylor (2002: xxii) recounts a breakdown that William James was said to have experienced in 1869 which plunged him 'into a near-suicidal depression'. This experience pre-empted his ongoing interest in 'the penumbra or margin of the normal everyday waking state' (Taylor, 2002: xxxi). He was interested in finding a principle of unity that would allow these anomalous experiences to be explained, including 'unconscious cerebration, dreams, hypnotism, hysteria, inspirations of genius, the willing game, planchette, crystal-gazing, hallucinatory voices, apparitions of the dying, medium-trances, demoniacal possession, clairvoyance [and] thought transference' (Murphy and Ballou, 1960: 219). His interest in religion and mystical experiences, as well as his interest in hypnosis, psychic research and psychopathology, led him to develop a 'dynamic psychology of the subliminal' (Taylor, 2002: xxxvi). He was influenced by subliminal psychologists such as Binet, Janet, Breuer and Myers, and although he has often been aligned to process philosophies, was equally interested in the problem of unity. Rather than draw a clear bifurcation between the one and the many, or even between perception and feeling, he was interested in synthesis. As he asks: 'do the parts of the universe "hang together", instead of being like detached grains of sand?' (James, 1902: 28). The focus on unity did not presuppose static psychological states or capacities, and importantly was not achieved cognitively. He likened synthesis to the experience of conversion which 'bursts through all barriers and sweeps in like a sudden flood' (James, 1902: 170). Conversion might be subconscious, unconscious or volitional, likened to different modes of attention, the experience of which often feels like a possession or a miracle.

Studies of telepathy and mediumship also became an important part of James's psychological theorizing (see Gitre, 2006; Murphy and Ballou, 1960). We will consider the relationship between James's writings and the theories of the subliminal psychologist, Frederick Myers (1903) in Chapter 7. This work will be discussed in relation to the continuities between subliminal psychology and the concepts of the double brain and bicameral consciousness. What it is important to state here is that James saw telepathy and hypnotic suggestion as subliminal thresholds aligned to the cosmic and the spiritual. The articulation of the one and the many took place within this context and shows the close relationship between mysticism and what was later to become 'the non-mystical theory of hypnotic suggestion' (Murphy and Ballou, 1960: 28). Gitre (2006: 3), in an important commentary on the centrality of psychical research to James's theories, suggests that what we find is an 'evolving, complex and contradictory cosmological realism', rather than a straightforward social constructionist or anti-foundationalist epistemology.

I argued in the previous chapter that the problem of 'the one and the many' was increasingly mapped onto differentiations made between the civilized and the primitive, the superior and the inferior, the simple and the complex, and the impulsive and the environmental. Thus, particular passions, affects and forms of psychopathology were distributed across populations such that they became attached or fixed to particular bodies and cultural objects. Women, the working classes, colonial subjects and children were all viewed as more suggestible and amenable to processes of social influence, which might result in what Guattari (1984: 36) has termed 'subjected groups'. This term was used by Guattari to describe the kinds of solidification of affect, ideas and belief which characterized individuals who were seen to become fixated in relation to a particular institutional object or figure. In other words, he reworked the very ideas of mass psychology and crowd psychology explored in the previous chapter, which had dominated the landscape of fear and anxiety at the turn of the last century. Guattari's (1995) work on subjectivity is interesting for some of the arguments that will be put forward in this chapter. As we saw in Chapter 1, the kinds of ontologies of subjectivity enacted within the psychological sciences are being overlaid by relational and quantum ontologies characteristic of work within affect studies. Rather than instigate a different ontology characteristic of the approach to the psyche and the psychological I am developing in this book, I rather seek to explore what different modelizations of subjectivity make possible in our theorizing.

The concept of modelization comes from the work of Guattari (1995) in *Chaosmosis: an Ethico-aesthetic Paradigm*. Guattari does not abandon the concept of subjectivity in this work, but does acknowledge the role knowledge practices such as psychology and psychoanalysis have played in producing normative ontologies of personhood. Guattari develops what he terms a 'transversalist conception of subjectivity' (1995: 4), which explores the role of material and *immaterial* processes within practices of subjectification. The concept of transversality produces what Guattari terms a machinic approach to subjectivity which removes the concept from psychological conceptions of personhood. Instead, it is recognized that the subject is always more than human and more than one. Therefore, the psyche cannot be reduced to conceptions of the unconscious housed within a human mind, nor to language or signification (see Chapter 6). The *imm*ate-rial in Guattari's work refers to those pre-verbal intensities that we might now associate with affect. Indeed, Guattari develops his approach to trans-subjectivity from work on infant psychology (Stern, 1985) which he argued emphasizes the importance of the ethology or ecol-ogy in the production of affective intensities and transfers. This approach which Guattari (1995) developed was enacted in La Borde clinic,[1] where he attempted to create 'collective subjectivation' in his work with people living with mental health difficulties (p. 6). The pos-sible creative invention of these practices was based on the assumption that they might extend and create modes of individuation based on process and the singularity of event (see p. 7).

The important insight that I take from this work is the need to approach conceptions of subjectivity and particularly the unconscious as *inventions*, and to think about these inventions ecologically. In other words, rather than replace one ontology with another – relational with quantum, for example – I seek to explore what conceptions of 'mental touch' allow us to think and do in relation to both affect and the problem of personality. I also take seriously Guattari's under-explored argument that most relations of discursivity rely upon a 'pathic' ver-sion of subjectivity (1995: 26) – that is, on conceptions of subjectifica-tion which are implicitly reliant upon hypnotic conceptions of the subject, even if they remain unexplored and underdeveloped. This is a similar argument to that made by Andriopoulos (2008) in relation to contemporary social theory's reliance upon hypnotic conceptions of power, which he equates to post-hypnotic suggestion. He particu-larly cites the work of Judith Butler and Michel Foucault as exemplary in this respect. I also argue that we need to examine some of the minimal theories of subjectivity that are implied within work on affect, even when at times it is presumed that affect does not need a subject to register (see Chapter 1). In this chapter we will start to explore 'mental touch' as it became enacted particularly in relation to the rise of new communication technologies at the turn of the last century. This will allow a consideration of how an engagement with a more (tele)pathic conception of subjectivity might extend and con-tribute to debates on affect and the problem of personality.

## Communication as the Communion of Souls

Telepathy was clearly a contradictory creature. Sometimes imagined as the path towards spiritual or earthly utopia through shared sensations, it could also be viewed as the mechanism behind a collapsing of all thought in the primitive, riotous, unthinking crowd mind. (Thurschwell, 2009: 194)

In the previous chapter we explored how suggestibility, as a mode of communication, was not based in the cogito, but *felt* through a body which might best be described as more processual. Spaces between bodies were not marked by gaps or intervals (mapped in terms of linear, spatialized time), but passages through which particular communication processes would flow. The individual was not bounded, but opened out to others through a more porous and permeable membrane, which might resonate or attune through a coming together of intensities. This description of communication, recast as psychic energy, and located within multi-directional movements of communication, is one which was central to more spiritual conceptions of communion in the nineteenth century (Porter, 2005). Peters's (1999: 1) illuminating genealogy of the modern idea of communication, or at least its dream of being about the 'mutual communion of souls', is one which draws its foundational status from nineteenth-century spiritualism. He argues that this tradition took ideal communication as happening best 'when bodies and language are transcended in favor of more ethereal modes of thought transference' (1999: 64). The idea of immaterial contact, which characterized the investigation and enactment of psychic processes, is one which as Peters argues, is also disembodied. That is, immaterial contact, as it came to be imagined within discussions of telepathy for example, was framed as a form of dematerialized transmission of communication, based often on fantasies of 'complete sympathetic union with the *mind* of another' (Thurschwell, 2009: 183; emphasis added).

This fantasy of melding is one that he suggests reappears in contemporary discussions of virtuality and cyberspace, where cyberspace, and the more utopian dream of leaving the 'meat' or 'flesh' behind, borrows 'from the mother lode of angelology' (Peters, 1999: 75). The angel, much like Haraway's (1991) cyborg, is a hybrid figure who fuses the psychical and the physical and the divine and the human. The angel represents a dematerialized version of communication where communication is not located within language and cognition, nor requires proximity of bodies for transmission to take place. Drawing from more telepathic conceptions of communication, transmission was seen to work 'at a distance', through light, sound, heat, gravity, magnetism, odours and affections, through a kind of 'sympathetic transmission' (Peters, 1999: 78). David Howes (2009) argues

that the concept of sympathy was also related to a particular conception of the imagination related to telepathic conceptions of communication. We encountered this notion of sympathy in the previous
chapter, explored in relation to Connor's (2003) discussion of 'maternal impressions'. This concept related to new conceptualizations of
the imagination in the nineteenth century aligned with the emotional, the psychic and the affective (Moscovici, 1985).

Peters (1999) charts the genealogy of telepathic conceptions of
communication through its inception in the work of Franz Anton
Mesmer (1734–1815). Mesmer was credited with promulgating the
idea of animal magnetism. Magnetism was seen by Mesmer as referring to a force which flowed within and between individual subjects.
This imponderable fluid could arrest within a body causing disease
and could flow between actors through a force which became
known as the *ether*. Although Mesmerism was wildly popular,
Mesmer and his practices became the subject of a Royal Commission
investigation in Paris in 1784, in relation to possible fraud (see
Riskin, 2009). The results of the investigation were interesting.
Accusations of fraud remained unfounded; what was challenged was
the idea of a *fluid* flowing within and between subjects. Instead, the
effects of mesmerism were attributed to the principle and faculty of
the imagination. Its mysterious and immaterial workings were
aligned to a kind of placebo effect (Riskin, 2009).

Although this seemed to resolve the matter, as Riskin cogently
argues, the imagination was 'a subject of profound ambivalence'
(2009: 130). Imagination took up a place within late eighteenth- and
early nineteenth-century thinking, which resonates with the profound ambiguity that describes experiences such as suggestion, voice
hearing, attention and related processes which I have termed 'threshold phenomena'. These phenomena disclose the subject's affective
openness but also articulate cultural fears and fantasies about the
danger of possession or automatism. In a similar way, imagination
was seen to reveal the possibility that 'a body exercises an action
upon another without an intermediary being' (Riskin, 2009: 138).
The body's capacity for mediation through this faculty was also seen
to offer up the potential danger that the subject would 'turn
inwards', 'away from the sensory channels that opened it to its sur-
roundings' (p. 131). This capacity was therefore seen to make possible both the possibility of manipulation by another (later to be
reconfigured through crowd psychology), and for the subject to lose
contact with their milieu, becoming subject to imagination misleading the senses. Thus, the problem of personality was articulated in

relation to this capacity, which was opened up by the investigation of Mesmerism within this context.

Peters utilizes a historical account of the emergence of dynamic psychiatry, written by Ellenberger (1970), to discredit Mesmerism and to close down an engagement with the principle of the imagination which replaced this view. He subscribes to a particular logic of scientific invention and discovery, by reproducing the view of Ellenberger (1970) that Mesmerism was superseded by the birth of psychoanalysis. Ellenberger's treatise is indeed titled *The Discovery of the Unconscious* and charts the unfolding of a psychic space, now recognized as a space of the unconscious or intrapsychic, as being the modern forerunner of old abandoned ideas, such as the idea of hypnotic suggestibility. Ellenberger (1970: 69) recasts Mesmer as an odd, eccentric fellow whose scientific investment in the idea of magnetism could be linked to his own morbid sensibilities, or psychopathological personality:[2] 'The frustrations of his personal magnetism were perhaps subordinated to certain more basic psychopathological features; a morbid oversensitivity, moodiness, and alternating elations and depressions. During his periods of success he showed a restless, almost hypomanic, activity.'

This is a familiar tenet underpinning historiographies of science. These kinds of historiography present scientific psychiatry as a modern enterprise. It is presumed that with the benefit of hindsight, and the application of the scientific method, the past can now be reinterpreted in light of truth and rational understanding. Ellenberger (1970: 69) repeats this logic by considering Mesmer's doctrine as containing 'the seeds of several basic tenets of modern psychiatry'. The logic of her treatise follows a similar direction to the fate of suggestion within the psychological sciences. As we saw in the previous chapter, suggestibility was refigured as a problem of will rather than being viewed as a normative capacity of personhood. In a similar manner Ellenberger refigures some of the concepts central to Mesmerism, spiritualism and studies of hypnosis. Thus, the idea of rapport (a tuning in with the patient), hypnotic suggestibility, and spiritualist practices for investigating psychic phenomenon, such as automatic writing, crystal ball gazing and so forth, all became redistributed in relation to a notion of the unconscious. She argues that a concept of mental energy replaces (or supersedes) magnetism and suggestibility is replaced by the psychotherapeutic notion of transference. Hypnotic suggestibility is recast as a problem of will. Experimental studies of hypnosis within psychology have continued this transformation into the twentieth century. The problem of feigning, duplicity and compliance have become the central circulating terms within this new assemblage (see Overholser, 1985)[3]. Similarly, some of the practices central to nineteenth-century spiritualist traditions were seen to be modified by psychotherapeutic practices and used as techniques for analysing unconscious psychic processes. Ellenberger concludes that hypnosis is effectively abandoned and repudiated, with the birth or discovery of the unconscious flourishing between 1906 and 1910.

Practices such as hypnotic suggestion have a much more complex history and have not simply been superseded, either within the psychological sciences or psychoanalysis (Blackman, 2010a; Campbell and Pile, 2010; Chertok and Stengers, 1992). Indeed, Ellenberger is mindful of the multiplication of ideas of suggestibility that circulated within understandings of mass psychology at the turn of the last century. She also charts the modulation of these ideas in the writings of key nineteenth-century philosophers such as Henri Bergson in his published works, *Essai sur les données immediates de la conscience* (1889), and the study of mysticism in his final book, *The Two Sources of Moral and Religion* (1935/1977). Similarly, Peters (1999: 93) also recognizes that although Mesmerism seems to have had a short shelf life, it still circulates within understandings of mass psychology, and charts the strong influence of hypnosis on some of the theorists of the psychology of the crowd and the public in the work of Le Bon, Tarde and Freud (see Chapter 2).

Peters (1999) also reproduces a similar logic of invention and discovery in his dismissal of the grounds and validity of ideas of suggestibility. He does, however, provide a much more interesting account of the birth of modern communication technologies in relation to related telepathic modalities of communication. Many authors have highlighted the close relationship between the emergence of new communication technologies in the nineteenth and early twentieth centuries with understandings of communication derived from telepathy and psychic research more generally (Andriopoulos, 2005, 2008; Kittler, 1990; Sconce, 2000). That is, despite the discreditation of Mesmerism, the attribution of imagination as a possible capacity for explaining so-called Mesmeric effects is one that endured. It was articulated in a new way in relation to emerging media technologies in the nineteenth century and their intimate connection to telepathic conceptions of the subject (see Andriopoulos, 2008; Sconce, 2000). Telepathy was seen to be a mode of communication which could not be aligned to a specific sense organ. As David Howes (2009) argues, we often think of the sensorium within Western cultures as being made up of five senses (vision, hearing, smell, taste and touch) which are aligned to the five sense organs (the eyes, ears, nose, mouth and skin). Telepathy, or what Howes also subsumes under the concept of a sixth sense, is interesting because there is no corresponding sense organ. Indeed, telepathy is more akin to a 'psychic' 'perception of one form or another' (Howes, 2009: 6); this was often equated to the idea of 'acting at a distance', where processes of transmission which did not require physical proximity were seen to result in some kind of (psychic) modification.

Communication technologies, such as radio, the telegraph, cinema and the telephone, were all seen to transmit ideas, beliefs and emotions through these immaterial forms of contact which were equated to a form of 'mental touch' (see also Sconce, 2000). Peters argues that telepathy represented an interesting cross-fertilization and reworking of older ideas of Mesmerism. He charts this cross-fertilization through the ways in which the idea of the ether carrying thought, gesture and image in immaterial and intangible ways, became a central metaphor for exploring the significance and reception of radio broadcasting in the early twentieth century. The 'wireless rays of radio' were equated to the ether and its ability to *touch* people across distances (Peters, 1999: 108). Similarly, the overcoming of space and distance in the medium of the telegraph, and the overcoming of time, and even death and loss, in the medium of photography and cinema, allowed these technologies, he argues, to embody our dream of immaterial contact. This dream would simultaneously assuage our anguish and fear that distance, death and loss are what indeed characterize our finitude.

He argues that the chasm or gap which opens up between this interchange of hope and anguish are what circumscribe the dream of modern communication. It is in this chasm or gap that he locates all the mishaps, hesitancies and misunderstandings which characterize communication as an embodied process. He argues that the solution to these gaps or misunderstandings is often better communication, conceived as dialogue, where one listens and applies practices of empathy to the voice of the speaker. The idea of successful communication as dialogue is one which, Peters argues, falls woefully short of what it actually means to communicate. Communication is not about connection (a meeting of minds), as one's words are always polysemic and slippery. 'There are no sure signs in communication, only hints and guesses. Our interaction will never be a meeting of *cogitos* but at its best may be a dance in which we sometimes touch' (Peters, 1999: 268).

## The Body of Spiritualism

We can see in the above discussion of communication some of the fantasies and desires which are articulated through concepts of mental touch and the replacement of an imagined dematerialized form of communication with the importance of voice, presence and dialogue. In other words, what is effectively cast as a disembodied form of communication is replaced with an understanding of communication as an embodied, enacted process. This is about touch as the seeking of a physical, material presence, where the notion of touch as a mode of sympathetic action is recast as a kinaesthetic sense. Peters (1999: 270) argues that the sensient body has a bodiliness, a materiality which cannot be transmitted or transported in a more immaterial sense:

> People who care for each other will seek each other's presence. ... And the bodies of friends and kin matter deeply. The face, voice, and skin have a contagious charisma. There is nothing so electric or unmanageable as touch: we feast our eyes on each other, kiss, shake hands, and embrace.

He argues that presence, rather than action at a distance, is what matters, and literally that bodily matter and its proximity to others becomes 'the closest thing there is to a guarantee of a bridge across the chasm' (p. 271). Although the replacing of one mode of perception with another – mental touch with physical touch – seems to settle the problem of how to attempt to achieve successful communication, concepts of mental touch and suggestibility have not simply been superseded and left behind. As we saw in Chapter 1, and throughout the book so far, the subject of affect returns to modalities of communication which cannot be contained by concepts of physicality, unless we are willing to conceive of physicality or materiality as having its own lively dynamism which cannot be contained by the communicating self-present subject.

Rather than adjudicate between two rather different conceptions of touch, I will explore later in the chapter how these concepts return and have been reinvented in work on televisual affect, for example. This work emphasizes the concept of 'action at a distance' embodied in mesmerist and telepathic conceptions of communication, and explores the flow of sensation, intensities and energies through the concept of the flow or transmission made possible by technological mediums such as television and film, for example. This work emphasizes movement between self and other, human and non-human, inside and outside as being central to understanding our consumption of media forms. This problematizes the forms of dichotomous thinking that have characterized some work within media studies, which has framed the audience and the medium, subject and object as being separate entities which are subject to interaction effects. It is the ideas of separation and interaction that are potentially displaced within reformulations of mental touch within media and cultural studies. This directs our attention to the potential value of the modelization of subjectivity enacted within this work as being central to approaching the problem of mediated communication. In the next section we will start to explore this in relation to the concept of the *flow* and the ontologies of personhood that were becoming instantiated, particularly in relation to emergent communication technologies of the time.

## Movement and Flow

In *Batteries of Life: On the History of Things and Their Perception in Modernity*, Asendorf (1993) argues that a particular ontology of movement and affect has become one of the defining features of modernity. He links this new ontology to the rise of communication technologies in the nineteenth century, 'which infinitely increase the capacities of people and information to move' (p. 57). He connects this emergent relational ontology with new vitalist conceptions of movement. These ontologies circulated terms which foreground sensation, mobility, motion and discontinuity and create 'continuity, habit and sequence' as markers of social and individual pathology (p. 5). This ontology was connected across a number of contexts which included city planning, literature, philosophical theorizing and under-standings of nervous life. Asendorf describes how the city planning conceived by Haussmann in Paris, and particularly the construction of the boulevard, enabled or engendered the movement of the pedestrian. He also cites the literature of Baudelaire, and his position of the *flâneur*, as being one who circulates within the crowd, but also remains apart from it. The privileged position is the *flâneur* – the one who can move, observe and set himself apart. He 'exists only in his distance from it – in that he observes, reflects on the accidental con-stellations in the crowd, preserves his seclusion ... All of this demands a mobile psychic disposition, the preconditions of which are the love of masks and disguises, ... the hate of home and the pas-sion of travel' (p. 63). Fixity and habit became the inferior psychic disposition attributed to the masses. Asendorf also cites the vitalist philosophies of Bergson, Simmel and Dilthey as being based in a set of contrasts between habit and duration, custom and movement, and conformity and transience. The capacity to be open to continual change is what defines aliveness and life.

Asendorf (1993) argues that the connection, combination and recombination of this new relational ontology drew life from concepts and metaphors which framed the reception of electricity and spiritualism in the nineteenth century. The concept of the *flow*, the idea of an 'invisibly flowing force' (p. 153), was central to spiritualism, and to practices, such as Mesmerism, which attempted to 'know' this force through the concatenation of medicine, science and spiritualism. A flow does not have a definable beginning and end, it appears to not have discernable boundaries and moves across and between spaces which cannot be mapped through linear, spatialized, measurable co-ordinates. Thus a flow denotes passages, movement and social influence processes which do not act by force, prohibition or repression. As well as being a very energetic relational model, it is also rather elemental. A flow is often countered to all those elemental processes which cause petrifaction. This is matter which once flowed, but has now been arrested, carrying the traces of life in its contours, textures, depth, colours and surface. Although these petrifaction processes exist as life forms which bear the traces of agrarian-cyclical time (here I am thinking of petrified lava fields which exist on volcanic islands such as Lanzarote), they act as dynamic points of intersection and interchange with other elemental flows, such as the wind, water, and what we might term 'life itself'. Petrifaction is not static and carries an aura, an energy which is not dissolved. Thus, the concept of the flow and petrifaction, in terms of organic and elemental matter, are always in a complex relationality.

This interchange between flows and stasis is a central contrast which Asendorf ties to understandings of nervous life in the nineteenth century. There was seen to be a connection between understandings of electricity as an invisible flowing force, and the idea of an 'extrasensory, electromagnetic force that influences and steers the course of an individual life' (Asendorf, 1993: 155; Nye, 1990). This force might cause bodies to attract or repel, and was seen to be capable of 'acting at a distance'. Here, again, we encounter ideas of mental touch and sympathetic action and attraction. Electric light was seen to be an invisible force, but one which tended to give out a very stiff, bright light which was contrasted with the flickering and varying intensities of gas light. According to Asendorf (1993), the constancy and brightness of electric light, its uniformity and homogeneity, lent a kind of aura or unreality to shapes, objects and people. Electric light was seen to flatten and create an immaterial presence or feel to things. Asendorf (1993: 163) argues that 'electricity, energy and life were synonymous'. He argues that the idea of bodies as conductors, as having currents flowing through them, was aligned with the idea of 'electricity as a life force' which not only illuminated, but also could create new life. The idea of flows, forces, immaterial energies, and bodies that acted as lightning rods or conductors for these forces was related to the new definitions of life, the human and bodies that were part of this assemblage. This took the idea of non-verbal communication processes out of a material body and into the realm of the spiritual telegraph.

The notion of the self-enclosed, bounded subject, and the distinction between the inner and the outer, created a fiction of unity which Asendorf (1993) argues was untenable within this assemblage. Understandings of the 'nervous body' and its conduction by invisible electromagnetic forces became a way of conceiving of bodies and bodiliness which was 'non-corporeal, immaterial, arbitrarily subject to being charged with tensions' (Asendorf, 1993: 176). The capacity of the body to affect and be affected was tied to the movement of processes which would continuously flow through bodies, causing variation and discontinuity in terms of sensation and affect:

> Just as the contours of things disappear in impressionist art, so do the boundaries between day and night disappear in social life; the permanent flow of currents of goods and traffic in the large city, lit first by gas and later by electric lights, give notice of the dissolution of the social body into an oscillatory field, in which everything individual and bounded evaporates. (Asendorf, 1993: 173)

The concept of the flow is one that is central to how the movement of affective processes is often conceived within studies of affect and embodiment. In Chapter 5 we will consider approaches to movement which cannot be contained or conceptualized through the concept of the flow. In the next section I want to consider some of the limitations of the concept of the flow, specifically in relation to the vexed question of technicity. We will encounter the limits of conceiving of flow through a mentalist conception of immaterial communication as it was derived particularly from telepathic modalities of communication. We will specifically develop this in relation to recent work on affect, mediation and embodiment within media and cultural studies.

## Televisual Affect

There is an increasing literature within television studies which is beginning to consider the role of televisual affect within our consumption of media forms and practices (Gorton, 2009; Kavka, 2008; Skeggs, et al., 2008; Wood and Skeggs 2008). This work recognizes the importance of the registers of emotion, feeling and affect within televisual engagement and problematizes the binary that has framed audience reception studies between those considered passive and those considered active. Historically this binary has been class-based, with the mindless (working-class) masses considered overly suggestible to media influence and the ideal middle-class media consumer considered able to resist and engage critically with what is presented to them on the screen or over the airwaves (see Blackman and Walkerdine, 2001). Kristyn Gorton's (2009) re-evaluation of this historically sedimented binary argues that the audience(s) must be considered both active *and* passive, and that a focus on emotion discloses the criticality of audiences whilst at the same time acknowledging their emotional involvement. The recovery of emotion as an important yet neglected, or even denigrated, aspect of media consumption also works to revalue media forms and practices which have been associated with working-class tastes and habits, such as reality TV (see Blackman, 2011b; Wood and Skeggs, 2011). The focus on affectivity within these processes of subjectification reframes reality television as an important process of 'government by suggestion' and repositions suggestion as in need of serious rethinking and conceptualization.

This work rearticulates understandings of mental touch central to understandings of mediated communication in the nineteenth century and repositions television as a medium of tele-presence – that is a medium that brings things close. As Kavka (2008) argues, 'television fulfils its function as a technology of intimacy; by bringing things spatially, temporally and emotionally close, television offers to re-move the viewing subject'. This is primarily through its 'collapse of distance and time through the production of affective proximity' (Kavka, 2008: 7). The functioning of television as a technology of intimacy is of course not new. Stefan Andriopoulos (2005: 622) cogently illustrates through a cultural history of the emergence of television the 'fundamental interrelationship of television and clairvoyance' as it developed during the twentieth century. He shows how archaeologies of media forms such as television, that we might find in the work of Frederick Kittler (1990) for example, overlook or deny the cultural discourses that were intimately tied to such technological innovations. He shows how psychic research into mediumship was a necessary condition for the technological development of the medium. We might recognize the historical link to psychic research through the prefix *tele*, linking the television to processes of affective transfer tied to psychic phenomena; this might include telepathy, telekinesis, telephony and telegraphy, for example. Television was considered by psychic researchers to be an occult domestic medium that allowed clairvoyance to increase across distances. Although we might be inclined to dismiss such formulations now as outdated, or forms of quackery, I have shown in other work that formulations of affective transfer found in telepathy, for example, have a lineage to current work on affective transmission across the humanities (see Blackman, 2010a).

What is important about the historical link that I am making between television as a technology of intimacy that we find in Kavka's work, and television as a technology that facilitates and produces the possibility of 'psychic actions at a distance' (Andriopoulos, 2005: 628), is that both formulations introduce a rather different set of concepts for thinking about media consumption; these include the concepts of sympathy, attunement, mediation, emotional involvement, amplification, and television as a technology of suggestion. These concepts can be found within contemporary affect research as well as appearing within twentieth-century psychic research (see Blackman, 2010a). The link between media technologies and psychic research has been recognized in relation to the emergence of cinema and its positioning in the early twentieth century as primarily a hypnotic medium (Andriopoulos, 2008; Valiaho, 2010). As Andriopoulos argues, possession and hypnosis were prevalent themes in the newly emerging medium, both in terms of the subject matter of many early twentieth-century films, such as Maurice Tourneur's *Trilby* (1915) and Robert Weine's *The Cabinet of Dr Caligari* (1919), but also in relation to how the medium was taken to function (see Andriopoulos, 2008, for a development of this). In early film theory, the new medium itself was seen to exert 'an irresistible hypnotic influence over its spellbound audience' (Andriopoulos, 2008: 4). Andriopolous (2005: 637) terms this the 'half-hidden borrowings' that were a necessary condition for the emergence and development of both television and cinema. The idea of television being a suggestive technology is captured in both Gorton's (2009) and Kavka's (2008) examination of the centrality of emotion and affectivity to media consumption.

## Telepathy, Synaesthesia and Kinaesthesia

One direction of work across the humanities in relation to the senses and mediated communication is to turn to the concepts of synaesthesia and kinaesthesia to understand the role of the body and embodiment in the management of sensation and perception. This work extends the sensorium to consider both how the senses always work in tandem or co-ordination, captured by the concept of synaesthesia (see Chapter 1), and how the movement of intensities, energies, sensations and affects between bodies are felt and registered through the perception of bodily movement. What is emphasized in much of this work is the non-cognitive or non-conscious, that is, all those perceptions which are felt in and through bodies, usually registered through the central nervous system, and which are seen to act autonomously from cognition. This registering is not simply the registering of the internal actions of the nervous system, but rather that of the flow of sensation *between* bodies, which finds its passage through the attunement of nervous systems with the other, human and non-human. This attunement opens the subject to the other and also directs attention to technicity, to the forms and practices which mediate and modulate this passage (see Hauptmann and Neidich, 2010).

One of the predominant models of subjectivity related to mental touch and telepathy during the nineteenth century was characterized though conceptions of the double or doubling (see also Chapters 6 and 7). The concept of automatism captured the concept of the double or subliminal self, which related to the sense one might have of being governed by imperceptible forces compelling one to act beyond one's control. One of the problems with the way in which automatism was conceived within telepathic conceptions of communication was its apparent *mentalism*. Howes (2009) suggests that the mentalism associated with telepathy, with its focus on the action of one *mind* upon another, subsumed within the concept of psychic projection, has been one of the conditions which has led to neurobiological reductionism in many understandings of the sensorium within contemporary approaches. Although telepathy and psychic research more generally have been focused upon '"psychic" perception of one form or another' (Howes, 2009: 6), this occludes or obviates the importance of understanding the role of technical mediation within studies of psychic phenomena. Howes suggests that the way in which psychic research was extended and developed within parapsychology, or what is now more commonly referred to as 'anomalous psychology', has added to this problem.[4] As he argues, the parapsychological laboratory is

> only interested in 'spontaneous' expressions of psychic powers, not ritualized ones; and they privilege measurement (or 'statistical significance') over meaning. Most critically, because of the extreme mentalism of their

position, they seek to *eliminate* sensory cues, rather than investigate their role in the production of other states of consciousness. (Howes, 2009: 27)

Howes (2009) suggests that studies of psychic phenomena have always been technical, modulated and mediated through particular techniques, practices and processes of experimentation. This was embodied in the mission and aims of the Society for Psychical Research established in the UK in 1874 which was to subject psychic and related phenomena to scientific forms of investigation and experimentation (see Blackman, 2010a; Thurschwell, 2009; see also Chapter 5). However, one of the problems with this research was that it was bound up with particular fantasies that were to become enacted within the scientific experiments that took form. Thurschwell (2009) explores how the Victorian thirst for the séance as a form of scientific investigation of mediumship, as well as a popular entertainment, particularly in the middle-class drawing room, was structured by a particular erotics. The erotics of the séance centred specifically on the proximity of upper middle-class university men to their subjects, mainly working-class women who were subjected to physical investigation and interrogation. The anxieties that accompanied these erotic and highly charged encounters were replaced by the rise and validation of 'thought transference' experiments that increasingly were to take place within the scientific laboratory and were to eschew the forms of physical touch and investigation that the séance invited. Thus, as Howes (2009) argues, a *mentalism* became circumscribed and enacted within the parapsychological laboratory which endures to this day (see Chapter 4 for a development of this).

The mentalism often associated with psychic research and telepathy also enacts another set of fantasies that we have explored in Peter's account – that is, fantasies that originate with 'the desire for complete sympathetic union with the mind of another' (Thurschwell, 2009: 183). Thurschwell refers to this as the 'erotics of mind melding' (p. 198), which she goes on to argue is based on the 'desire for absolute knowledge and melding with another' (p. 198). As we have seen, some of the fantasies enacted within telepathic conceptions of communication centred upon the overcoming of distance, space, time and even death, where the mind was viewed as porous and permeable to the other and not bound by structural constraints, including finitude and loss (see Thurschwell, 2009; Wake Cook and Podmore, 1903). However, as we have also seen, threshold phenomena such as telepathy, suggestion and voice hearing, which we will go on to explore in Chapter 6, were also structured by an ambivalent duality; mind melding or openness to the other could also represent a 'dangerous proximity' (Thurschwell, 2009: 199).

These fears and anxieties were articulated in the literature of the time, including the fascination in gothic fantasies with doubling, such as Dr Jeckyll and Mr Hyde, Oscar Wilde's *The Picture of Dorian Gray*, as well as a fascination with the vampire in Bram Stoker's *Dracula* (see Thurschwell, 2009). We can see the way the fantasies which structure 'threshold phenomena' repeat anxieties of proximity which co-exist with the potentialities enacted by more processual accounts of attention, perception and the senses, for example (see also Andriopoulos, 2008; Crary, 1990). As Thurschwell (2009: 201) cogently argues, 'telepathy both promised and threatened that the mind was not necessarily a sealed and protected space'. It is the recognition of the ambivalent duality which structures openness and the importance of mediation that the historical antecedent's of contemporary discussions of affect, such as telepathy and mental touch, bring to the foreground. Arguably it is the fantasies structuring some of the promissory hopes and desires surrounding the 'turn to affect' across the humanities which clearly show their lineage to conceptions of telepathy and mental touch as discussed in this chapter.

## Conclusion: Subjectless Subjectivities

This concluding section's subtitle, 'subjectless subjectivities', is taken from a chapter by Paul Bains, in a collection of essays edited by Massumi (2002b), discussing the significance of Deleuze and Guattari's ontology of bodily expression, and its discontinuity with referential and constructionist approaches to language and communication. The subject is conceived as a conduit for virtual and affective flows and forces which are pre-individual and do not require a subject to register. Indeed, one of the assumptions often made in this and related literature, as we saw in Chapter 1, is that the psychological subject, reconceived through self-presence and cognitive capacities, is unaware of the very flows or forces which they conduct. Because of the split made between affect and cognition, psychomaterialist explanations are often proffered to explain how such flow occurs. Thus the nervous system, aligned to affect, becomes a kind of black box and analogy for explaining affective transmission. I want to consider in the conclusion to this chapter what genealogical research on threshold phenomena add to these discussions.

Threshold phenomena, such as telepathy and hypnotic suggestion, disclose the ambivalence surrounding proximity, connection and openness to the other, human and non-human. Telepathy, like Mesmerism, imagination, hypnotic suggestion and related phenomena, all articulate fantasies and anxieties about liminality. The modulation and augmentation of such openness, whether fantasized about in the Svengali-like figure of the hypnotist acting as a secondary personality guiding the actions of another, or in the mediation of such potentialities in the development and functioning of communication technologies, is something that refuses to go away. Rather than deny the importance of telepathic conceptions of subjectivity to modernity, this book will go on to consider how these conceptions of the subject might extend and contribute to debates on affect and the problem of personality. How might the psychological subject, or more importantly modelizations of the psyche, be reconceived and reinvented on this basis? How can we model and imagine the relations between the psychological and the biological or mind and matter which do not presume separate objects or entities interacting?

Cultural histories and genealogies which have taken threshold phenomena as their subject, cogently show how the very distinctions between affect and cognition that are largely taken for granted in contemporary debates have very specific histories of condition and existence (see also Leys, 2011a). As one example, it is only when telepathy is reconceived as mind-melding that pathic subjectivity becomes modelled and enacted as 'thought transference'. This leads to and authorizes mentalist conceptions of communication that are dismissed in more embodied formulations and in accounts of affective transmission that are seen to bypass cognition. Affect is seen by some to supersede and replace conceptions of the psyche which are narrowly modelled on positivist forms of psychological experimentation. How we examine, investigate and enact processes of experimentation and mediation is central to understanding what affect is and could become. What I hope is clear from the reflections in this chapter is that minimal theories of telepathic subjectivity lie in the background to contemporary accounts of affective transmission. This is particularly so in those theories that presume affect does not require a subject to register.

In the subsequent chapters of this book I will take such minimal theories of subjectivity seriously, rather than dismiss them as psychologization. This will open up the subject of affect to the importance of genealogical investigation, and also to more trans-subjective conceptions of the psyche which rely upon more telepathic conceptions of subjectivity. One important aspect of this reinvention will be to consider the importance of mind–matter relations such that the psyche is not considered as a process disconnected from the body and embodiment. We will explore this particularly in Chapter 6, where we encounter the phenomenon of voice hearing as a trans-subjective modality of communication rather than an abnormal perception. As David Howes (2009: 36) similarly argues in relation to the concept of the sixth sense and its re-examination within sensory anthropology; this concept 'lies not in its promotion of this or that faculty, but in its power to open up the boundaries of conventional perceptual paradigms to new possibilities of perception'. We will explore this further in the next chapter where arguments put forward here will be situated within contemporary debates on affect and the problem of mimetic communication.

## Notes

1  La Borde was an experimental psychiatric clinic which was founded by the psychiatrist Jean Oury. Guttari worked there from 1953 to 1992. It became known as a centre for institutional psychotherapy, the principles of which rejected the analyst–analysand relationship and worked with forms of collective subjectification (see Reggio, 2004).

2  Ellenberger (1970: 68) pathologizes Mesmer as being 'a man dominated by a fixed idea which was rejected and scorned'.

3  Overholser (1985:3) cogently shows how the problem of fakery or duplicity has become one of the central problems of hypnosis. The problem of simulation, of how to tell whether a hypnotic subject is acting, or has entered deep trance, is engaged through the use of elaborate techniques of dissimulation. However, as anyone who has seen Sam Taylor-Wood's moving video portrait of David Beckham, which was originally hung in the National Gallery, London, will testify, 'it is entirely possible to simulate sleep and do a fairly believable job of it' (ibid.: 8). The question of whether he was or was not asleep is entirely un-decidable and possibly attends to the aura which surrounded him as he lay in repose.

4  Parapsychology is now more commonly known within the psychological sciences as the psychology of anomalous experiences and aligns a diverse range of phenomenon and experiences, including mediumship, electronic voice phenomena, magical beliefs, lucid dreaming, death-bed visions, miracle cures, paranormal beliefs, false memory, telepathy, near-death states, haunted experiences, hypnosis, the placebo effect and so forth. It is framed as a study of extraordinary or exceptional phenomena, but not restricted to those which might be delineated as paranormal. These phenomena are often framed and constituted through the neuro-psychology and cognitive psychology of perception and belief.

# 4

# The Re-enchantment of Materialism: Affect and New Materialisms

This chapter will explore the historical antecedents of contemporary work on affect by developing the implications put forward in the last chapter. That is, we take seriously matters spiritual, psychic and psychopathological and how these experiences were connected up through a particular set of terms and concepts. It is this lineage that for the most part is left out and occluded in contemporary theorizing. It continues to haunt cultural theory in terms of the practical and conceptual dilemmas it raises. It is not that these dilemmas are unrecognized, however; as we will see, they are often the starting point for work on affect that assumes that we are not singular and bounded, but rather permeable and open to being affected and affecting. However, what I want to do is look at what happens to suggestion within this work, and how a return to the spiritual, psychopathological and psychic might reinstate a rather different set of concerns for cultural theory and work on affect and embodiment.

I want to start with a contemporary approach to the question of the transmission of affect written by the late feminist scholar, Teresa Brennan (2004). Brennan's work has become often cited within affect studies (Ahmed, 2010; Gibbs, 2010). We will see how the terms within which this project was conceived highlight the conceptual and practical difficulties that studies of affect are pointing towards, but also how the disavowal of the spiritual, psychic and psychopathological is an important component of this reformulation. Because suggestion is eliminated from the analysis, and effectively refigured as a neurophysiological phenomenon, the analysis is in danger of reinforcing the very neuro-reductionism that it is at pains to avoid. This, I will argue, is characteristic of much work in cultural theory that plunders from the 'hard' edges of psychological and biological theorizing in order to offer up suggestions for the possible mechanisms that will explain the transmission of affect (see also Callard and Papoulias, 2010). These attempts, as we will see, retreat to the *singular* neurophysiological body in order to explain the transmission of affect *between* people. Thus, an understanding of the psychological complexity that would make the transmission of affect intelligible is reduced to the brain and the central nervous system, sidelining, what I see as one of the issues that is far from resolved: the problem of suggestion, or what Ruth Leys (2000) terms the 'problem of mimetic desire'.

## Emotional Contagion and Affective Transmission

Brennan begins her discussion by asking the following question: 'Is there anyone who has not, at least once, walked into a room and felt the atmosphere?' (2004: 1).

The assumption that this is commonplace, and one that we have all felt, even if we little understand how this occurs, is the starting point for Brennan's analysis. Although she refers to the idea that affect can be passed and transmitted between people as a 'conceptual oddity' (p. 1), it is one that has been documented in a burgeoning empirical literature within the psychological sciences devoted to investigating the phenomenon of emotional contagion. Brennan takes a very specific literature derived from the experiences of therapists in the clinic, to open out for the reader why emotional contagion poses problems for cultural theory. She argues that psychiatry and psychoanalysis work with the assumption that the healthy person is self-contained and clearly bounded. They know where they end and the other person begins. This is viewed as the capacity of conscious deliberation – that is, forms of sympathetic identification that are conscious, cognitive and perceptual (Leys, 1993).

However, what marks the experiences of many therapists and health care professionals is not distance and deliberation, but rather a felt sense that affects are being passed from the client to the therapist. Of course, different forms of therapeutic training have ways of identifying this affective exchange, and provide strategies for transforming it into information that is crucial for successful outcomes. Within more psychoanalytic therapies affective exchange is recognized through the concept of transference. The relational connection between the analyst and analysand is identified through the kinds of feelings, sensations, emotions and thoughts that register with(in) the analyst during the therapeutic encounter. They might have an acute sense that these are not their own. The development of analytic distance by the analyst is a strategy for making this exchange more visible, and helping to prevent the merging of their own affects and feelings with those of the client. This is recognized as a process of counter-transference that is also viewed as a valuable aid in interpretation.

In the context of the therapeutic relationship, Leys (1993: 285) argues that the presumption made is that transference processes help to refigure the analysand as one who can be 'distanced from the scene, can see herself in the scene, can represent to herself "as other", and hence can distinguish herself from the model'.

This presumption of separation and unified boundaries as the goal or endpoint of the therapeutic process is one that Leys (1993) traces back to the problem of suggestion that puzzled Freud and other nineteenth-century writers. This puzzle framed various attempts to theorize affect and forms of behaviour and experience that were marked by automaticity and appeared to be involuntary and non-conscious. The interest in hypnotic suggestion, as we have seen in this book so far, provided a psychic mechanism for explaining the nature of these processes, with some such as Tarde arguing that suggestion was the basis of sociality itself. Gabriel Tarde became one of the key proponents of the importance of what Leys (1993) terms a 'mimetic paradigm', positing a form of complex imitation derived from studies of hypnotic suggestibility and psychic phenomena to explain how fads, fashions, traditions and forms of affect and emotion would spread throughout populations. What marked the human subject was not their separateness or boundedness, but rather a radical relationality that opened out the subject to being continually permeable to the influence of others.

However, from the assumption of radical relationality that framed early attempts by psychologists and sociologists to explain the basis of sociality, both Leys (1993) and Brennan show how these ideas have been marginalized and excluded in favour of what Brennan (2004: 2) terms the idea of 'affective self-containment. In previous work I have traced the refusal of a mimetic paradigm in the work of early social psychologists, such as McDougall (1910) and Ross (1909) – see Blackman (2007b). They both refigured suggestion through a contrast between will and compliance. This translation reified the normative psychological subject as one who could exercise will and habit in order to resist social influence. Suggestion did not simply disappear but, as we have seen in Chapter 2, was refigured as a capacity that was inferior, lower and associated with the bodies of those who, within an evolutionary paradigm, were increasingly aligned with animality and primitiveness. This contrast allowed suggestion to be inscribed within the brain and central nervous system, associated with what were considered 'simpler' instincts. These were viewed as less amenable to modification through the action of habit and discipline. This instinctual paradigm allowed theorists to account for forms of behaviour and experience that seemed to by-pass reason and criticality, and that were characterized by their spontaneity, fixity and repetition.

Leys (1993: 295) traces a variant of this translation within the work of the anthropologist George Herbert Mead. She argues that he appears to have been driven by a desire to eliminate suggestion from social theorizing and to replace it with a form of conscious imitation. Imitation was accepted as a form of copying or mimesis, but one that was based upon a conscious comprehension of other selves. As Leys (1993: 295–296) summarizes: 'Mead makes imitation a phenomenon of discrete pregiven elements (or mechanisms), not the dissolution of boundaries; of temporal delay, not instant communication; of distance, not merger; and of cognitive self-representation, not blind emotional identification'.

We can see here the identification of the key concepts that were to link up and transform suggestion, such that conscious deliberation would become the marker and expression of the normative subject. What was to be stressed, and actively managed and produced within governmental, social and scientific practices, was a self who could exercise restraint and inhibition; who could recognize the distinctions between self and other and inside and outside; and was therefore able to maximize and reinforce what was considered their inbuilt or pre-existing potential for rationality and criticality. Hypnosis as a technology of suggestibility was considered a dangerous practice that in Mead's words explained nothing. It was considered a technique of coercion and manipulation that undermined these latent potentials. This led Mead to denounce hypnosis as 'a short-circuiting of deliberation' (Leys, 1993: 300). It was considered a lower state of consciousness that could be found within inferior forms of 'mob psychology' that were considered a threat to democratic freedom and responsible action.

What we clearly have here is a redistribution of automaticity, the involuntary and forms of unintentional communication within the body – and particularly the central nervous system (cf. Wilson, 2004), such that the problem of suggestibility or mimetic desire appears to be resolved. Leys (1993: 282) relates this to what was perceived as one of the chief problems with the concept of hypnotic suggestibility or imitation which Tarde's account of becoming had been derived from: 'its inability to impose limits on change, its threat to an ideal of individual autonomy, its challenge to an existing social order based on hierarchy and difference'. The apparent limitation of suggestion to explain the limits or obstacles to change was resolved through the action of the instincts. Suggestion within Tarde's account seemed to be a model of a free flow or exchange between individuals that in its most ideal form, conversation, would enable the constant modification of ideas, thoughts and beliefs. In one of the few considerations of the importance of Tarde's work to sociology, Hughes (1961) argues that Tarde's *inter-psychologie* and *inter-spirituel* conception of communication is based upon a utopian and theoretical fantasy: 'The theoretically pure society would be that in which the conversation of minds would be uninhibited by all the barriers which now prevent the free movement of ideas from one mind to another' (p. 556).

This was certainly the view that united the work of many early sociologists and psychologists who engaged with the work of Tarde, but adapted the concept of suggestion through much delineation and speculation as to how the instincts were the site of blockages or obstacles to change and movement. Tarde preferred to locate obstacles to change and movement, or the orchestration of particular lines of movement within the concept of invention. This concept referred to those individuals who were credited with prestige and authority, and who were enabled to instil certain forms of acceptance and compliance within populations. This was not due to their will or creative genius but due to the position the inventor or leader was able to take up within a particular relational configuration. Thus invention was accomplished by 'lines of force which came to traverse the individual person' (Barry, 2005: 54). This might result in a particular association of ideas, practices and human and non-human actors. This 'social' conception of invention was distinctly different from the route that social psychologists such as McDougall and Ross were to take, which was to pave the way for the privileging of an instinctual economy as a key site for social psychological investigation (see Blackman, 2007b). This effectively constituted one of the conditions of possibility for the emergence of the anti-mimetic turn which takes a number of forms across the disciplines of social psychology and sociology at the turn of the last century.

This early work in many ways prefigures contemporary work on affect that is reactivating the kinds of questions that dominated and puzzled scientists and philosophers who have been considered founding figures of social psychology and sociology. Brennan (2004) frames this explicitly in relation to the 'transmission of affect' that she argues undermines the idea of self-containment that has persisted within the psychological and biological sciences into the twenty-first century. However, although many subdisciplines of psychology do operate with a notion of containment, there is a burgeoning subdiscipline of social and personality psychology that is concerned with the 'puzzling incongruity' of emotional contagion (Hatfield et al., 1994: 183).

There is a vast array of empirical studies which describe and document instances of affective transmission, but that lack a conceptual coherence in terms of explaining the possible mechanisms of transmission. In an article in the *Journal of Motivation and Emotion* that is characteristic of many, it is recognized that 'social contagion' and cognitive negotiation of another's affect often seem to occur in parallel (Doherty, 1998). These ideas are distributed throughout the experimental literature (see Van Kleef et al., 2010, for an overview). The opposing paradigms are presented as competing hypotheses, which of course the psychological sciences hope they will one day be able to resolve. Hatfield et al. (1994) characterize these competing hypotheses by making a distinction between emotional mimicry and synchrony. This is a distinction between the idea that emotions can be 'caught' in different ways and the idea of synchrony that privileges the 'conscious processing of information' (p. 9). We have seen the way that this distinction has its lineage within debates that were attempting to resolve the problem of mimetic desire at the turn of the last century (between Mead and Tarde, for example). Mimicry refers to what is viewed as the *automatic* imitation of another's facial expressions, gestures, voice, posture and movements. In the sense that one can be said to have 'caught' another's emotion or affect within an exchange or encounter, this relies upon the presumption that much of this exchange occurs on a non-conscious level that is not always 'accessible to conversant awareness' (Hatfield et al., 1994: 10).

This is also described as a form of attunement that is marked by a synchronization of one's rhythms of communication with those around you. This is not about conscious recognition but about forms of bodily affectivity that are seen to involve the sending of rapid and automatic or involuntary forms of non-verbal information to other people. A good example of this explored by Vincianne Depret is the case of Hans the horse (Despret, 2004a). Hans was seen to confound the scientific community by apparently being 'in tune' with the minimal, involuntary bodily movements of the experimenter. These would manifest in slight twitches or movements so subtle and minuscule that they would not register to the so-called naked eye. This attunement created an experimental artefact where Hans appeared to be able to solve complex multiplication puzzles by stamping his hooves (see Blackman, 2008a, and Blackman and Venn, 2010, for further development of this).

These forms of affective transmission are contrasted with conscious cognitive processes that might be conditioned or unconditioned. The use of a behaviourist paradigm to explain synchrony foregrounds the importance of habit within this conception. Conditioned emotional responses are those associative responses that originate within a learnt habitual response. There is a distinction here between unconditioned affective responses and those that become assembled into particular patterns of response due to past experiences. Conditioned affective responses are particular patterns of association between the senses and muscular, glandular and visceral responses such that, although learnt, they appear automatic and involuntary. Hatfield et al. (1994), like Brennan (2004), cite many examples that point towards the startling and incontrovertible evidence of emotional contagion or affective transmission. These include some of the examples that we have already explored in this book so far, including evidence from studies of mass and crowd psychology, non-verbal communication and 'hysterical contagions'. They also consider the distinction that led suggestion to be eliminated from social and psychological thought at the turn of the last century. Mimicry was viewed as an instance of 'primitive emotional contagion' (Hatfield et al., 1994: 10) found in animals and infants (and those considered inferior). Mimicry ideally is kept in check or superseded by the development of conscious deliberation or conscious forms of sympathetic identification. Thus Hatfield et al. (1994: 79) cite evidence from ethology to suggest that imitation is a 'phylogenetically ancient and basic form of intraspecies communication'.

The intractability of affective transmission has forced a rethinking of this problem for contemporary cultural theory and for more marginal areas of the psychological sciences. Although considering the phylogenetic distinction that has led to this refusal, Hatfield et al. finish their book by likening emotional contagion to a form of magic or rapport that is still little understood, but has profound implications for public policy, a knowledge that they argue will be hugely important for lawyers, psychotherapists, doctors and others who would benefit from a knowledge of the subtle processes through which emotional contagion might operate. This concluding statement is not a far cry from the proclamations of Boris Sidis, a nineteenth-century psychologist considered in Chapters 2 and 3, who argued that an understanding of ordinary suggestibility would provide solutions to problems encountered in schooling, the legal system and the therapeutic relationship. It seems that we have not moved so far away from the concept of suggestion as it at first seemed. But what does this recognition mean for contemporary engagements with affect within cultural theory?

## Affect and the Neurophysiological Body

Brennan (2004) plunders the area of neuroendocrinology to provide possible answers to the puzzle of affective transmission. She does recognize that early work on mass psychology was an area where 'there once nearly was a theory of the transmission of affect', but that the mechanism of transmission was not effectively explained (p. 51). Much like McDougall and other early social psychologists such as Floyd Henry Allport (1924), she dismisses suggestibility, although she also derides McDougall for even considering suggestion in his translation of the concept as a form of primitive sympathetic response: 'With this principle, McDougall came very close to my argument, although it is unclear what his "primitive sympathetic response" consisted of, partly because he did not free himself from the rhetoric of "suggestibility"' (Brennan, 2004: 55).

Brennan suggests that the biochemical literature on entrainment within the area of neuroendocrinology would be a better place to consider the problem of affective transmission. The concept of entrainment is one that has its place within a conception of affect that inheres within discussions of non-Western spiritualist traditions. Ann Game (2001), the Australian sociologist, uses a more energetic conception of entrainment to explore the relational connections between herself and her horse (KP), such that an experience of these connections helps her to understand how she was implicated in the rehabilitation of her horse following its paralysis due to an accident. Like Brennan, Game refuses the idea of separation and boundary, in this case not simply between human and human, but between human and animal. She argues that an attunement to the exchange and mixing of affects between horse and human, in this example, allowed her to literally bring her horse back to life: 'To help her to remember canter, my body had to take up this movement. The between horse-and-human movement of canter had to be generated for KP to entrain with it, to get in the flow' (Game, 2001: 6).

The concept of entrainment or attunement that Game is mobilizing is one that is distinctly different from the concept of entrainment that is central to Brennan's arguments. Brennan removes any trace of its spiritualist lineage, equating the concept of energetic exchange to an exchange or transfer of chemicals. Chemical or nervous entrainment is likened to the effect one nervous system can have on another. The vibrations or frequencies that are transmitted to another are explained through the action of hormones and pheromones that are 'literally in the air' (Brennan, 2004: 69). Although Brennan does not want to reduce affects to hormones, she seeks to explain unconscious processes through their conversion into hormonally produced effects. As she suggests:

> If olfactory communication turns a hormone into a pheromone and changes another's affects, does it also change their hormones in a way that (temporarily) changes their habitual affective disposition? Are such changes, in turn, communicated by additional pheromones? If such cycles can be shown to hold in groups, then the contagion of affects has been explained. (Brennan, 2004: 72)

Brennan suggests that the only factor preventing science from considering the place of endocrinology in the transmission of affect is the foundational fantasy of self-containment that excludes the very anomalies of communication that Brennan seeks to explain. The concept of entrainment that Game refers to is one that is linked more to a vitalist conception of human and psychological life. Life is defined by the flow or exchange of a vital force- an *élan vital* – that connects rather than separates and is felt and registered within the body through a subtle sensing. Game cites the work of R.D. Laing (1985), the famous British psychiatrist who was linked to the anti-psychiatry movement in the 1960s and 1970s, which so inspired the work and practices of Deleuze and Guattari (Guattari, 1984). Laing was interested in the idea of energetic connections and the relationship of energetic connection to rhythm. Game cites an example of entrainment taken from Laing that describes a synchrony of rhythm that often occurs in the presence of someone that you are open to – that your breathing will synchronize: 'you entrain your rhythm' (Game, 2001: 3; see Chapter 5).

Game relates the notion of energetic entrainment to a more relational way of being that involves what she terms a 'sensitive feel' (p. 8). Although she describes the origins of this sensing within more Eastern psychospiritual traditions, she also refers to a body of work by contemporary philosophers and cultural theorists that is indebted to this 'magically mimetic relation' (Taussig, 1993). This includes the work of the anthropologist Mick Taussig, the philosopher Gaston Bachelard (1971), Michael Serres (2008) and the feminist theorist Marie Clement (1994). Despite this body of work Brennan (2004) suggests that we need a 'non-occultish explanation' (p. 68) of entrainment that brings the study of affect 'down to earth' (p. 95). Indeed, she goes as far to argue that hypnotic suggestion, through an understanding of the olfactory system, will be explained through a form of chemical attunement: that 'electrical entrainment and hypnosis are probably the same thing' (p. 184, n. 9). The 'hard' edges of the psychological and biological sciences are seen therefore to provide a body of knowledge and evidence that can be used to further our understanding of affect within the humanities and related disciplines.

## The New Paradigm

Although work on affect is often posed as a counter to the priviliging of discourse, language and signification across the humanities, it is also a response to psychoanalysis, and psychoanalytic concepts of fantasy and desire. The supplementing of Foucaudian work on discourse with accounts of desire was an attempt by many to consider our investments in particular normalizing practices, fictions and fantasies (see Butler, 1993; Henriques et al., 1984). Although this was a way of investigating agency and resistance, the body was often sidelined, leading to a problem with accounting for more embodied forms of agency (see Burchill et al., 1991; Csordas, 1994; Hoy, 1986; Rose, 1996, 1999; Shilling, 2003). The problem of embodied agency and the potential functionalism of cultural inscription has been raised in different ways by authors concerned with the reification of the subject as a dupe, positioned at the intersection of relations of force, power, and ideology with little room for manoeuvre (Blackman and Walkerdine, 2001; Hoy, 1986; McNay, 1992). One of the key questions is how bodily or material processes are implicated in the attachments subjects' might have to particular practices – governmental, aesthetic, clinical, political and so forth. Why do certain technologies of the social and practices of the self have such an affective force? How are instinctual, affectual and involuntary registers mobilized by particular practices? These questions recognize that practices of social and self formation do not simply work with a docile body, but they organize, marshal and channel particular energies or affects that cannot be explained without a serious engagement with the affectivity and dynamism of matter.

Connolly (2002) frames this relationship as one between culture, the brain and the body, and turns to cognitive neuroscience to explore the potency of particular techniques of self-cultivation. His main focus is on how to account for the 'affective energies' of cinema and cinematic techniques in relation to brain composition

(Connolly, 2002: 13). Nigel Thrift (2004) argues that the turn to affect consolidates a number of problems that have beset cultural theory in its attempts to analyse the relationships between government, regulation and subject formation. As we have seen, one of the insights from this shift is the recognition that language is not the only meaningful way in which communication takes place. One of the other key assumptions of this work is that 'distance from biology is no longer seen as a prime marker of social and cultural theory' (Thrift, 2004: 57). In fact, this appears to be the driving force of much of the work on affect that has turned to the psychological and biological sciences for inspiration. In different ways physiological, neuroscientific and cognitive scientific accounts have been mobilized to inject life and vitality into the inert docile body that has come to characterize much of sociology and cultural theory (Blackman, 2008a; Brennan, 2004; Connolly, 2002; Massumi, 2002a; Wilson, 2004).

The key question, then, is how to understand the performative force of particular practices of self and social formation, and what work outside the humanities can be brought to bear upon this question. Connolly's (2002) account is interesting from the perspective of 'affective transmission' as he is assembling work from cognitive neuroscience that is attempting to explain the role of affect within thinking and judgement. This work, often aligned with the theories of the cognitive neuroscientist Antonio Damasio (1994, 2000) is interesting because affect is located within a realm of rapid, non-conscious perception. This realm of perception is a parallel form of processing that allows us to take in a complex range of information that is 'much more' than we can explicitly or consciously register. These are what Damasio terms 'somatic markers' that operate below the threshold of conscious experience and are registered in the body through a visceral sense. This is what we might term 'gut feeling' or intuition, which for Damasio helps us to make decisions and operate effectively in the world. Although 'affective energy' is located within a rapid realm of non-conscious parallel processing, part of it becomes available to consciousness through the action of the autonomic nervous system:

> Part of the affective energy mixed into thought becomes available to consciousness as feelings and concept-imbued emotions, but other thought-imbued energies find symptomatic expression in the timbre of our voices, the calmness or intensity of our gestures, our facial expressions, the flush of our faces, the rate of our heartbeats, the receptivity, tightness or sweatiness of our skin, and the relaxation or turmoil in our guts. (Connolly, 2002: 76)

Connolly also links his 'neuro-politics' to the work of nineteenth-century philosophers and scientists, such as William James and Henri Bergson. He frames their concerns as part of a minor tradition which, along with more contemporary philosophers of science, such as Isabella Stengers (2008), has reflected upon 'biolayering': the layering of culture with nature such that they mutually co-constitute each other. Although Connolly highlights the interest of Bergson and James on the nature of memory, thinking and so forth, an important dimension of their work is occluded. Although they all paid attention to the biological theories of the day, they also paid close attention to theories of psychical constitution that might animate the more porous and permeable aspects of the self. A key focus, as with one of their contemporaries, Gabriel Tarde, was on the psychological or psychic mechanisms that could explain movement and change, as well as fixity and habit. They did not simply focus on the movement (of flows, intensities, forces, sensations, energies, etc.), but on how movement is registered in ways that must take into account differential psychic dynamics of self and sociality. These dynamics might not necessarily involve boundary-making; the specificity of such taking form requires an attention to what Whitehead (1938, 1979) called 'actual occasions' or what Simondon termed the 'associated milieu' (Venn, 2010; see Chapter 7).

The concept of occasion is related to the process philosophy of Whitehead, a mathematician and physicist writing in the early twentieth century (see Stenner, 2008). He was committed to developing modes of thinking about phenomenon designated as biological or psychological which did not bifurcate subject–object, nature–culture, material–immaterial, inside–outside, and psychological–social (see Brown and Stenner, 2009; Stenner, 2008). The concept of occasion and event has been taken up in studies of affect to refer to the singularity of affect taking form; the actualization of an always already remainder of autonomic and virtual potential (see Clough, 2010a; Chapter 1). What is given less attention to in this work are the mattering processes (Kavka, 2008), which include processes which cannot simply be designated as somatic (involving the nervous system for example), unless we are willing to conceive of materiality as being psychically attuned in ways we little understand. Paul Stenner (2008) makes a similar argument in his consideration of Whitehead's work for developing the importance of *process* for understanding psychological entities and concepts. Stenner (2008) argues that although Whitehead's work has been taken up to refigure matter, there has been much less attention to how Whitehead's work reframes the 'psychosocial interface' (p. 91). This often leads to 'a rather too hasty dismissal of the concept of subjectivity as such and there is a related tendency to "flatten out" any would-be distinctions between human and non-human entities' (p. 92). This importantly directs our attention to the complex relationship between mediation, experimentation and the body's potential for mediation which will be developed in Chapters 6 and 7. Although there has been much work on quantum ontologies and how this refigures matter (understood as dynamic and lively – see Chapter 1), there has been much less attention paid to psychological concepts and their refiguring through quantum mechanics which was also evident in the writings of Niels Bohr (1963; see Radin, 2006).

## Mind and Matter

The importance of modelling mind–matter relations such that the psyche is also approached as an embodied trans-subjective process can be found in Sidis's (1898) work, one of the inspirations for William James's process psychology. For Sidis, an understanding of the psychical mechanisms revealed through a study of suggestion, telepathy, mediumship and related phenomena would provide an 'insight into the nature of social forces' (p. 3). As we know, Sidis was particularly interested in hypnotic suggestibility, and argued that although certain techniques could produce a state of hypnotic suggestibility, likened to somnambulism, the 'suggestible element' is always with us. He identified certain features of technologies of governance and self and social formation that repeated the common features that would induce a state of hypnotic suggestibility. This included the fixation of attention, the distraction of attention, monotony, the limitation of voluntary movements, the contraction of the field of consciousness, inhibition and immediate execution. Sidis argued that the potency of these characteristics became heightened through indirect rather than direct means.

Sidis did not subscribe to the emergent psychological view explored in Chapter 2, where suggestion was increasingly understood and aligned to the lack of will. As we have seen, this had led will and inhibition to be considered higher capacities located within the mind, whereas suggestibility was viewed as a more inferior capacity located within the reflex ideomotor centres of the nervous system. This was considered to be the site of more automatic, involuntary and simple processes that bypassed rationality and criticality. Sidis argued that this effectively reduced unconscious cerebration to a kind of physiological automatism. He rather argued that hypnotic suggestibility revealed the 'coexistence of two streams of consciousness' or two selves, manifested through cleavages (p. 91). These cleavages for Sidis could be observed in the study of psychopathology and spiritual matters. Thus the study of 'double selves', or what we might now refer to as multiple personality disorder (Hacking, 1998), might reveal how these two selves could become disaggregated: 'Under favourable conditions the sub-waking self wakes from the deep trance in which it is immersed, raises its head, becomes completely conscious, and rises at times even to the plane of personality' (Sidis, 1898: 131).

However, in the normal waking state the 'secondary self' still communicated and transmitted impressions. This created what Sidis termed a 'highway of suggestion' (p. 179). Thus the selves could 'blend into one' as well as 'flowing apart' (p. 162). Sidis, like James (and Bergson and Tarde) was interested in studies of psychic phenomena reported by the Society of Psychical Research. Thus the impressions transmitted by the secondary self did not simply inhere within a singular body, but also breeched the boundaries of the apparently self-contained body. This was observed through their expression in particular psychic phenomena and practices, including automatic writing, crystal gazing and mediumship.

What is interesting about this work was its attempt to account for subjectivity; for how the self was able to synthesize the different selves together such that one could be said to have a personality. However, the personality or 'problem of personality', as James framed it, was not a singular entity or 'thing', but rather a process which was reified as an entity. This was the 'holding together' or aggregation that characterized the personality or self. Rather than distinguish the plural self through a hierarchy between the higher and lower, Sidis turned to physiological explanations of subconsciousness that could account for the two key processes that linked the selves: association and aggregation. I will discuss the physiology of this account later in the chapter when we turn to more recent work within feminist science studies that is refiguring the nervous system by refusing the distinction between the higher and the lower (Wilson, 2004).

Although Sidis's work had a huge impact on both William James and Gabriel Tarde, the focus on suggestion as a mechanism that is psychic and physiological, and simultaneously material and immaterial, has been written out of both Brennan's and Connolly's accounts. Instead the 'psychic' is replaced by either the endocrinological system

(Brennan, 2004) or the neurophysiological (Connolly, 2002) such that the problem of suggestion appears to have been resolved. This is curious as both scholars are attempting to account for that which occurs beyond conscious awareness, and yet is seen in both cases to have a profound motivating force on action, thought, feeling and so forth. Connolly does at least acknowledge James's interest in hypnosis and the idea of a subliminal self but assumes that this register of life can be explained through contemporary neuroscientific research. This is a central presumption of much affect theory which should be approached with some caution and circumspection (see Callard and Papoulias, 2010). Much of the language assembled in what has come to be known as a 'new paradigm' refigures concepts that had a key place within the kinds of imaginaries that were circulating at the turn of the last century. However, these imaginaries linked concepts that took form within particular spiritual and religious imaginaries and were indebted to the kinds of occultish and energetic explanations that both authors are at pains to discount or translate into a 'neurophysiology of affective thoughts' (Connolly, 2002: 170). It is the reactivation, rather than silencing, of these background versions that might allow a rather different set of concerns to emerge for humanities and social science scholars interested in theorizing affect.

## The Nervous System, Affect and the Body

Affect is part of biology, if anything is. (Connolly, 2002: 67)

The above statement is one that, as we have seen, is uniting much of the work on affect within this new paradigm. In this section I want to consider the work of the Australian feminist psychologist Elizabeth Wilson, who explores similar themes and issues in her book, *Psychosomatic: Feminism and the Neurological Body* (2004). Wilson suggests that much feminist work in cultural theory has repudiated the biological, and focused its attention on the role of ideation and cultural inscription to the detriment of considering what biological processes would allow social practices to take hold of the body. Again the focus in this work is on the performative force of certain practices, and how a serious and detailed engagement with biology and neurology would allow a greater understanding. As she says: 'how many feminist accounts of the anorexic body pay serious attention to the biological functions of the stomach, the mouth or the digestive system? How many feminist analyses of the anxious body are informed and illuminated by neurological data?' (p. 8).

Wilson returns to the work of Freud and brings to the foreground his early interest in physiology and the nervous system that she argues has been silenced in contemporary accounts of his work (which are usually aligned to his early interest in hypnosis and telepathy, for example). This work, she argues, has focused attention on the role of ideation in the therapeutic process, sidelining the mechanisms of biological conversion that translate hysterical symptoms into bodily perturbations. Her key focus is on the relationship between biology and psychology in understandings of depression (see also Wilson, 2011), psychosomatic symptoms, sexuality and emotion. In line with work discussed so far in this chapter, Wilson adds weight to the argument that language is not the only meaningful mode of communication. The psychological and biological are not two discrete entities that somehow interact, but enter into relational connections such that they exhibit a 'relational complexity' and mutual co-constitution (2004: 20). Wilson challenges one of the key presumptions that she suggests has guided the anti-essentialist mantra that has framed critical psychology, some feminisms and cultural theory – that is, that biology is inert mass. This presumption is organized through a distinction between the higher and the lower, where the body is considered lower and aligned with automaticity, and the higher realm incorporates the mind and rationality. In the case of psychosomatic symptomatology this has framed understandings that suggest that the psychological origins of psychosomatic experiences lie in the mind. Thus, they are viewed as accessible via language and ideation where the psychological is located within cognition and so-called higher processes.

This organizational distinction misconstrues the realm of the psychological or the psyche, which Wilson seeks to take out of the mind and distribute throughout the central and peripheral nervous systems (such as the enteric nervous system). In line with work on affect discussed so far, this is an attempt to consider phenomena that subjects might experience as involuntary, non-conscious and spontaneous or beyond conscious control. However, rather than reduce these experiences to some kind of physiological automatism – as in the idea of an instinctual economy, for example – she instead considers the communicative aspects of the nervous system such that it can be said to be psychological. Wilson suggests that most psychological events are unconscious or involuntary and do not simply take place in the head but are embodied and enacted throughout the nervous system. Thus, Wilson suggests that the nervous system is psychologically attuned in its relationships to self and other(s), where our embodied relationships are 'enacted enterologically' (p. 45). Thus, 'bloatedness, nausea, vomiting, constipation, diarrhea are modes of distress enacted enterologically' (p. 46). Wilson suggests that psychoanalysis is one area that could be more sensitive to neuro-logical data as it works primarily with non-conscious or unconscious perception. However,

> neurogastroenterology and psychoanalysis have become too interested in the central nervous system and the head as the focus of their treatment regimes. The nervous system extends well beyond the skull, and as it so travels through the body it takes the psyche with it. The transferential nature of the nervous system (i.e., its obligatory relationships to other systems: biochemical, psychological, enterological) has yet to be grasped in either psychoanalytic or gastroenterological frameworks. (p. 47)

This is a call for psychoanalysis to consider the biological and neu-rological dimensions of affect, as opposed to its privileging of the relational connections between ideation and affect. For Wilson it is not simply that affect is biological, but rather that materiality exhib-its an affectivity. To this end her work echoes work on affect that we explored in Chapter 1. She argues that this insight demands a differ-ent conceptual language and turns to work on genomics and the chiasmus as a 'means for diagramming complexity' (p. 58). This work allows her to conceive of the organization of the brain and nervous system as being both dimorphic and distributed in complex ways (divergent). The challenge is to think the relational connections (or reticulation) between the dimorphic and divergent, other than see-ing them as separate entities that somehow interact. Rather than seeing the brain or central nervous system in either/or terms, Wilson uses the chiasmus to frame their relationships as both/and allowing a greater degree of neurological complexity to emerge. This allows Wilson to challenge the view that physiology is automatic and invol-untary, such that the autonomic nervous system has the potential to be 'attuned to and held captive by, the thoughts and actions of oth-ers' (p. 76). Thus the psychological and cultural are entangled with the physiological such that they cannot be said to exist in a func-tional hierarchy. They are twisted, folded and reticulated rather than hierarchical and suppressive. This has some similarities with work on brainhood that we will explore in Chapter 7.

Arguably Wilson's work also re-enacts some of the issues and questions that drove Sidis's work on suggestion. As we have seen, the concept of suggestion that Sidis articulated similarly worked with the reticulating connections between association and aggregation (which could be transposed onto Wilson's relationships between the dimorphic and divergent, for example). Sidis (1898) equally rejected the kind of functional hierarchy of the physiological systems that guides Wilson's work, and instead explored how nerve cells existed in relationships of complex association with other nerve cells (which were also accompanied by psychic content), as well as becoming synthesized into particular aggregates or constellations. Sidis saw these reticulating relationships as being governed by duration and intensity rather than any distinction between the higher and the lower. These relational connections exhibited a remarkable plasticity and in their chameleon-like character could disaggregate and reveal gaps and cleavages. These gaps and cleavages extended and incorporated the social and psychic such that the nervous system, the social and the psychic were entangled in complex ways: 'The social psychical scalpels are big, powerful; their edges are extremely keen, and they cut sure and deep' (Sidis, 1898: 299).

Sidis incorporated particular views about sociality that were derived from the particular context within which he was writing. Thus much of the final chapters of his book is devoted to discussions of so-called 'mob psychology' and mental epidemics or forms of hysterical and emotional contagion that dominated discussion within early psychology and sociology. Sidis concluded that 'Man [*sic*] is a social animal no doubt; but he is social because he is suggestible' (p. 310). What is curious about the body of work that I have examined thus far in this chapter, is the features it shares with this early work on suggestion, but also how this work has been silenced, occluded and in some cases explicitly rejected. What is interesting in both is what has been highlighted and what simultaneously has been obscured and placed within the background. I share a concern with other writers who are raising doubt over whether the elimination of suggestion and the mobilization of biology and neurology to articulate affect is the only direction to go (Borch, 2006; Leys, 2000; Orr, 2006; Thrift, 2008). Christian Borch has argued that what is interesting about the way that suggestion took form within early sociology was its relationship to 'a complex interplay or in-between of rationality' that, as we have seen, dissolved boundaries between self and other (2006: 3). Rather than simply assume that the problem of mimetic desire has been resolved in the contemporary turn to affect, it might be wise as Borch (2005, 2006) has argued, to open suggestion up to new theoretical horizons.

The new interest in the philosophy and sociology of Gabriel Tarde offers much promise in this respect. However, the psychical mechanisms that underpinned Tarde's account of sociality have largely been obscured and silenced within actor network theory (see Blackman, 2007b; Latour, 2002, 2005). What we effectively get is a flattened account that is informed by an ontology of movement and change. This assumes somehow that the problem of suggestion is over. The emphasis in much of this work is on how to account for flux, becoming and movement, and the 'problem of personality' as James (1890) conceived it is viewed as a misnomer or reductionism that should be ignored. As Fraser et al. (2005) argue, the 'new vitalism' that much of this work subscribes to emphasizes becoming over being and movement over inertia. This is an approach that privileges 'process as a mode of being' (p. 1). Although, as we have seen, the historical antecedents of this 'new vitalism' were concerned with process and radical relationality, there was also simultaneous concern with aggregation, synthesis and 'hanging together'.

## Massumi and Affect

The work of Brian Massumi (2002a) is important in this respect. In his book, *Parables for the Virtual: Movement, Affect, Sensation*, Massumi defines the body as being characterized by its capacity for movement and change. This definition is counterposed to approaches to the discursive body that have freeze-framed the body within a range of social positionings that 'subtract movement from the picture' (p. 3). The shadowy other to this ontology of movement and flux is the realm of habit, fixity and inertia. Massumi has become one of the seminal theorists of affect and, although aligning affect with movement and change, laments the lack of a conceptual framework within cultural theory to address its logic. This logic is related to the non-conscious and imperceptible vital force that traverses between and distributes human and non-human actors within a field of potential. The body is thus a 'conversion channel' or transducer that can modulate or amplify this intensive force through a kind of sensing feel, rather than a conscious calculation.

Massumi draws a lineage with the work of William James and Henri Bergson to specify the importance of a vital force but, as with much work within this tradition, also silences their interest in psychopathology, hypnotic suggestibility and psychic phenomena that engendered this set of terms and concepts. Massumi turns to cognitive neuroscience to find a conceptual language for cultural theory that will allow affect to take form. The body within this formulation is both a transducer of potential but also an interrupter to the system of flow that becomes lodged through the action of habit: 'Habit lies at the hinge of nature and these divergent process lines of culture. Habits are socially or culturally constructed. But they reside in the matter of the body, in the muscles, nerves, and skin where they operate autonomously' (Massumi, 2002a: 236).

Thus capture and containment are explained through the formation of habits that interrupt the flow of this intensive vital force. Although this is an attempt to account for the relationship between being and becoming, the invocation of habit as an explanatory concept brings with it its own set of problems (see also Blackman, forthcoming). What I want to do here is sketch out one of the key problems by exploring the genealogy of habit in the work of early social psychologists such as William McDougall and Floyd Henri Allport. We will see then how the retreat to habit to explain *being* sets up a particular model of social influence that creates more problems than it solves. The invocation of the importance of habit was part of an anti-mimetic turn across the social sciences that attempted to relocate the non-conscious or suggestibility within a set of conditioned physiological automatisms. Although this might seem to account for capture and containment, it relies upon a view of sociality that is organized through particular schedules of punishment and reinforcement. The psychological actor within this work was one seen to be guided by conscious deliberation and sympathetic identification, rather than the very non-conscious modes of perception that Massumi wishes to privilege. It was this view of the subject that was incorporated into particular practices of self and social regulation, such as Victorian self help (Smiles, 1864) that emphasized the importance of drill, routine and repetition in the remaking of working-class men's subjectivity (see Blackman, 2008c, for a development of this).

## Old Habits Die Hard

As an example of the importance of subjecting habit to genealogical investigation I want to consider the work of the social psychologist William McDougall (1910), who was very influenced by the writings of Gabriel Tarde (see Blackman, 2007b). His reflections and engendering of habit as a particular social-psychological concept are illustrative of the anti-mimetic turn which characterized social psychology at the turn of the twentieth century. McDougall developed the concept of 'disposition' which he viewed as a development of the general psychological principles which underlay manifold activity. This term was used to bring together a notion of the inherited with the acquired, as a means of addressing the degree of assimilation between the actor and the acted upon. McDougall (1910: 19) placed a study of the instincts at the heart of social-psychological enterprise, which he defined as the 'essential springs or motive powers of all thought and action'. However, although McDougall is often credited with championing nature, his account weaves together nature and nurture in ways which are an interesting precursor to contemporary theories of affect in social theory (cf. Blackman, forthcoming; Ahmed, 2004; Sedgwick, 2003; Wilson, 2004).

Although instincts were considered the springs of thought and action, they were not strictly or simply located within the biological. They are always 'organized in systems of increasing complexity' (McDougall, 1910: 17), but are often performed without deliberate action. The invocation of forms of action which might be enacted without conscious reflection was for McDougall a way to close the question of mimetic desire. These forms of action were not to do with non-conscious suggestion, but rather were located within a bodily unconscious understood through the concept of habit. Habits were patterns and regularities of behaviour, motor skills, reflex actions and responses which were engrained within a kind of bodily memory. However, although these forms of bodily memory lay outside the subject's conscious reflections and deliberations, the accomplishment or performance of the involuntary was a complex psychophysical process which involved the cognitive, the affective and the conative – the co-constitution of knowing, feeling and intention.

'Conation' is a term which is taken to refer to the motivational aspects of behaviour; that which is seen to propel us towards certain kinds of action. Conation within psychology has largely been forgotten within studies of habit. What has been emphasized is what has come to be seen as the non-intentional aspects of habit and the separation of both affect and habit from cognition and conation (see Leys, 2010a, 2011a). When we look at the history of conation within the psychological sciences the complexity of how to think habit becomes apparent (see Huitt, 1999). McDougall used the concept of conation to refer to the *intentional* aspects of behaviour, including possible psychic motivations, seeing the cognitive, affective and conative as co-constitutive processes. However, increasingly and throughout McDougall's body of work, what became emphasized was the importance of conscious deliberation. Intentional aspects of habit were recast as conscious, rational, cognitive processes, allowing for a separation between habit and cognition and between affect and cognition. As I argued in Chapter 1, the supposed non-intentionality of affect is one aspect of contemporary debate that should be subjected to genealogical inquiry (see also Leys, 2011a; Chapter 7; Blackman, forthcoming).

Ruth Leys (2000: 7) suggests that the invocation of habit as a kind of bodily unconscious, encoded beyond 'verbal-semantic-linguistic representation', provided the conditions for refiguring suggestion as having a 'mechanical-causal basis'. Although habit is a relay point between what is considered inside (in this case 'simple' instincts) and what lies outside (the social), the focus becomes the singular body. As we have seen the retreat to the singular body to explain the performative force of practices has led cultural theorists such as Brennan, Wilson, Massumi and Connolly to the neurohormonal body, the nervous system, the perceptual system and the brain. The very inside–outside distinction that the mimetic paradigm displaces is replaced by a singular body, and by knowledge practices like the 'hard' edges of the psychological and biological sciences concerned with what is taken to be located within the boundaries of the person. It is true to say that even the 'hard' edges of the psychological and biological sciences recognize that there is more to the subject than what is inside. However, the problem becomes a perennial one: how to explain how the outside gets in. The framing of this question presumes a clear distinction between the psychological and the social, the inside and outside, and tends to draw on behaviourist models of socialization as in the work of Damasio (2000), for example. This reifies the very model of social influence, embodied in the dualism between nature and nurture that has beset the psychological and biological sciences since at least the turn of the last century. It engenders some of the very paradoxes and dilemmas that cultural theory is attempting to move beyond, that is, the problem of structure and agency and the individual and society. As Leys (2000: 71) argues:

> the malleability and radical heterogeneity of the 'subject' that is internal to the mimetic theory will be countered by an antimimetic concept of the self as the sum or aggregate of more or less fixed component parts (Prince's 'traits' or 'dispositions', Janet's psychical 'elements', McDougall's 'instincts', etc.) that can be shuffled together in a variety of different combinations … . And whereas the mimetic paradigm expressly holds that no 'real' self exists prior to mimesis, the concept of the self as a multiple of component traits or dispositions tends itself to the commonsense idea that there exists a 'real' or 'normal' self that can be identified and recuperated.

The reliance of theories of brain plasticity such as we find in the work of Damasio on proto-theories of the self is exemplary in this respect. As we will see in the epilogue to this book, although Damasio's work assumes that the brain is plastic, subject to modification and transformation, his work also relies on minimal theories of subjectivity to make such claims (see also Malabou, 2008). We might conclude, therefore, that mimesis and anti-mimesis are never as far apart as they might at first seem. This work importantly also draws attention to the importance for humanities scholars of taking a more critical approach to neuroscientific and psychological forms of experimentation. My argument is that these forms of experimentation do not simply disclose or reveal psychological entities and objects, but rather are performative. They have complex genealogies which are important to take into account in any dialogue or engagement we might have with the sciences to authorize accounts and theories of affect.

## Conclusion

I am not suggesting, however, that we should choose mimesis over anti-mimesis. As Leys cogently argues, this would assume that suggestion is a continuous object that simply needs to be recovered. As she shows in her consideration of hypnotic techniques in relation to the rehabilitation of trauma, hypnosis itself takes form as a very different kind of object across a range of practices and techniques. However, reifying the subject as an information-processing machine or a neuro-hormonal subject does not resolve the practical difficulties of refusing suggestion. Rather than attempt to resolve on one or other side of the dichotomy, I seek instead to explore what suggestion might become if we allow the work to interpenetrate each other. I will start in the next chapter by utilizing what has been placed in the background in contemporary work – that is, the psychopathological, spiritual and psychic – to see how a re-engagement with these background versions might enrich cultural analysis. I will also keep very much in the foreground some of the insights from discursive analysis that have attempted to provide a more complex form of sociality than that produced within behaviourist models of socialization (cf. Henriques et al., 1984). What I will emphasize in this analysis are some of the terms that circulate within approaches to affect within cultural theory – that is, the concepts of energy, attunement, flow and transmission. These will be complemented by turning to work that is beginning to explore the relationship between rhythm and becoming. We will see that this work offers up a body of knowledge that refuses the idea of the singular body from the outset, and allows an invention or modelling of subjectivity that does not rely on what are often taken to be transhistorical concepts, such as habit or instinct.

# 5

## Affect, Energy, Rhythm and Transmission

> One is inside
>
>   then outside what one has been inside
>
>   One feels empty
>
>   Because there is nothing inside oneself
>
>   One tries to get inside oneself
>
>     that inside of the outside
>
>     that one was once inside
>
>     once one tries to get oneself inside what
>
>     one is outside:
>
>     to eat and to be eaten
>
>   to have the outside inside and to be
>
>     inside the outside (Laing, 1970: 83)

I have started this chapter with an excerpt from R.D. Laing's poetic translations of some of the relational dynamics that he observed in his clinical practice. He famously referred to them as knots, tangles, fankles, impasses, disjunctions, whirligogs and binds. The *knots* refer to those relational connections that circulate between people that are characterized by a kind of rhythmic repetition. This rhythmic repetition is not simply a fixity of habitual thought, but rather forms of dialogue and reflection that displace the very idea of a clear and distinct separation and boundary of self from other and inside from outside. Laing (1970) also referred to them as 'webs of *maya*', disclosing his interest perhaps in forms of energetic exchange or interchange that have a kind of psychic pull. We get caught up in these webs, perhaps losing our way or being unable to navigate. They are not us, but equally reveal the positions we try to invest in to resolve or rid ourselves of the unbearable tension these webs might create. The knots also reveal the complexity of how we might become an unwitting host, expressing a relational dynamic through the singular body as depression, neurosis, psychosis, paranoia and so forth. What is interesting about the dialogue scenarios that Laing dramatizes in the book, *Knots*, are the ways in which the dialogues mutate, converge and overlap, taking on a chameleon-like property. What characterizes the characters is less their ability for conscious deliberation, and more the affective intensity that pushes and pulls them into what might be described as forms of habit and repetition.

Laing, like many of his contemporaries, was interested in the relationship between energetic transmission and rhythm. Laing was writing in the same anti-psychiatric context that inspired the work of Deleuze and Guattari (Guattari, 1984). He drew on a contagion model, but this was a model that foregrounded the subject as a particular kind of host. The host would act as a kind of concealed carrier of relational dynamics which he or she was positioned within and could not necessarily articulate, except in some cases through extreme forms of bodily affectivity. Laing famously described one such *double-bind* in the context of a family member who expresses, through a psychotic episode, the connections or relational dynamics which bind the participants. What we have here is an extreme state of bodily affectivity linked to a particular set of relational dynamics or connections which might usually remain invisible or occluded. This state of bodily affectivity is not simply a felt sense of intensity, but a numbing and blinding repetition of bodily tics, obsessions, fixed ideas and compulsions which tie the subject to repetition and rigidity.

Laing's work foregrounds forms of psychopathology that are marked by rigidity, but which should not simply be dismissed or confined to habit or immobility. These forms of *secret madness*, usually expressed through a singular body, could be thought of as enactments of a disharmony or attunement of the subject to relational dynamics which are hidden or covered over. This is a kind of *rhythm analysis* which explores how some subjects might resonate with and through these energies, resulting in blockages or forms of inertia. Laing was interested in the concept of entrainment that had been developed in the work of geophysicists such as Shumans, who had explored how brainwaves can become attuned to naturally circulating rhythmic signals (cf. Becker and Shelden, 1985). Shumans had argued that instabilities or disharmonies in rhythms could produce tics, compulsions, narcolepsy, panic attacks and so forth.

We saw in the previous chapter how the notion of entrainment is one that has been developed in more meditative spiritual practices, such as Buddhism. Ann Game (2001) uses this concept to discuss forms of embodiment that are thoroughly relational and characterized by experiences of being moved or impressed, which bypass conscious rational reflection. Similarly, the embodied relations that Laing discusses are those that are marked by non-conscious absorption, bodily affectivity and a radical (psychosocial) forgetting. What is passed between participants is a form of energetic exchange that is felt within an affective register, and which is not easily available for conscious deliberation. It is not that affect or emotion is simply 'caught' or transmitted between subjects, but that subjects get 'caught up' in relational dynamics that exhibit a psychic or intensive pull. What this work draws attention to is the complexity of the relationship between energy, transmission and rhythm. The concept of entrainment that Laing mobilizes is one that presumes the subject is porous and permeable, rather than being affectively self-contained. Laing's project was a map of the power relationships that governed these energetic exchanges, where certain people's rhythms were subsumed or blocked by others. These rhythms related to the person's own bodily and psychic rhythms that would resonate and attune with others in harmonious or disharmonious ways: 'The principle of *autorhythm* entails that each person has his or her own biorhythm and a right to this rhythm, and no person has a right to interfere with the rhythm and tempo of anyone else if it is doing anyone harm' (Laing, 1985: 27).

Arguably, this is a mimetic model of transmission that explores the complexity of rhythmic identifications, dis-identifications and affective transfer between subjects. The dialogues he observed in his practice were not 'simple affective transfers' (Brennan, 2004: 49), but complex affective cycles that Laing situated within family relationships. The 'familialism' of Laing's project was one of the main reasons why Guattari rejected Laing's model of energetic exchange, framing it as a broader problem with how Freudian psychoanalysis specified the problem of madness (Guattari, 1984: 54). Guattari argued that Laing was simply reifying the family or Oedipal relations as an 'interpretive machine' that was simply replacing one set of repressive social relations with another (p. 56). As has been well documented, the project of Deleuze and Guattari, from *Anti-Oedipus: Capitalism and Schizophrenia* (1983) to Deleuze's later writing in the *Logic of Sense* (1990) and *A Thousand Plateaus* (1987), develops an energetic model of affective exchange or *becoming*. Deleuze and Guattari's notion of becoming was indebted to modes of psychopathological experience, such as delusions and hallucinations that were characterized by 'a considerable disordering of conventional subjectivity' (Goddard, 2001: 54). As we have seen, Laing saw the production of psychopathology, expressed through particular psychic and bodily symptoms, as tied to complex relational dynamics that were difficult to see.

In contradistinction, Deleuze and Guattari argued that psychopathology was a form of becoming or creative breakdown that allowed one not only to see repressive social structures but also to escape them (Goddard, 2001: 54). Thus, Guattari's description of femininity or 'feminine becoming' as an escape from the norms of an established order was equated to the 'sex of children, of psychotics, of poets (note the coincidence in Ginsberg, for instance, of a fundamental poetic mutation of a sexual mutation)' (Guattari, 1984: 233). Thus psychopathology was refigured as a form of *creative becoming* that would become a model or figuration for how to think about energetic exchange and vitalism. As we saw in the previous two chapters, what this tends towards within contemporary understandings is the development of a new vitalist politics that privileges movement and flow. Life is characterized as movement 'understood in terms of constantly shifting relationships *between* open-ended objects' (Fraser et al., 2005: 3).

In this chapter I want to consider in more detail some of the assumptions that are being imported into this new vitalist politics, and focus upon what is being occluded or placed firmly within the background. By taking matters psychic, spiritual and psychopathological as case studies we will see that a consideration of the occlusions makes for the emergence of a rather different set of concerns. I want to suggest that these concerns offer up a radically different figuration for thinking about vitalism in the context of the psychological and psychopathological. This will enable us to think about the relationship between affect, energy, rhythm and transmission in ways that do not require a retreat to the *singular* neuroendocrinological or neurophysiological body to explain the mechanisms of transmission. As I argued in the previous chapter, although distance from biology is no longer a marker of work in the humanities, a focus upon research in the biological and psychological sciences that works with a singular body is problematic. There is an assumption from the outset that you can separate the inside from the outside, the psychological from the social, and the natural from the cultural. Although, of course, there is a commitment to displacing these dualisms, the problem of social influence creeps in through the back door and refuses to go away.

The engagement with the 'hard' edges of the biological and psychological sciences is an attempt to deal with the flattening out of the subject that is characteristic of much of this work. If we simply see energy as flowing between individuals, how can we explain the mechanisms of transmission? However, if energy can be converted into hormones or pheromones, then the mystery is revealed and we can explain sociality. This does not resolve the problem of mimetic desire (Leys, 2000) or suggestion and is in danger of reducing the psychological complexity of becoming to chemical or neurophysiological information exchange. What we have here are forms of embodied materiality that reduce the enactment of being 'one yet many' to biological and neurological processes. Although the subject within these formations has a body (rather than being patterns of information, for example), what we end up with are forms of materialism that distribute the psychological throughout the nervous system, the brain and the hormone system. This 'setting in the flesh' arguably produces new forms of determinism that are not dissimilar to the forms of distributed cognition characteristic of molecular biology (Hayles, 1999: 57). As we have seen, these approaches all eliminate suggestion from their theorizing, and particularly forms of suggestion that were not simply located within the mind or produced within a contrast between will and compliance (Sidis, 1898). The occlusion of this work has led to particular models of the psychopathological and the spiritual being mobilized within many contemporary approaches to affect with little reflection or consideration of their complex conditions of emergence and formation. I will start this chapter by considering what models of psychopathology have been mobilized within some of these accounts and what the implications are for theorizing *becoming*.

## Psychopathology and Becoming

In *Mass Hysteria: Critical Psychology and Media Studies*, I argued with Valerie Walkerdine (2001) that cultural theory regularly uses overgeneralized psychological and psychopathological categories in order to theorize subject formation. These have included the concept of schizophrenia in the work of Frederic Jameson (1991) and autism and melancholia in the work of Baudrillard (1983), for example. One model of psychopathology that is preferred by many contemporary philosophers and cultural theorists is mania. Emily Martin (2007) has suggested that manic experience has come to be seen as a productive, creative force within neoliberal cultures. It is seen to 'produce an immense and potentially creative liability of mind' and is becoming highly valued in the work place and increasingly viewed as a positive state within late capitalism (p. 188). In this section we will consider why this psychopathological category has had such a use value and has become a taken-for-granted concept in much theorizing. The relationship between mania as a form of creativity and ways of understanding sociality and subject formation has been a long and complex one. I will start with debates that have a more recent history and relevance for later discussion in this chapter. This is a permutation of the idea of mania as a creative force that links it more firmly to the notion of genius.

## Outsider Art

The mythology of creative genius and its relationship to psychopathology has a long historical lineage. In the early part of the twentieth century one variant of this discussion took place in relation to the value and significance of what has come to be known as 'outsider art'. This is art that has been made by psychiatric in-patients, mediums, visionaries, criminals and others who were considered eccentric and existing outside of social norms. As the supplementary catalogue accompanying an exhibition of 'outsider art' termed, *Inner Worlds Outside*, at the Whitechapel Gallery, London (28 April – 25 June 2006), recounts, the definition of outsider art by artists such as Paul Klee and Pablo Picasso was art that was taken to be 'spontaneous and unadulterated by knowledge'. This assumption brings together two key ideas: that 'outsider art' is produced out of an experience of 'social isolation and an autonomous creativity' (Spira, 2006: p. 7). One of the key problems that have been identified with this definition is whether individuals are able to exist outside of cultural norms and, if so, what this means for how we understand sociality and the nature of art practice.

These questions might seem strange when we consider work that has come out of a constructionist and post-structuralist tradition across the humanities that has understood the subject as formed in and through the workings of language, discourse and signification. In fact, what the exhibition describes as a postmodernist sensibility is one that problematizes the very idea of social isolation and autonomous creativity. From this vantage point it seems strange to see certain individuals or groups as creative geniuses able to escape regulation and put images and ideas together in ways that create diversion, distraction and new ways of seeing, being and experiencing. However, it is precisely this mythology of creative genius that Guattari (1984) mobilizes in his definition of becoming. The focus upon a micropolitics of desire in Guattari's (1984) book, *Molecular Revolution: Psychiatry and Politics*, saw a dispersal of groups and individuals, including women, children, 'psychotics' and artists, as engaging in forms of revolutionary struggle that could render impotent or immobilize repressive social structures. In other words, the mad were true revolutionaries who have escaped social control and would provide a model of becoming that could inspire political struggle:

> What this means is unleashing a whole host of expressions, and experimentations – those of children, of schizophrenics, of homosexuals, of prisoners, of misfits of every kind – that all work to penetrate and eat into the semiology of the dominant order, to feel out new escape routes and produce new and unheard of constellations of a signifying particlesigns. (Guattari, 1984: 84)

Thus molecular desire is equated to movement and flux that is blocked by the molar; the molar are arrangements and constellations of relational elements that become grouped or territorialized, preventing the movement of machinic desire. These are crystallizations of systems of intensity that delimit becomings and prevent or block the possibility of movement. We can see through the terms that Guattari uses in his discussion of creative becomings that the model is very much an energetic model of flux, flow and intensive relationships. It operates according to a bipolar logic that privileges flow and movement and views modes of subjectification (in the Foucauldian sense) as tending to 'block the fluxes' (p. 102). This bipolar logic privileges particular forms of psychopathology; that is, those characterized by mania. The psychiatric definition of mania refers to what is taken to be a pathologically elated and elevated mental state, characterized by rapidity of thinking, euphoria, agility of cognition, lack of inhibition, talkativeness and so forth. This is a hyperrhythmic state that is constantly in movement, resulting in some cases in an inability to sleep, impulsiveness and sometimes psychotic delusions and hallucination.

Catherine Dale (2001) has explored this logic through an engagement with Deleuze's fascination and entrancement with the work of Antonin Artaud. Artaud was a poet, writer, actor and theatre practitioner who struggled with and against the psychiatric system that had incarcerated him for his experiences of psychopathology. What was important to Deleuze and Guattari about the performativity of Artaud's (1958) well-documented mania (and psychiatric incarceration) in his theatre of cruelty was the importance of gesturality (Kristeva, 1989). The theatre of cruelty has been described as a form of 'in yer face' theatre that 'grabs the audience by the scruff of the neck and shakes it until it gets the message' (Siertz, 2006). Siertz discusses the characteristics of 'in yer face' theatre that have produced a new aesthetic sensibility that works with affective transmission, preferring audiences to feel shocked, upset and offended on a deeply visceral level. It tries to engage audiences in an affective register such that they are unable to position themselves as detached spectators. Artaud used theatre as a form to explore this affective transmission. He did not simply recount his experiences of mania in either a poetic or literal sense, but rather enacted their felt intensity through the materiality of his body. The intoxicating sounds, images and thought which leaked in often quite brutal and violent ways pointed to the impossibility of deciding whether they were real or imagined; whether he was recounting through a strategy of performative deliberation, or allowing the audience to witness the process of a further breakdown which would end in his 'histrionic collapse' (Dale, 2001: 85): 'Artaud bases his theatre of cruelty upon a model of movement, which, like the movement in Balinese dancing, in which Artaud was keenly interested, is not narrative but affective' (Dale, 2001: 134).

Thus we can see here the relationship between movement and energetic force that has become the foundation of the Deleuzian approach to becoming. For Artaud, theatre was a site for disclosing the life force that flowed through and between people, where the theatre of cruelty was

> designed to wake the audience and actors alike from the sleepy voyeur-
> ism of contemporary theatre and its reliance on representation and
> psychology. In attacking the spectator's sensibility, the theatre of cru-
> elty seeks to scare the audience, so that, on leaving, they feel as though
> they have just left the dentist's chair. (Dale, 2001: 132)

Blockages within this bipolar logic were equated to habits and automatisms that would prevent the movement of what Dale (2001: 134) equates to 'the first force of man, his *élan vital*'. This model of energetic flow was based upon a very particular model or version of psychopathology that would equate madness to a form of creative insanity or 'poetic fire' (Porter, 1987). The condition of madness as a form of poetic fire relates to a nineteenth-century version of moral insanity that viewed madness – or 'cracking up', to use Deleuze's terminology – as a condition of error or deception. Moral insanity was thus a (mis-)association of ideas, accidental (and often creative) connections and unnatural associations. The mind was delirious, 'going off the tracks' (Donnolley, 1983: 111) deluding judgement and will. As Porter (1987: 86) discusses, whilst considering the profound influence of Locke's theories on this version: 'Madmen, he wrote, do not appear to have lost the faculty of reasoning but having joined together some ideas very wrongly, they mistake them for truths, and they err as men do that argue right from wrong principles.'

Within this reconfiguration of the mind as a creative reasoning apparatus came a restructuring of those elements of mind seen to play a part in this active process. The assemblage of elements which made up this discursive space included a fascination with 'twilight states', such as reverie, illusions, somnambulism, hypnoticism, and sleep and dreaming. One key distinction which was mobilized was one that differentiated the imagination from the intellect, and linked the creative action of the imagination with both madness and genius. The imagination was constituted therefore as a fantastical space of 'creative reverie' where new and novel associations could be made. Within the psychiatric nomenclature of the time forms of moral insanity were differentiated from other forms of madness that were considered congenital, where intellectual and creative powers have either decayed, weakened or been entirely obliterated. These distinctions were mapped onto distinctions which were gendered, sexed, raced and classed, and were to be radically reconfigured with the shift to molecular psychiatry at the turn of the last century, which unified madness as an expression of degeneracy (see Blackman, 2001, for an extended discussion).

The exaltation of the 'schizophrenic' as a 'sensitive type' able to free the imagination and explore an illusory, expansive space was also part of a reconfiguration of madness that took place within a set of reverse or counter-discourses in the 1950s, 1960s and 1970s within Anglo-American culture. These ideas were also taken up in humanistic psychology and referred to as the 'third force' (see Blackman, 2001). The 'schizophrenic' was seen to possess an exceptional gift or sensitivity that, in common with other 'ecstatic' states, would lead to a loss of sensibility (Laski, 1961). This state was seen as providing access to a range of creative experiences. Texts such as Gowan's (1975) *Trance, Art and Creativity* viewed hallucinatory phenomena as providing access to a prototaxic mode – a trance state that was viewed as necessary for creativity.

Hallucinations appear to occur under all types of trance experience, spirit possession, mediumship, shamanism, hypnosis, psychoactive drugs, and sensory deprivation. They also appear to occur rather uniquely outside of trance to 'normal' persons where there is sufficient psychic pressure (such as the death of a friend or relative). Whether one is dealing with the voices of spirit possession, and mediumship, the magical lights and other out-of-body experiences of the shamen, the induced hallucinations of the hypnotist, the psychedelic colours of the drug-user or similar visual imagery in sensory deprivation, the diversity and universality of such imagery is evident. (Gowan, 1975: 128)

In a similar vein, Laski (1961) redefines Virginia Woolf's writings as accounts of ecstasy, where she is viewed as having an extra-special sensitivity. The dissolution of the mind was seen as the first step in attaining mental health (Gowan, 1975; Huxley, 1961; Leary, 1968, 1973; Ouspensky, 1968). These ecstatic states were also linked to mystical experiences that were seen to reveal other dimensions to life to that which was viewed as the 'everyday technological world view' (Greeley, 1974: 7). These ideas became connected up in a counter-movement that used psychedelics and mind-expanding drugs such as mescaline to provide a glimpse to these other dimensions of life (Weil, 1973). These ideas were reformulated within humanistic psychology in the 1960s and 1970s, emphasizing the importance of adaptation, growth and development as a life-enhancing process (Maslow, 1954; Rogers, 1961). The mystical-religious framework that underpinned this discussion was reworked within a particular psychological landscape.

In her book, *Transpositions*, Rosi Braidotti (2006) recognizes that the Deleuzian energetic conception of the becoming subject is one that has a lineage through the work of Spinoza to forms of mysticism, spirituality and psychopathology. Deleuze was particularly entranced with the notion of the 'crack' that was so elegantly described by F. Scott Fitzgerald in his novel, *The Crack-Up*. This novel recounts his experiences of eventual (alcoholic) breakdown and nervous exhaustion. Deleuze relates this to contemporary attempts of artists, writers and intellectuals to think through and with 'the crack': the profound and ineluctable limit of one's tolerance for the intensities which 'push the subject to deferral' (Bradotti, 2006: 261). Bradotti discusses key female literary authors and writers, including Virginia Woolf and Sylvia Plath who suffered with forms of psychopathology that would exemplify this historical and, some might say, mythological link between madness and creative genius. These forms of creative madness or mania were viewed as complex forms of psychopathology that were linked to the fine-tuning of an intellect which might go awry. These were forms of madness linked to the mind and thought or 'thought-energy' (Dale, 2001: 131) producing associations and mis-associations of ideas.

However, these forms of madness were also the privilege and province of the middle-class intellectual or literary figure, and were usually aligned to conditions of life seen to be peculiar to men, such as work, wealth, business and family responsibilities (Maudsley, 1879). Thus, 'simpler' forms of insanity were more usually aligned with the working classes, colonial subjects and women, viewed as the expression of inferior psychic and biological constitution (see Blackman, 2001, for an extended discussion). It is interesting that what has been authorized within more Deleuzian versions of contemporary approaches to affect is a disembodied vital force which flows through the social body. The subject is a conduit for such forces, which are felt with an affective intensity, and open and extend the subject such that they are always 'in transport' (Massumi, 2002b).

I have tried to show in my argument so far that the energetic model of becoming which Deleuze develops is inflected through the deployment of a particular model of psychopathology: creative mania. This romantic framing of the problem of psychopathology is one that sees the very groups who would be viewed as degenerate within molecular psychiatry in the nineteenth century refigured as creative, revolutionary heroes providing philosophy and political struggle with their true vanguards. A similar romanticism might be detected in the work of Braidotti (2006), who equates the intensity of the interrelationships which the becoming subject is located within as an awareness (if at times painful and untenable awareness) of this flow and distribution of forces. She cites Deleuze's discussion of his own alcoholism and eventual suicide as central to the bringing of death into life characteristic of his non-dualistic philosophy of bodily affectivity. Her focus upon death (*zoe*) as well as life (*bios*) is a welcome excursion from forms of vitalism which she aligns with neoliberal strategies of governmentality. These are those that would render pathological some of the practices that might help you cope and endure; what she reframes as 'whatever gets you through the day'. As she argues: 'Happiness, in this scheme of thought, is a political question and the role of the state is to enhance and not hinder humans in their striving to become all they are capable of' (p. 230). However, what is perhaps overlooked in Braidotti's figuration are the implications of mobilizing particular models of psychopathology that are deployed with little caution or reflection. What I want to do in the next section is focus upon and explore in more detail what is occluded, hidden and disqualified by this model (in terms of psychopathology). This would point towards other kinds of figuration that would still foreground energetic connections and a rhythmic approach to affect refracted through a rather different set of concerns.

## Rhythm Analysis

Christian Borch (2005: 2) has argued that Gabriel Tarde's thought raises two important issues for contemporary theorizing: 'crowds and rhythms'. As we have seen throughout this book, Tarde's account of sociality relied upon a particular psychical constitution or process to explain the spread of social forces – a complex concept of imitation that was derived from particular understandings of hypnotic suggestibility. Tarde (1969: 22) believed that inventions were always 'heavily dependent on antecedent ideas' and that ideas and practices developed, mutated and spread due to 'increasing imitations, oppositions and inventions'. In the foreword to Tarde's book, *On Communication and Social Influence*, Clark draws an analogy between imitation and 'the ripples on a surface of a pond',

> regularly progressing toward the limits of the system until they come into contact with some obstacle. The obstacle, however, is likely to be the imitation of some earlier invention, and when the two collide, from their opposition is likely to emerge a new product – that is, a new invention – which in turn is imitated until it too meets further obstacles, and so on, ad infinitum. (Tarde, 1969: 21)

Tarde's concept of imitation was one which was not about mechanical reproduction, but a more complex form of imitative desire which was *thought* through concepts derived specifically from hypnotic trance and psychical research. This allowed for spontaneity and repetition to exist in close proximity, and to trouble any notion of a simple stasis of reproduction, which he attributed to the work of Durkheim (see Blackman, 2007b, for a development of this). Borch (2005) recasts this process as one which foregrounds rhythm as an important component of Tarde's ontology of suggestion, and suggests that this aspect of Tarde's work has been given much less attention. One commonality between Tarde's approach to rhythm and R.D. Laing's is the presumption that these rhythms are conditioned or engendered by relational connections that often remain occluded or are difficult to see. The emphasis on rhythm for both writers is not one of simple repetition, but one that recognizes the contingency of rhythm; they change, mutate, converge and overlap. They often depend upon some kind of repetition, but it is not repetition itself that is the defining element. Borch turns to the work of

Nikolas Rose to explore the materiality of rhythm, and how rhythms can be conditioned, structured and produced by particular architectural, governmental, cultural and scientific practices. He argues, following Rose (1990, 1996, 1999), that

> as the individual does not exist prior to the rhythms but, on the contrary, is produced by them and their momentary stabilized junctions, and since the subjectification of the individual therefore changes, rhythmanalysis is not merely a perspective on imitations per se, but equally a tool to demonstrate a society's dominant ways of promoting subject positions. (Borch, 2005: 94)

Although this is an important component of any rhythm analysis, the focus upon practices of self and social regulation reintroduces many of the problems that are guiding contemporary approaches to affect within the humanities. That is, the question still remains why certain practices have such an affective force or psychic pull. Why do subjects have a subjective commitment to certain practices rather than others? How might we understand and analyse what Connolly (2002: 20) frames as the forms of 'subliminal attachment' that connect bodies, brains and culture? These are the very questions that inaugurated the mobilization of more psychodynamic theories to complement what was seen to be the overly deterministic approach to discursive constitution in the work of Michel Foucault, for example (cf. Blackman and Walkerdine, 2001; Butler, 1993; Walkerdine, 1990; Walkerdine et al., 2001). What we can take from the long tradition of work in critical psychology and cultural theory that has spanned at least the last three decades is that techniques of self and social regulation marshal, organize and choreograph affective attachments. We are not simply voluntarist, cognitivist subjects who move freely across practices. Rather what characterizes the possibility of change is the subject's very resistances to that process (cf. Walkerdine, 1990; Butler, 1993).

What is characteristic of some contemporary approaches to affect across the humanities is a retreat to the neurophysiological body in order to explain the mechanisms of affective transmission. Although this work is bringing the body back into discursive analysis, it relies upon work that has already presumed a split between the individual and the social. It also reduces psychic or psychological complexity to the neurophysiological. The problem is one that Riley (1983) identified many years ago when she argued that biological explanations of social life and social explanations of psychological life were both equally deterministic. In some ways, the very terms of this pendulum-like swing are not overcome by revalorizing work in the biological and psychological sciences. What we need are approaches that can recognize the problem of 'the one and the many', but also be sensitive to relational connections that cannot easily be seen.

In Laing's approach these relational connections were most visible in disruptions of rhythm that were both contingent (they were identified by shifting and modulating patterns of repetition of thought, feeling and so forth), and revealed through a cleavage or gap between the relational constellation and the affective intensity or psychic pull of the members within it. The rift would disclose the complex basis of the affective attachments which might bind the participants, often through the registering of extreme forms of psychic and bodily affectivity (usually by one of the participants). I want to take this as a model for beginning to think about the relationship between rhythm, energy and affect. In the next section I will consider the seminal work of the British playwright, debbie tucker green, in order to illustrate what I think is at stake.

## Handprint

debbie tucker green is a black feminist playwright who has already been compared to Sarah Kane, the enfant terrible of the theatre establishment whose work has also been characterized as part of 'in yer face' theatre (Siertz, 2006). Like Kane (2001), who wrote a series of plays dealing with emotional, physical and sexual abuse and her own experiences of psychiatric incarceration, debbie tucker green also deals with difficult and complex emotional issues. She has been described by Lynette Goddard (2007: 182), in the book, *Staging Black Feminisms: Identity, Politics, Performance*, as the 'most significant Black British playwright of recent years'. *Dirty Butterfly*, *Born Bad* and *Stoning Mary* all deal with examples of familial abuse 'told' through a theatrical form that discloses the complex relationships between affect, rhythm and energy (see Goddard, 2007, for an extended discussion). I will concentrate on a radio dramatization of her play *Handprint* that reveals some of the issues that I wish to foreground in my discussion of psychopathology and its mobilization by cultural and philosophical theorizing.

*Handprint* was broadcast on BBC Radio 3 in the UK on 26 March 2006 and is described as an intense encounter between a man and a woman in a bar one evening. The play is made up of a series of vignettes that move between a number of background stories that illuminate what might usually remain in the background. This movement reveals something of what compels the man and woman to keep talking to each other. Their compulsion is framed through a frustrating cycle of affective dynamics that see the man and woman taking up the position of tormentor, persecutor and victim at different moments throughout the dialogue. The dialogue is multi-layered and open, with the man and woman appearing to become different characters    characters who are never specified by name so that the issue of who is being exploited and exploiting can never be resolved. The characters return again and again to the same assertions that are recast in slightly different permutations each time, revealing the psychic or affective pull that keeps them in movement.

As Goddard discusses, tucker green has been inspired by rhythm; both the rhythmic forms of some black poetry, music and performance, including the songs of American and British black artists such as Lauryn Hill, Beverley Knight and Jill Scott, and the sound and rhythm of black urban speech. As Goddard argues, what characterizes much black urban speech, particularly within black urban street culture are 'short simple sentences replete with repetitions, backtracking, interruptions, overlaps, silences, stammers and stutters' (p. 185). The affectual force of the dialogue is carried through the relationship of rhyme, rhythm and repetition that, she argues, allows 'intense personal dynamics' to be 'conveyed by focusing on the verbalization of the characters' banal and trivial internal and unconscious thoughts' (p. 188). It is certain that affect is being passed between subjects, but what is made visible is how the characters are literally driven to tears, violence and anger by relational dynamics that they do not understand and cannot clearly articulate. As one of the characters played by a woman states in *Handprint*: 'Are you doing it on purpose, what you don't know you doing?' The play is about feeling *and* not feeling cast not as opposites, but in close relational proximity. The characters feel with an affective intensity, but they do not understand the psychic or affective pull that produces this intensity. In many ways the vignettes in *Handprint* as well as the oeuvre of tucker green's plays share many characteristics with the dialogues poetically dramatized by R.D. Laing (1970) in *Knots*. Characters literally go round and round tied to dynamics that are not repeated in mechanical form, but mutate, converge and overlap such that it is difficult to see where one person ends and the other begins.

Goddard ends her discussion with the implications of tucker green's work for developing black feminist futures. She focuses on the opening speech from tucker green's play *Born Bad* that deals with a young daughter's resentment of her mother:

DAWTA:  If you actin like a bitch

I'm a call you it

If you looking like a bitch

I'm a call you it

If you looking like a bitch as you looking on me – I see yu and yu bitch ways – mi a go call you it again mi noh business

Watching yu watchin me like the bitch bitch you is

(tucker green, 2003: 4 quoted in Goddard, 2007: 181)

Goddard's discussion of the play focuses upon how the characters are 'trapped in the intensity of tackling the issues that have created their family dynamics' (2007: 181). Similarly, Laing's dialogue-scenarios in *Knots* reveal the frustrating intensities that bind the participants together and literally tie themselves and others up in their energetic interchange. To continue the dialogue-scenario that opened this chapter:

But this is not enough. One is trying to get

the inside of what one is outside inside, and to

get inside the outside. But one does not get

inside the outside by getting the outside inside

for;

although one is full inside of the inside of the outside

one is on the outside of one's own inside

and by getting inside the outside

one remains empty because

while one is on the inside

even the inside of the outside is outside

and inside oneself there is still nothing

There has never been anything else

And there never will be (Laing, 1970: 83)

The image of the handprint taken from the title of tucker green's play of the same name is a beguiling mnemonic for remembering what might be covered over by the mythology of madness as a form of creative genius. What tucker green explores are forms of psychic and bodily affectivity that confine, trap and tie the subject to inertia, habit, depression, distress, paranoia and so forth. These forms of psychopathology are those that are made 'other' to the ontology of movement and flow privileged in many discussions of affect and becoming that we explored in Chapters 1 and 4. These are forms of psychopathology that are about movement, but movement that returns to the same frustrating point, albeit in a slightly different configuration each time. The subject becomes defined by their body, where, in many contemporary explanations of psychopathology, habit, rigidity and inertia point towards the inability of the subject to engage the capacity for conscious deliberation and flexible thinking that would allow them to self-organize in light of these recursive loops (Blackman, 2005).

Similar kinds of assumption also appear in some work aligned with affect theory across the humanities. Bruno Latour presumes that subjects can be articulate through learning to be affected, 'put into motion by other entities, humans or non-humans' (2004: 205). This proposition assumes that subjects embody the potential to be affected, and that this potential is maximized or diminished through the way one is linked and articulated through relationships with others, again human and non-human. The body is 'a dynamic trajectory', and can become more or less sensitive to the elements which mediate this potential (Latour, 2004: 206). In a similar vein, Brennan (2004: 117) argues that a knowledge of affective transmission can be developed through what she terms 'practices of discernment' (equated to psychoanalytic practices) such that 'affects pass from the state of sensory registration to a state of cognitive or intelligent reflection' (p. 120). These are similar arguments to those being made within forms of psychological theorizing that are drawing from complexity theory (Marks-Tarlow, 1999) and discursive and critical psychology in the context of dialogical psychology (Lewis, 2002). These arguments reframe what I have termed James's 'problem of personality' (the problem of how we 'hang together') as a problem of dialogicity (Blackman, 2005). The problem of dialogicity identifies the cognitive and linguistic capacities that allow subjects to be both 'one yet many' (Lewis, 2002: 150).

The dialogical self is a self which is characterized by its flexibility; its ability to be open to change, to be dynamic, experimental, creative and innovative, but also to enact its own self-regulation and control. As Josephs (2002: 162) argues, 'the self is regarded as a plurality of different, including even opposite, voices, rather than a uni-dimensional, monological entity'. The flexible self is able to embrace change and movement, whereas the habitual self is aligned to rigidity, routine and tradition, viewed as the enemy of dialogicity. As Lysaker and Lysaker

(2002: 213) state when discussing the collapse of the dialogic self in schizophrenia, 'we would find a rich and lively internal world, one replete with affect but lacking in organization, coherent interconnections and therefore accessibility to others'. The curative process that Lysaker and Lysaker (2002) advocate is one which should focus on the renewal of dialogical processes where the therapist becomes a 'cognitive prosthetic' (p. 217). These accounts that traverse cultural theory and the psychological and biological sciences assume that the self is a process, not an entity, but that a healthy 'self' is one who is capable of flexible reorganization and conscious discernment or deliberation. To be moved implies an awareness, and as Latour (2004: 205) suggests in the context of what it means to have a body, to be put into motion requires a registering of this motion as 'if you are not engaged in this learning you become insensitive, dumb, you drop dead'.

What is interesting about the becoming subject of Deleuze, as developed by Braidotti (2006), Latour (2004) and Despret (2004a, 2004b) is that the subject is reified as having or being able to develop the capacity for attunement, described as a becoming aware of the intensities and relational connections that are articulating her. What is missed by these accounts is how the concept of entrainment developed by Laing, Game and tucker green is a sensitivity to a relational process that is marked by non-conscious absorption, bodily affectivity and a radical (psychosocial) forgetting (see Chapter 6 of this book for a development of this). tucker green's focus upon the relationship between rhythm and affect is inflected through a gendered and racialized politics. She recognizes that what is expressed through a singular body is that which often the subject does not know or feel, but that locates her within a set of complex political and relational dynamics. This was the thrust of Laing's work that, although rejected for his familialism, still offers some interesting tools for theorizing. This is particularly urgent given the overgeneralized ways in which psychological and psychopathological concepts have tended to be used within cultural theorizing. I will turn to a development of these ideas in the next chapter. To conclude this chapter we will turn to a related discussion of the relationship between mysticism and becoming within Deleuzian-inspired work that identifies a rather similar set of concerns.

## The Body of the Medium

In an edited book, *Deleuze and Religion*, Bryden (2001: 1) highlights the 'contact zone' between mysticism and the Deleuzian notion of

becoming that has resonances with the argument I made in the preceding discussion. In the same volume, Goddard (2001) argues that
mysticism as 'an existential practice of subjectification' (p. 53) is
based upon an 'ecstatic experience of the outside' (p. 54). This was
central to Deleuze's notion of becoming. He suggests that mysticism
in Deleuze's account is aligned with other forms of creative breakdown, such as psychopathology, that disaggregate or disrupt conventional modes of subjectivity. Goddard suggests that Deleuze
distinguished between ecstactic forms of mysticism and those that
become institutionalized, thus becoming static. The flow of an *élan
vital* engendered by mystical practices was contrasted with the
blockages instilled by religious practices, doctrines and techniques
that crystallized this force and 'turn back the flow of creative evolution' (Goddard, 2001: 58). Goddard (2001: 57) suggests that
Deleuze equates this *élan vital* to Bergson's (1911) discussion in
*Creative Evolution* that characterizes it as a 'virtual creative force that
propels life forward, to develop ever new forms in a process of per-
petual invention and becoming'. Goddard clearly shows the mystical
component to Deleuze's thought (inspired by Bergson), that is
dependent upon a very particular conception of the spiritual.
Goddard argues that although Bergson's thought was indebted to
research into the psychic and paranormal, it is a good deal more
controversial to make this claim about Deleuze. However, he argues
that without an understanding of the historical antecedents to this
work it is hard to fully grasp how Deleuze was mobilizing energies
and affect in relation to cinema, for example. As he argues:

> Nevertheless, as in the case of the mystic, cinema, in its crystalline
> forms can become a spiritual tool, capable of facilitating an experience
> of ecstatic subjectification in which spectators experience cinema as a
> pure optical and sound formation, a vision and a voice, a scattering of
> time crystals that leads them beyond the boundaries of their static
> selves and into profound contact with the outside. (Goddard, 2001: 62)

Keith Ansell-Pearson (2001) also shows the lineage between
Deleuze's notion of creative becomings and the Bergsonian notion of
creative evolution. He argues that Deleuze's focus was on invention, on
the unthinkable and unseeable, that which has not been actualized but
exists as a creative possibility. Thus the mystical as well as the psychopathological create 'zones of indiscernibility' (p. 150), which have the
potential to give birth to new modes of existence. As he argues (p. 141):

> 'God' stands for a centred universe, a fixed hierarchical order, and a
> substance that is outside of an immanent becoming or evolution; in

short, it stands for transcendence. Deleuze, then, is a thinker of the infinite: of infinite movement and infinite speed precisely because he is a thinker of immanence.

This relationship is based upon an ontology of flow and movement that arguably obscures and elides other ways of framing the relationships between affect, energy and transmission. In order to consider this and inaugurate a different set of concerns, I want to consider the body of the medium. As we already discussed in Chapters 3 and 4, nineteenth-century spiritualism was a religious imaginary that was centred upon practices which aimed to demonstrate and open up the possibility of communication with the dead. The body of the medium was likened to a lightening rod, channelling forces which would manifest in voices, images, sensations and bodily performances, which were made available for inspection, verification, interrogation and delegitimation or authentication. So what other figurations might we take from the link between spiritualism and contemporary approaches to affect that might foreground a related but also rather different set of concerns?

I want to sketch out a number of concerns that I hope might contribute to a rather different kind of project. The first is that what became important within scientific studies of spiritualism and suggestibility were the bodies of particular subjects. Whether it was the shellshocked soldier who so occupied Freud and his technique of abreaction and cartharsis, or the feminine body of the medium and the veridicality of the voices she spoke, what was authorized was the study of suggestibility within a singular body. Although early crowd psychology was concerned with the way in which a complex set of social, affective and economic connections could be modified and amplified, what was instated was a concern with the pathological characteristics of crowds which were likened to the feminine and the abnormal (cf. Barrows, 1981). With the translation of suggestion as a mechanism for understanding affective transmission into a set of capacities located within a singular body, suggestion was increasingly to be specified through the action of the central nervous system. For social psychologists, such as Allport (1924: 245), suggestibility mobilized 'prepotent reactions'. These were viewed as 'deep-lying reaction tendencies [which are] already present' within individuals and groups (p. 245). Allport (1924: 246) mobilized this notion of suggestibility, defined as a sympathetic reaction brought about by conditioning, to explain the popularity of spiritualism between the two world wars in Britain:

Persons deprived of loved ones by the late war have developed an attitude of yearning expectancy concerning some future contact with the souls of the dead. Spiritualistic mediums and *ouija* boards have provided suggestions for the release of these tendencies, and an international craze for things 'psychic' has been the result. Yawning when others yawn is not sheer imitation. It occurs principally when we are tired and on the point of yawning ourselves.

The affective intensity of such responses was linked to the action of the central nervous system. Prepotent responses, although learnt and acquired, were, for Allport, accompanied by the preparatory setting of the synapses which would be augmented, intensified and discharged by certain forms of social facilitation and stimulus. Thus, the experience of affective transmission was one which could be explained through the action of the central nervous system which would produce 'bodily changes' (Allport, 1924: 304). These were distributed to muscles, the senses and other parts of the nervous system, creating a felt sense of affective intensity. With this move from ordinary suggestibility (as a form of invisible mental touch) to the examination of suggestibility within a singular body, habit becomes the location for automaticity, non-intentional communication and bodily affectivity. For Freud, of course, the instincts became the site of affective intensity, and repression became the logic of connection and transformation. But what might happen if we foreground instead spiritual communication as a figuration which does not simply point towards invisible energies, but also to connections between the self and other, human and non-human, past and present and physical and ethereal, which can only be spoken and felt by some people and not others; or at other times may not be spoken at all. In other words, those carnal, relational connections which circulate and position people and that are usually occluded and covered over. These are connections which are felt affectively, and which circulate between the self and other, the human and the non-human, the physical and the ethereal, and which make it difficult to establish borders and boundaries. This does not mean that the subject is a mere node, a lightening conductor for such forces; but rather that these connections and capacities are felt and expressed in registers which might not be easily available for conscious reflection, or for academic cartography (of the kind practiced by proponents of actor network theory, for example).

I want to take the figure of the medium as an example to foreground what I think is important in this transfiguration. What was considered vulgar about spiritualism, according to Daniel Cottom (1988), was not only the way in which spiritual modes of communication were open to everyone, including and especially so-called ordinary folk, but also how one could be impressed or moved by the words of the medium and by the sounds emitted by everyday domestic furniture. One such object, which became an emblematic figure of such lowly perturbations, was the table. As Cottom (1988: 765) amusingly recounts:

> Soon after modern spiritualism announced itself with the 'Rochester knockings' of 1848, tables took on a new and controversial life. No longer were they content to live out their days impassively upholding dishes and glasses and silverware, vases, papers and books, bibelots, elbows, or weary heads. They were changed: they began to move. Tables all over the United States and then in England, France, and other countries commenced rapping, knocking, tilting, turning, tipping, dancing, levitating, and even 'thrilling' – though this last was uncommon.

It was not of course the table, or other 'homely devices' (p. 770) such as cabinets, musical instruments, curtains and drapery which became the subject and object of scientific enquiry. Rather, men of philosophy and science, such as William James, Henri Bergson and Gabriel Tarde, were interested in the veridicality of the words and information 'telegraphed' by the (female) medium. The very definition of mediumship was one in which the medium did not know the words she spoke. She was a mere conductor to be judged by the audience, which increasingly was to be assembled within the middle-class domestic drawing room, made up of eminent and distinguished men (this included Robert Owen, the founder of modern socialism) and women of notoriety (cf. Lamont, 2004). Thus, one of the most celebrated mediums was Daniel Dunglas Home (one of only few male mediums) who was seen to be of unquestionable status and respectability, and whose demonstrations and testimonies were taken very seriously (Lamont, 2004). As Pels (2003) highlights, what became of interest, within a distinction made between the so-called higher and lower senses, was the voice or cognition of the medium. This logocentric and *mentalist* approach to occult phenomena literally took the voice out of the body of the medium, which was then subjected to various and increasingly institutionalized forms of scientific inquiry, including various experimental activities formalized through the establishment of the Institute for Psychical Research in 1882 (see Chapter 3). As Lamont (2004: 915) argues, 'research was concentrated primarily on ostensibly mental phenomena such as clairvoyance and telepathy'. What was ignored and sidelined was the role of the so-called lower senses in spiritual communication, and, as we have seen, the actions of furniture as manifestations of such communion. This concern was inflected through a hypnotic paradigm that increasingly presumed that only certain people (women, children, etc.) were susceptible to the ideas, thoughts and feelings of other minds, mortal and immortal.

The ordinariness and accessibility of spiritualism, with its humble origins in the testimonies of ordinary people, such as the Rochester sisters in New York (Murphy and Ballou, 1960), was to become transformed through a scientific, logocentric gaze. This gaze linked telepathy and mediumship to particular forms of psychopathology, such as hallucinations and delusions, and saw these experiences as having a common element. It is the shaping and emergence of this particular linkage that transformed the notion of energetic connections as a very particular kind of assemblage. It is this assemblage which provides one of the conditions for the emergence of creative mania in the energetic approach to becoming developed by Deleuze.

However, if we take the figure of the medium as a prototypical feminist subject, she spoke of connections that could not easily be seen, recording events that 'resounded with portentous significance' (Cottom, 1988: 771). Like other homely devices that were seen to act as spiritual telegraphs, the medium, much like the nineteenth-century table that Cottom refers to, 'speaks of more than the other world. It tells of contemporary conflicts over people, objects, and language that otherwise are *apt to go unnoticed*' (p. 766; emphasis added). Although it was men of science and philosophy who were to become interpretive authorities (including William James), what this exposed, according to Cottom, was 'an apparatus of institutions, traditions, texts, practices, personal relationships and common sense' (p. 775) that characterized scientific reason. Thus, men of science would only allow themselves to be moved by 'the sorts of "spirits" they happened to prefer' (p. 777).

Although there is a significant body of work exploring the proximity of spiritualism to cinema, first-wave feminism, the reception of media technologies in the nineteenth century (Sconce, 1998, 2000), and the framing of cyberspace at the beginning of the twenty-first century (Waters, 1997), more attention needs to be paid to the kinds of figurations that have been used to enact these relationships. Sconce discusses the paranormal discourses that surrounded the reception of the wireless and radio in the early decades of the twentieth century, showing how they mobilized an oceanic metaphor to describe the ether. Attempting to destabilize the taken-for-granted nature of this metaphor, he asks: 'Why did so many contemporaries liken the ether to an ocean, initiating a practice that continues even today in the metaphors of "flow" that inform theories of television technology?' (Sconce, 1998: 217).

## Conclusion

Waters (1997) suggests that one reason for the enduring, haunting presence of a particular spiritual assemblage within cultural theory is that it foregrounds permeability (of the subject), and the idea of a constantly shifting and mutating network of relationships. As she frames it, 'spiritual and virtual technologies alike operate as forms for the enactment of some rather resilient tensions – tensions above all about the capacity of subjects to overspill and transgress the cultural and psychic limits which construct and constrain them' (p. 437). As we have seen, it is the idea of creative becomings, of subjects being able to 'see through' and overcome the limits that block them, that has become the mainstay in cultural theorizing. Although this notion of becoming is based upon a very specific way of enacting the significance of psychopathology and spirituality to discussions of becoming, it is the specificity of this framing that largely remains in the background.

In the next chapter we will consider some rather different ways of modelling what often passes as psychopathology. These models will be located in debates surrounding the intergenerational transmission of trauma, which suggest rather different ways of understanding affective transmission. The focus of the chapter will be on the problem of divided attention, the phenomenon of voice hearing, and work on mediated perception and diasporic vision (see Cho, 2008). The relationship between voice hearing and trauma and abuse is one that has been well established within user movements, such as the Hearing Voices Network (see Blackman, 2001, 2007a). Although there is a body of work exploring the relationship between voice hearing and trauma and abuse within the context of a person's autobiography, the relationship between voice hearing and historical trauma is much less developed. This work offers some exciting and challenging ways of thinking about the voice which take discussion beyond the singular individual. This work will be situated within discussions of a subliminal archive enacted primarily within William James's Harvard Psychological Laboratory which in different ways contribute to the genealogy of anti- or non-intentionalism which is central to my argument. The experiments and practices I will consider work with suggestive topologies in ways which challenge the separation between affect and cognition. This will allow me to make an intervention into affect studies which does not reduce affect to pre-individual, autonomic processes, and which works with a subliminal or even transliminal ontology of subjectivity in ways which open affect up to genealogical inquiry.

# 6

## The Problem of Automatism: Divided Attention, Voice Hearing and Machinic Vision

### Listening to Voices: An Ethics of Entanglement

I want to start this chapter by positioning and situating myself and my own interests, academic, personal and political, in relation to the phenomenon of voice hearing. My academic and intellectual interests were informed by my own experiences of growing up with a mother who hears voices. I was aware at a very young age of the power of psychiatry, having experienced my mother being sectioned and hospitalized cyclically, and witnessing her reliance, since the age of 18, on a repeat prescription of Largactyl. In times of crisis this did nothing to lessen the distressing voices that she heard. I had a rich fantasy life as a child, and my mother's voices and delusions became part of my world. As with psychosis, the distinction between fact and fiction was blurred in my own experiences of my mother's voices. I responded to her accounts and engagement with them as real, as real as they were for her, and as meaningful communications. There were patterns to her voices, particular voices visited each time, particularly her granny who offered comfort and reassurance, and other voices which were more abusive and distressing. These voices also had a pattern and rhythm and became familiar interlocutors. I have and always felt that I got to know much more about my mother and her life when she was psychotic. What was confusing to me at a very young age was why her experiences then were not listened to and not considered as having any meaning. They were predominantly to be suppressed by drugs and electroconvulsive therapy. The voices were ignored, silenced and forgotten as she returned to a far from acceptable version of normality.

My encounter with psychiatry was to return as a teenager when my mother, prompted by her psychiatrist, suggested that I might have genetic counselling. I had already read all the books on psychiatry in my local library and was aware of an established narrative: that if you have one or two parents with mental health difficulties (read 'illness') you have a higher chance of developing mental illness (read 'difficulties') as 'it', whatever 'it' was, could be passed on genetically. This narrative had terrified me as a teenager and I can remember when I reached my 25th birthday feeling palpable relief that I had managed to escape, not my mother's experiences, as I had felt deep depression and anxiety about my own potential 'risk', but the 'psychiatric system'. I had, however, been told by a counsellor I saw whilst doing a psychology degree that I probably would not finish the degree as I had 'a lot of trauma in my life'. She recommended that I saw a male psychiatrist who was also a vicar. I declined and went on to get a first-class honours degree. I tell this story because my PhD, which I went on to do in the early 1990s, was very much driven by my own anger and sense of injustice at the biogenetic model within psychiatry. However, my experiences and motivations were written out of the PhD. It was presented as an academic study, informed primarily by the historical approach to the human sciences developed by Michel Foucault and extended in the context of psychiatry and the psychological sciences by Nikolas Rose – what he refers to as the 'psychological complex'. The PhD was later written up as a book, *Hearing Voices: Embodiment and Experience* (Blackman, 2001).

My PhD question was an exploration of how it had become possible historically for hearing voices to be predominantly understood as a pseudo-sensory by-product of the brain, to be responded to with neuroleptic drugs and primarily to be ignored by the voice hearer, professionals, family and friends. Whilst doing the research I became aware of the beginnings of the emergence of the Hearing Voices Network in Manchester and collaborated with many people who went on to become key members as it developed nationally and internationally. This included Mickey and Sharon De Valda, Ron Coleman, Terry McClaughlin and Julie Downs. Mickey, Sharon and Terry are sadly no longer with us. One of the fundamental premises enacted by the Hearing Voices Network is that voices are meaningful modalities of communication. This assumption is one that has pioneered work and practices challenging biological psychiatry and improving the lives of many (including my mother, who now regularly attends a hearing voices group run by her local primary care trust).

This chapter will contribute to the subject of affect by focusing on the phenomenon of voice hearing. Primarily within the psychological sciences, voice hearing is usually considered an irrational perception aligned to a disease process. As I have argued in previous work, hearing voices is generally considered a first-rank symptom of schizophrenia predominantly treated within biomedicine through the use of neuroleptic drugs (Blackman, 2001, 2007a). Although there is much contestation around the reliability and validity of the concept of schizophrenia (Boyle, 1990), the view that voices are simply a meaningless epiphenomenon of a disease process is one that endures, although challenges to this view have been multiplying, particularly with the rise and success of the Hearing Voices Network across the UK and Intervoice across Europe. The Hearing Voices Network is an international network of alliances between service users, professionals and families, carers and friends of voice hearers, which originated in the Netherlands and is linked to the pioneering work of two Dutch psychiatrists, Marius Romme and Sandra Escher (Romme and Escher, 1993).

The beginnings of the network are linked to the appearance of Marius Romme with one of his patients, Patsy Hague, on a popular Dutch television programme. She talked about her experience and theory of why she heard voices. The response to the programme was overwhelming, with over 700 voice hearers contacting Romme. He established that there were many people who heard voices and who had never been in touch with psychiatric services. Romme's interest shifted to a focus upon the kinds of non-psychiatric explanations and coping strategies these individuals had developed to manage their voices. One of the main shifts in the status of voice hearing to emerge from this reorientation away from a disease model, with its corresponding language of deficit and pathology, was that voices have something to say, that they should be listened to (see Romme et al., 2009). They might be thought of less as irrational perceptions and more as forms of embodied memory or modalities of communication that challenge both our understandings of madness and how we might approach memory and perception (see Blackman, 2001, 2007a, for a development of this). Once we start to listen to voices our conceptions of madness and the limits of understanding perception through a singularly bounded and distinctly human psychological subject might also be subject to challenge (Cho, 2008).

The phenomenon of voice hearing presents particular challenges for understandings of affect. As we saw in Chapter 1, many approaches to affect across the humanities subscribe to the belief or view that affect is non-intentional – that is, that affect can be separated from cognition, and in that separation primarily be located within a material substrate of a more lively and processual body (Gregg and Seigworth, 2010). Although this view of bodily matter views bodies as open to the other, where distinct separations between self and other, inside and outside, and human and non-human are destabilized, what remains a problem is the status of the psyche within such perspectives. As we saw in Chapters 1 and 4, the invocation and authorization of biology as lively, dynamic and responsive are often seen to solve the problem of seeing bodies as psychically attuned. The psyche for many is seen to constrain understandings of affect to a closed psychological subject. However, what of phenomena such as voice hearing, which reveal our fundamental connection not only to the other, but to pasts that cannot be articulated, and to distributed forms of perception which might be described more as machinic (Cho, 2008; Johnston, 1999).

Machinic perception or vision is a form of mediated perception which, Cho (2008) argues, allows one to see through another's voice. Machinic perception distributes perception across a range of actors and agencies, rather than confining understandings of perception to a human sensory perceptual apparatus. The distribution of perception might allow us to see or hear what voices might embody; what perhaps cannot be articulated, known or heard. We explored this proposition in the previous chapter in relation to a different figuration of the medium as speaking what cannot be spoken. In other words, mediated perception might direct us towards a social trauma that has been foreclosed. Cho's study is a way of linking up what Davoine and Guadilliere (2004) term 'histories beyond trauma' – that is, connecting up those histories that have never been told, authorized or documented within official histories, such as the forgotten Korean War, with microhistories of trauma and shame. Davoine and Guadilliere are analysts who have worked for over three decades with psychosis. Many analysts are reluctant to work with hallucinatory phenomena, preferring instead to work within the confines of language and ideation. Davoine and Guadilliere have pioneered work within studies of the intergenerational transmission of trauma, particularly approaching psychosis as an attempt to bring into existence a social trauma that has been foreclosed. This is an attempt to explore precisely those carnal generational connections that exist genealogically but which cannot be articulated. For Davoine and Guadilliere the subject is always a subject of history, even though those histories may have been cut out of what they call 'the sanctioned social narrative' (p. xii).

## Transmission

In order to understand Cho's concept of machinic vision, which comes from the work of the Deleuzian scholar John Johnston (1999), an example might be instructive. Machinic vision is characterized as the distribution of perception across space and time, carried by mediums other than the speaking subject. This has resonances with Paul Connerton's (1989) work on remembering and memory. Connerton argues that memory is not an individual faculty, but rather something shared and collective. The question is where the operations of collective/social memory are to be found. Connerton's focus is particularly on what he terms non-inscribed memory; that is, memory that is transmitted through non-human actors and agents, and includes those that are embodied in habits, rituals and traditions (see also Blackman and Harbord, 2010). Johnston's (1999) distributive and mediated approach to perception is central to how Cho understands the trauma of the forgotten Korean War and its articulation primarily through patterns of secrecy and silence. My own experiences of growing up with a mother who hears voices have parallels with Cho's work, and connect me with listening to my mother's voices as both a child and adult. Cho's (2008) encounter with secrecy and silence starts in the intimate dyadic space of her relationship to her mother and the gaps in her own understanding of her mother's migration from Korea to America as a GI bride. Her mother's migration story is never told, although her journey is one emblematic of many narratives of Korean diasporic women who settled in the USA after the Second World War. These narratives, which Cho finds in social work literature, for example, are characterized as a journey from rural poverty to psychosis. Cho's mother's experience is hallucinatory; she hears voices. Cho witnesses the significance of the voices primarily through the gaps, silences and contradictions which provide the elusive context for the voices' existence and circulation. Cho cannot recover her mother's life story, for it is a story that cannot be articulated by a subject who can be self-present to herself.

The memoir that Cho stages shows up the limits of autobiography and even autoethnography and requires a different technology and method for thinking about how we might listen to voices, and how we might see through another's voice. As Cho (2008: 66) argues, following the work of Johnston, 'what is perceived is not located at any single place and moment in time, and the act by which this perception occurs is not the result of a single or isolated agency but of several working in concert or parallel'. This might include agencies and actors such as media technologies including film and television, art practice (see also the work of the artist Shona Illingworth, 2011), memoirs, social science accounts of migration found in social work literature, and second-generation Korean Americans' experience of growing up within a Korean diaspora. These migration stories might be surrounded by patterns of shame, secrecy and silence. Cho invokes the idea of the 'assemblaged body' to consider how a voice might become distributed across space and time, where the voice crosses borders and boundaries to take residence or find a home. The voice hearer may hear the voices of others, of people they do not know or cannot understand. This moves discussion of voice hearing beyond the function of the voice within the context of a person's autobiography, to the role of the voice as a ghost distributed across space and time, revealing perhaps the entanglement between past and present, living and dead, fantasmatic and real, self and other, and human and non-human (see also Clough, 2010b).

This work has parallels with work on culture and performance which has looked at embodied forms of memory enacted through dance, for example. I want to refer to an article published in an edited collection, *Internationalizing Cultural Studies: An Anthology* (Abbas and Erni, 2005). One theme that the anthology takes up is how to understand performance (which might include drama, ritual, show and spectacle) as ways of 'knowing' the past and therefore intervening in the future through enacting different versions of the present. Hamera's chapter focuses on what she terms the 'performance of amnesia', enacted through embodied forms of performance (in this case Cambodian dance) which allow bodies to 'speak what they can't' (Pollack, 2005: 76). This is about the communication and transmission of intergenerational forms of trauma that appear to be 'unrepresentable' (if we remain at the level of signification), and that are usually contained through a logic of silence. The family that Hamera attempts to interview have been displaced through forced migration to Los Angeles following the genocides carried out by the Khmer Rouge in the 1960s in Cambodia. What characterized the Sems family was their unwillingness or inability to articulate the trauma surrounding these events, which Hamera links to their survival and sanity. Indeed, Hamera (2005) suggests that the 'relational amnesia and aphasia' (p. 96) that surrounded their refusal to 'confess' was a form of 'strategic forgetfulness which kept them alive' (p. 97). One could see this as a form of stuckness, where the family could not process the trauma which foreclosed the possibility of conscious deliberation and expression. Indeed, one version of trauma that Ruth Leys (2000) identifies in her genealogy of trauma is that trauma is a wound that cannot be registered and therefore cannot be integrated into consciousness. It remains as a disorder of memory or form of dissociation which prevents the processing and working-through which might allow the trauma to be acknowledged and the suffering accepted and communicated.

However, what is interesting about the significance of the practice of dance in the Sem's family life was that the Khmer movements that were performed by the parents allowed them to embody the traumas and communicate with those who did not survive, and therefore to afford the possibility of intergenerational communication and transmission. The Sems talked about the voices they heard whilst dancing who communicated the traditional Khmer dance movements to them. In this context the dance was a relational practice that afforded a 'with-ness', and that allowed connections of lineage and continuity to be forged and embodied. Hamera (2005: 98) describes the voices as 'ghostly interlocutors' that, although experienced as 'other' (they were not experienced as internal dialogue but as coming from those who did not survive), nevertheless were integrated and enacted through forms of embodied practice. Thus, the dance was not the expression of an individual psyche-in-trauma, but rather a form of affective symbiosis which allowed a reaching toward the unrepresentable and unknowable.

This reaching toward was not characterized by a singular body reaching out to another singular body through a discrete sensory motor system. Rather, the dancing bodies were always in excess of themselves and importantly communicated with 'others' through the embodied experience of voice hearing (see also Blackman, 2011a). Affective transfer within this context is not just the circulation of forces or intensities, but rather directs us towards psychic dynamics of sociality and subjectivity which reveal an intergenerational exchange, where the 'other' is embodied as a voice or trace registered corporeally. The forms of intergenerational connection communicated through the Khmer dance and embodied as a voice(s) draw our attention to the complex affective and relational dynamics that circulate intergenerationally and intercorporeally and which cannot be reduced to a lively and processual materiality, unless we can also take account of psychological processes which are not bound by a singular, closed psychological subject. Distributed perception thus engenders what Johnston (1999) terms 'a new form of collective psychic apparatus' (Cho, 2008: 174).

The argument I want to make is that imagining this new collective psychic apparatus takes us back to conceptions of the psychological subject (understood through the concepts of subliminality and transliminality), which we find in telepathy and hypnotic suggestion in the nineteenth and early twentieth centuries. As we have seen throughout this book, it was the rise of the psychological sciences that led to the translation of suggestion into an abnormal capacity located in those considered 'other' to particular conceptions of normality (see Chapter 2). Thus the capacity to be affected became refigured as a psychological lack, primarily understood through concepts derived from evolutionary biology. As I have argued in Chapters 2 and 4, the psyche is replaced by the nervous system aligned to the actions of habit and instinct. In other words, particular social norms allowed for specific conceptions of human nature to be enacted, leading to the kinds of ontology of subjectivity that we now regularly encounter within discussions of affect (see Chapters 1, 4 and 5). One of the implications of this, as I argued in the last chapter, is that the overgeneralized accounts of psychopathology and spirituality that find their way into affect theorizing require analysis and situating genealogically. We saw in the last chapter how one such figuration, related to madness as mania or creative genius, is central to Deleuzian accounts of becoming. I want to now turn to the work of Emily Martin who has done much to displace the romanticism of such claims within contemporary discussions of psychopathology.

## Bipolar Logics

Emily Martin, a Professor of Anthropology at New York University, had for years lived under a diagnosis of manic depression. She experienced this as one of shame, secrecy and silence. She felt the need to keep this diagnosis secret from colleagues and even some friends and family. She chose to 'come out' as living with manic depression (her preferred term) in her book, *Bipolar Expeditions: Mania and Depression in American Culture* (2007), in which she explores the experience, both of herself and others, of living under a diagnosis of bipolar disorder. She makes the important point that conceptions of sanity and insanity are always based on regulatory ideals or normalization processes which become naturalized within the psychiatric and psychological sciences. As Martin argues, 'what it means to be rational or irrational depends on what notions of personhood are in play, notions that must be understood in cultural context' (p. 37). She goes on to argue that, 'in the United States in the late nineteenth century, psychic states that might erode the edges of the disciplined and aware self, make its borders permeable to other selves, or allow it to drift into discontiguous psychic states were given positive value' (p. 38).

She contextualizes the shifts in normative conceptions of personhood, particularly within neoliberal forms of governmentality, by exploring what kinds of values and capacities are now valued and valorized within normative conceptions of personhood. Now workers and citizens primarily must be self-governing, lean, agile, quick and constantly able to change and transform themselves. She argues, within a context prior to the financial crash of 2008, that emotional lability, particularly within the workplace, became valued. This, she argues, is one of the conditions which have led mania to be recast as an experience that if harnessed can allow one to be extremely productive and successful.

The book is based on an ethnography of seven support groups, which were conducted over a five-year period. These groups were set up and run by people living under a diagnosis of bipolar disorder. Martin also attended conferences run by pharmaceutical companies for patients and professionals, as well as conducting over 80 extensive semi-structured interviews. Her experience of stigma and shame seems very at odds with the alignment of creativity with mania which we find across popular and celebrity cultures, as well as scientific and academic theorizing. The linking of mania with creativity, for example, has been endorsed by celebrities such as Robin Williams, Jim Carrey, Richard Branson and Stephen Fry; it has been backed by mental health campaigns in the UK run by *Time To Change*. Throughout the book she focuses on the cultural shifts which have led bipolar disorder and particularly mania to be recast as an object of desire, aligned often to abnormally high levels of achievement and success. Although this might be one way to normalize mental health difficulties and reduce public fear, prejudice and stigma, it primarily reduces the experience of psychosis, mania, voice hearing or depression, for example, to neurochemical processes, primarily seen to be amenable to neuroleptic drugs. This is no more so than in areas of neuroscience and psychiatry that have recognized voice hearing, for example, as a potential modality of communication, but who aim to find and image the so-called pathological deficits within the brain which are seen to produce such phenomena.

In the next chapter we will consider an area of neuroscience concerned with the 'double brain', which cannot be exhausted by the predominant preoccupation of neuroscientists with imaging, spatializing and locating particular experiences within specific parts of the brain. Work on the double brain arguably is a contemporary manifestation of some of the beliefs, concerns and questions which dominated subliminal psychology throughout the late nineteenth and early twentieth centuries. The ontology of personhood which was enacted within subliminal psychology, and which travelled across literature, philosophy, cinema and even the legal system (see Andriopolous, 2008), was a belief in multiplicity rather than singularity as being a defining characteristic of personhood. However, the idea of multiplicity, of being open to being affected and affecting others, was not simply celebrated as a generic capacity of human and non-human actors. There was a hesitation surrounding permeability that was cross-cut with cultural fantasies, beliefs and desires. Andriopoulos's (2008) cultural history of possession makes the cogent argument that studies of possession and hypnotic suggestion, as enacted across film, medicine, literature, law and science in the late nineteenth and early twentieth centuries, are central to genealogical studies of modernity. In a breathtaking analysis he constructs a fascinating archive, which includes early twentieth-century cinema's preoccupation with hypnotic suggestion (Maurice Tourneur's (1915) *Trilby*, Robert Wiener's (1919) *The Cabinet of Dr Calgari*, and Fritz Lang's (1922) *Dr Mabuse, The Gambler*, for example); hypnotic crime and suggestion as enacted in literature (particularly Kafka and Broch); the legal system's preoccupation with hypnotic crime; debates about hypnotic suggestion across subliminal psychology and psychoanalysis; as well as discussions of suggestion, mimesis and imitation within philosophy and the social sciences (particularly Tarde and Durkheim, for example). He argues that possession must be inserted into cultural histories of modernity if we are to fully understand the cultural fears and fantasies related to this, which resurface in remarkably similar ways in the present.

Grace Cho (2008) recognizes this paradox in relation to the concept of double consciousness (Du Bois, 1903; Gilroy, 1993). The implication of a split or double self that the concept of double consciousness engenders was not simply about multiplicity or permeability. It is not just about being open to connections. The idea of the split or double self could also imply a sense of being governed through another's gaze, a gaze which might produce shame, 'the desire for whiteness, and psychotic imaginings about the symptoms of social disease' (Cho, 2008: 163). Developing a similar argument, Andriopoulos (2008) argues that cultural histories of hypnotic suggestion, and its centrality for understanding permeability in the late nineteenth century, were also governed by fears, fantasies and desires about possession and control. These fantasies were enacted in the popular cinema and literature of the time, with the undecidibility of the value of suggestion oscillating between the capacity of subjects to extend beyond themselves, overlaid with anxieties about being controlled by an other, either human or non-human. We have seen the centrality of the ordinariness of suggestion as being the key tenet of Tarde's mimetic sociopsychological paradigm. We have also seen how Tarde conceived of the limits to suggestion by invoking evolutionary concepts, showing that permeability and affective transfer were not simply evidence of free-flowing forces or intensities, but were governed by other psychobiological dynamics which Tarde argued needed to be specified (see Chapter 5; Blackman, 2007b).

This debate or oscillation, which I have termed throughout the book the problem of 'the one and the many' or the 'problem of personality', is one that I have argued resurfaces in contemporary debates about affect. This is not simply about openness to affect, and certainly problematizes some of the generic definitions of affect which revolve around this subscription. As I argued in Chapter 1, and with Couze Venn in a special issue of the journal *Body & Society* on affect (Blackman and Venn, 2010), the definition of affect as the body's capacity to affect and be affected is too broad. It could also be interpreted as some 'thing' that bodies have, a quality, a vital element, a capacity existing independently of relationality, that is expressed through affect, or is a substratum for it (see Blackman and Venn, 2010). This often relies upon invoking the nervous system, endocrine system, or a particular neuropsychological concept, such as the mirror neuron, in order to animate the body's lively processuality.

This is not to say that engagements with science and embodiment are not important to understanding affect, but that the status and authorization of scientific accounts within work on affect do need some circumspection and caution (see also Chapter 1). In the next chapter some of this work will be carried out by engaging with marginal work in the neurosciences on the 'double brain' and bringing to bear some of the genealogical work developed in this book on suggestion, voice hearing, telepathy and so forth, on how we might deploy and extend some of these arguments across both science and the humanities. I will argue that the problem of personality is one that can be reposed in relation to this work, and also that the more radical insights of work on the double brain might transform our understandings of affect. In the next section I want to focus specifically on the voice and voice hearing to tease out some of the texture and timbre of what a focus on the voice can bring to the subject of affect. I will orient this specifically to work on the intergenerational transmission of trauma, and the notion of the psyche that is presumed and enacted within this work.

## The Voice, Affect and the Diasporic Unconscious

Cho (2008) invokes the concept of the 'diasporic unconscious' to refer to affective transfer, in the context of voice hearing, as being more than sensation, intensities, bodily or kinaesthetic feelings. She refigures the voice as an entangled process that speaks what might elude our gaze. In order to listen to the voices, she turns to film and art practices, often those of second-generation Korean Americans who had grown up in similar patterns of secrecy and silence and had expressed their own experience of this through artwork, or what we might term 'artworking' (Blackman, 2011a; Ettinger, 2006). Ettinger's (2006) matrixial approach to communication is based on the concept of 'border-linking'. This concept is used to describe the way bodies become linked at a psychic level, where affects are shared, which include the trauma and desires of others. These affects can be bound through particular practices which circulate through inter-subjective relations. For Ettinger, we are never fully self-contained nor exist in affective symbiosis, but become weaved together in complex ways. Ettinger, through her practice as an analyst and in her artwork, is interested in these 'invisible' relations, those that are felt and registered through an infra-language and primarily in a non-optical register as 'nonverbal intensities' (p. 51). Certain practices function as affective carriers of trauma, and Ettinger is particularly interested in the intergenerational communication of trauma through the unsaid and unrepresentable. She uses the term 'artworking' rather than 'artwork' to move beyond a static representational logic. This is not about the articulation of narratives, but non-representational processes which attempt to present an experience that is primarily foreclosed and therefore arguably unrepresentable (see also Illingworth, 2011).

In a similar way, Cho (2008) attempts to reconstruct what her mother's voices might be saying by turning to secondary histories of the Korean War. She uncovers the profound shame of many Korean women who became GI brides, who had met their husbands while working as prostitutes for American soldiers on army bases in Korea. Sanctioned militarized sex-work was rife. The term for the militarized sex-worker in Korean is *yanggongju*, a term which embodies the deep sense of shame and denigration felt by the women involved. Cho approaches the figure of the *yanggongju* as an agent of transgenerational haunting. The traumatic secret that is concealed by many Korean women might take root as an unspoken history that can become transmuted into an hallucination and haunt the next generation. As we have seen, this might also include the social production of shame, which is carried by subjects in ways that might not be easily available for articulation. She draws on work on intergenerational haunting (Abraham and Torok, 1994) in order to explore this. One example of distributed or mediated perception that she draws on is the film *Souls Protest* (2000). This contemporary film dramatizes an event in Korean history that was never officially documented. Referred to as the Korean Titanic, this is the story of an event where a boat carrying Korean prisoners of war back from Japan to Korea was blown up, allegedly by the Japanese crew who had fled the boat just before an explosion was heard and the boat sank. The 'truth' of this event can never be known as there were only two survivors; a baby and an adult who had lost his tongue as a prisoner of war. What is important is not representational truth or accuracy, but how the distinctions between fact, fiction and fantasy are always blurred within forms of historical reflection and cultural memory (see also Walkerdine, 1990). Cho argues that media technologies, like film, can act as forms of distributed perception, allowing one to bring a trauma that has been foreclosed into the social, so that the voices can be listened to. This is not about historical accuracy but the staging of that which has never been spoken and to a certain extent is unrepresentable as official histories have never been documented of this event. It has literally been written out of history.

In some senses the approach to affect that underpins the diasporic unconscious is closer to understandings of telepathy and mediumship that we have encountered throughout the book so far. That is how to understand forms of affect transfer at a distance, such that phenomena such as voices, dreams, emotions and feelings can travel across space *and* time, between and across bodies in ways that take us back to nineteenth- and twentieth-century conceptualizations of telepathy. Cho's topology of diasporic unconscious similarly is a view of the unconscious which is ontologically trans-subjective and carried by mediums other than the speaking subject. However, the diasporic unconscious is a creative and political reinvention of the concept of synaesthesia, rather than telepathy. As we saw in Chapter 3, synaesthesia is a term which recognizes that the senses do not work in isolation and cannot be separated as if they are discrete senses located in particular parts of the body, for example. Synaesthesia challenges the hierarchization of the senses historically associated with the individualized body where the senses have been distinguished according to divisions made between the higher and lower, distant and contact, civilized and primitive, and even mind and body (see Blackman, 2008a; Falk, 2004).

The concept of synaesthesia has been important for work on the affective body and affective image, particularly in relation to the concepts of movement vision and body-without-an-image, which we explored in Chapter 1 (Featherstone, 2010; Massumi, 2002a). As we have seen, this work explores the non-visual and primarily kinaesthetic processes which register the workings and circulation of affect between bodies. What is emphasized in this work is haptic communication (Boothroyd, 2009); the way in which affective processes can be registered through a combination of the senses, where the visual is displaced, or understood as always co-existing and reoriented through sensing and perceiving. Thus one might talk about the 'mind's ear' or 'seeing' through a voice, for example. What is emphasized is the complex synaesthetic registering of sensation and intensities related to the passage of movement. However, as we saw in Chapter 1, Featherstone (2010) also makes the important argument that what is also important for understanding affect is how people move between different registers, between body-image and body-without-an-image, between 'the mirror-image and the movement-image, between affect and emotion, between the subject-object and the sensation of visceral and proprioceptive intensities' (p. 213). These questions will form one of the central focuses of the next chapter when we look at work on the double brain and bicameral consciousness.

If we take a different register of experience, one that is perhaps synaesthetic in a different way, we can start to consider how a focus on the voice and voice hearing, rather than the kinaesthetic bodily sensation and perception of the body-in-movement, might transform how we understand synaesthesia. I will argue that this takes our understanding of synaesthesia closer to nineteenth- and early twentieth-century discussions of telepathy. Indeed, in Boothroyd's (2009) engagement with haptic media, he moves beyond notions of synaesthesia to argue that haptic media – that is media that work non-representationally and cross-modally – might also be thought of as forms of telecommunication. The concept of telecommunication refers to the capacity of media to act at a distance and 'touch' audiences in ways that do not require presence or immediacy and are not about simple body to body transmission. This is what Gibbs (2010) characterizes as mimetic forms of communication. The prefix 'tele' importantly invites us to rethink the status of the psyche or psychological when considering what might be shared and transmitted between subjects. This cannot be reduced to a lively and processual materiality unless we are willing to conceive of bodies as psychologically attuned in ways which displace the singular, closed psychological subject. That work will be done towards the end of this chapter. In the next section I will focus specifically on the voice and consider what issues this opens up for the subject of affect.

## The Voice

In a recent article in the journal *Body & Society*, Schlichter (2011) argues that a focus on the voice transforms our understanding of the concept of gender performativity that we find in the work of Judith Butler, for example. As Schlichter (2011: 31) asks, what does it mean to 'ignore the performative aspects of the voice', what does it mean to 'think a body without a voice'? Schlichter argues that Butler's theorizing of the materialization of gender through iteration relies upon a visual logic. It is one that explores how gender is enacted through practices, including representational practices, such that gender becomes naturalized and normalized. She argues that although bodies speak (cultural norms, signs and symbols) their voices are muted. Drawing on Dolar's (2006) psychoanalytic work on the voice, she presents one of the central paradoxes of the voice. The voice is neither entirely inside or outside, self or other, material or immaterial. It is 'neither fully defined by matter nor completely beyond it' (Schlichter, 2011: 33). It is not simply the source of self-presence, and this is particularly so when we take as our focus the phenomenon of hearing voices. The voice, according to the musicologist Michelle Duncan, puts 'matter into circulation' (Schlichter, 2011: 33), and, as Jonathon Sterne (2003) argues, can only be heard through its exteriorization and mediation, including the vocal apparatus, sound technologies and so forth. However, what of voices that are heard but cannot be seen, or heard but which remain unintelligible? What of voices which to hear require a different kind of technology of listening based on seeing through mediated forms of perception, or what Cho (2008) terms, an ethics of entanglement?

The voice phenomena that I am interested in are not carriers of the 'self or identity' (Schlichter, 2011: 36). These phenomena are often experienced by voice hearers as coming from outside the self, as having an extra-personal dimension, which is often experienced as an assault on the person's psychological functioning. They are not, for example, experienced as internal dialogue or inner speech, and the extra-personal experience of the voices is that which often brings the voice hearer into contact with psychiatric services. However, although the source of the voices is one of the concepts used by psychiatry to ascribe the voices a pathological status (that is, are the voices experienced as coming from an external source?), this differentiation does not work in practice. When we examine the psychiatric architecture of concepts and techniques used to differentiate so-called pathological voices from those that it is acknowledged are possible across the population (following bereavement, for example) distinctions between the inside and outside and between the self and other do not hold up. Psychiatry supplements this distinction with a number of other concepts, such as duration, vividness and control, to articulate the problem of hallucination, but ultimately this conceptual armoury cannot contain or explain the myriad of contradictions and dispersals across the literature and within practice (see Blackman, 2001).

The idea that there is a taxonomy of natural disease, which corresponds to the experience of voice hearing, is itself a concept which has complex conditions of emergence, possibility and verification. This has been the subject of genealogical inquiry (Blackman, 2001). To that extent voice hearing might confound distinctions between the interior and external, past and present, self and other, material and immaterial, and even living and dead. Indeed, psychiatric practice is based on the presumption that voice hearing is pathological or an irrational form of perception because it is experienced as 'other', rather than as internal speech or dialogue, for example (see Blackman, 2001). However, the act of listening itself cannot be so easily differentiated according to distinctions between the inside (usually constituted as internal dialogue) and what is outside (seen as generated from sources that are experienced as coming from outside of the self). Indeed, Jean Luc Nancy (2007) draws out the paradoxes of listening, arguing that when listening one is 'to be *at the same time* outside and inside, to be open *from* without and *from* within, hence from one to the other and from one in the other' (p. 14). Listening does not necessarily engender the kinds of distinction between the outside and inside that psychiatric definitions of voice hearing rely upon. In this sense hearing or listening does not always 'consolidate the fragile modern self' (Ehlmann, 2004: 5).

Ehlmann's work on hearing cultures argues that listening is the source and production of relational knowledge, and is about proximity and connectedness rather than separation and singularity. Indeed, a more useful distinction might be made between hearing voices and listening to voices. As Carter (2004) argues, listening involves a more engaged form of hearing which is intentional. Where hearing might be considered monological, listening is always dialogical and relational, directed towards the other. This is a form of listening that might be described as 'telephonic' (Connor, 2004: 171), implying transmission and dialogicity. The other-directedness of listening is not simply about instilling or enacting the boundaries of a closed, singular psychological subject. Rather, listening implies 'communicational contact' (ibid.: 43) even when that contact remains elusive. This is where Cho's reconfiguration of the voice as machinic is important, as it directs our attention to the technologies of listening, beyond the capacity of individual psychological subjects that might allow the voices to be heard. Within this paradigm voice hearing reveals the possibility of articulation or voicing across bodies, human and non-human, separated potentially in both time and space.

As we will see in the next chapter, this trans-subjective nature of voice hearing is occluded within contemporary neuroscientific work on the double brain. This work, based on imaging the brains of people hearing voices, shows evidence of the double brain and particularly right hemisphere involvement in voice hearing. Right hemisphere involvement in voice hearing is seen to show evidence of how voices might be experienced as 'other' to the self. The right hemisphere involvement is, however, considered a pathological deficit aligned to aberrant activation of the right middle temporal gyrus. The conclusions drawn from such studies are that this brain region is responsible for the self-monitoring of inner speech and that this ability allows one to distinguish between speech that is internally and externally generated (Bentaleb et al., 2002; Dierks et al., 1999). It is this capacity for self-monitoring that is viewed as defective in the brains of those who hear voices, who are seen to mistake inner speech for externally generated speech.

In this framing of the 'double brain', the right hemisphere is viewed as capable of speech, but what is lacking is a particular property of mind – a cognitive capacity of self-monitoring – which would allow the subject to discern the inner from the outer and the internal from the external. This cognitive deficit is tied to what is taken to be the aberrant activation of certain regions in the right hemisphere, the right middle temporal gyrus, which give inner speech the experiential quality of externally generated sound. So in short, dysfunctions in brain are seen to underlie the pathophysiology of the phenomenon of voice hearing, which generates a cognitive deficit, taken to be a property of mind. There is a clear attempt here to localize brain and mind function in terms of the anatomy of the brain. The 'mental' in 'mental illness' is thus taken to be generated by abnormal brain function which creates cognitive disturbance and confusion, what we might recognize as a dissolution of boundary.

The posting of a particular mental operation – the cognitive capacity of self-monitoring – and the aligning of voice hearing to misinterpreted inner speech removes the more relational dimensions of voice hearing. This would potentially redistribute the 'mental' in rather different ways, more in line perhaps with Cho's (2008) concept of machinic vision. What is interesting about the experiential quality of voices for most voice hearers is their otherness; their experience as being other to the self and as not being tied to their own actions or words. This otherness is usually experienced as a dissolution of boundaries, which can be enacted and felt cross-modally – that is, the experience might involve all the senses, particularly touch (kinaesthetic), sight and smell. The experience often involves mixed modalities of perception, recognized within psychiatric terminology by the concept of psychasthenia. People often feel sensations under their skin; they might experience an overwhelming sense of being polluted or feeling contaminated or possessed, and experience accompanying visual distortions which contribute to their sense of dissociation. In other words, the experience is not simply aural, tied to the practice of listening, which as we have seen is reduced within contemporary brain-imaging studies of voices to a cognitive deficit – the inability to monitor and distinguish inner speech from externally generated sound. Thus voice hearing is constituted as a problem of attention, aligned to a cognitive deficit which produces a sense that the voice is 'extra-personal' or other to the self.

### The Problem of Divided Attention

The idea that attention discloses the problem of 'how a subject maintains a coherent and practical sense of the world' (Crary, 1990: 4) has itself been subject to genealogical investigation. Attention emerged and was constituted as a particular form of problematization in relation to the autonomous, affective self-contained subject in the late nineteenth century. Crary aligns this problem to the emergence of a range of new technological forms and practices which demanded a subject who could 'pay attention' in ways which were integral to new labour and educational practices. These practices, he argued required subjects who could 'effectively cancel out or exclude from consciousness much of our immediate environment' (p. 1). He refers to this as a new 'disciplinary regime of attentiveness' (p. 13). Distraction, dissociation and experiences of dissolution within these new practices of attention were remade as pathological states or phenomena diagnosed as a 'deficiency of attention' (p. 1). As he cogently argues, what became articulated as pathological was that which was viewed as a threat to social cohesion. As we have seen, within modern psychology and psychiatry these threats have become articulated as cognitive deficits grounded in the pathophysiology of the brain. The focus of much of this work is a concern with localizing the particular kinds of 'mental' operations that produce the coherence of conscious thought. In other words, attention is paid to the mental capacities, and their neurophysiological groundings, which allow subjects to 'hold together'. These so-called 'mental operations' can be visualized, quantified, measured and classified through various technologies of rationalization, and translated into particular kinds of digital and informational data.

Crary instead asks whether constituting attention in this way, as 'a faculty of some already formed subject', is a sign of the subject's 'precariousness, contingency and insubstantiality' (p. 45). One of the paradoxes that the nineteenth-century experimental study of attention within the psychological and behavioural sciences showed was that the problem was ultimately unrationalizable. As he argues, 'the more one investigated, the more attention was shown to contain within itself the conditions for its own undoing – attentiveness was in fact continuous with states of distraction, reverie, dissociation, and trance. Attention finally could not coincide with a modern dream of autonomy' (p. 45).

I want to extend this work by turning to forms of psychological experimentation which took place in what has been characterized by many as subliminal psychology. This archive, as I argued in the preface, was transdisciplinary, bringing together philosophers, scientists, writers, artists, legislators and so forth, including Henri Bergson, Gabriel Tarde, Boris Sidis and William James, to name some of the actors. In this section I want to focus on a series of experiments that took place in William James's psychological laboratory at Harvard University, between the avant-garde lesbian writer Gertrude Stein and Leon Solomons, both of whom were undergraduate students in psychology at the time. The experiments took place under the tutelage of the psychologist, Hugo Munsterberg (1893, 1916), exploring the phenomenon of automatic writing (see also Meyer, 2001). The experiments that Gertrude Stein (1874–1946) took part in during the 1890s explore what has come to be known as 'divided attention' (see also Meyer, 2001). The aim of the experiments was to explore the extent to which phenomena associated with hysteria could be created within the laboratory (Solomons and Stein, 1896). The backdrop to these experiments were some of the claims of subliminal psychologists, such as Myers (1903) and Sidis (1898), who, as we have seen throughout the book, were interested in psychic phenomena, such as telepathy and mediumship, as well as hypnotic suggestion and hallucinations, which they argued were evidence of other forms of consciousness, subliminal and supraliminal, which connected subjects to the other, human and non-human. Solomons and Stein, like many scientists of the time, remained ambivalent about the veridicality of such claims, but were interested in exploring associated phenomena, such as the concept of 'double personality', under experimental conditions.

One of my interests in this series of experiments is how we might theorize the links between art and science, particularly in relation to both experimentation and the role of the body in writing practices. It is perhaps not a surprise to imagine that Stein might have been interested in automatic writing and indeed many have drawn parallels between the phenomenon of automatic writing and her own distinct style and aesthetic that she later developed in her avant-garde literary writing. Meyer (2001) takes the argument about Stein's experimentation further, not just that her literary writing was modelled on these forms of scientific experimentation, but, as he argues, 'her writing turns out to be a form of experimental science itself. It is not just that her ideas about writing were influenced by science; she reconfigured science *as* writing and performed scientific experiments *in* writing' (p. xxi). It is argued that, for Stein, the experience of writing was about the *feel* of writing, perhaps equated to the experience of automatism produced within the laboratory, and for which she was an ideal experimental subject.

She never traded on the idea that her literary innovations were learnt as a student of psychology (an argument that the behaviourist B.F. Skinner made about her writing), although she also did not deny this. She did make the argument that automatic writing as produced and cultivated in the laboratory was meaningless and therefore did not qualify as writing, which she argued was always meaningful. In fact, talking about her experience of automatic writing, she argued that 'she had doubts about whether any of the writing was genuinely automatic' (Meyer, 2001: 225). This was because her focus was on how she could cultivate and produce automatic writing through developing certain habits of attention, which required discipline, training and the entanglement of human and non-human actors. As Meyer states, 'a refusal to attend to something, such as the actions of one's writing hand, required a great deal of concentrated attention' (p. 231). He goes on to argue that 'Automatic writing, produced in a laboratory context, required the same degree of attention that one needed to write a book' (p. 231).

My interest in this archive is what it might open up in terms of approaching experimentation as a performative practice, sharing links and connections across art and science. The concept of experimentation as simply revealing or disclosing entities or phenomena that pre-exist the experimental setting is one that ignores or elides the complex processes of mediation that allow phenomena to take form. We might think of practices of experimentation as inventive strategies for producing particular forms of entanglement. This is in line with work taken up across the sciences and humanities, which approaches experimentation as performative, and where the technical framing of an experimental event provides the setting for dynamic processes of enactment to take form. The complex ontologies of intra-action and contiguous processes are those aligning work across the sciences and humanities, particularly in relation to the subject of affect (see Chapter 1), and are often described as 'quantum ontologies' (Clough, 2010a) or relational ontologies (Blackman and Venn, 2010). As suggested, the ontologies connecting approaches across quantum physics, neuroscience and the humanities allow the phenomenal to be approached as fundamentally relational, but the question of exactly how relation enters into processes of mediation is one that sciences such as quantum physics are still debating and developing. Relationality should not be collapsed into mediation without serious consideration of how we might theorize the relationship between practices and processes of mediation and what I term 'threshold phenomena', such as attention, voice hearing, suggestion and even habit (see Blackman, forthcoming). I will take the experiment by Solomons and Stein (1896) as a way of working through some of these important issues, and of drawing out what a focus on threshold phenomena adds to discussions on affect.

## The Problem of Automatism

Solomons and Stein (1896) were interested in experiences which produce a sense of automatism; that is, experiences where a subject might feel that they are being directed or governed by an imperceptible force or agency, or even by a secondary personality. As we have seen, the experience of automatism is also one that is often experienced by voice hearers, where they might feel persecuted or commanded to action by a voice that is fundamentally 'not-me' (see also Chapter 8). The experience of automatism reveals how permeability can be experienced as connection but also as possession (see Andriopoulos, 2008). Automatism is a phenomenon that describes experiences which are threshold phenomena; that is, they operate across and between the self and other, material and immaterial, inside and outside. These experiences direct our attention to the body's potential for mediation, and the dangers of aligning this potential to a lively and processual materiality, unless we are willing to conceive of bodies as also being psychically or psychologically attuned in complex ways of which we still have little understanding (see Chapter 1). Solomons and Stein, like many scientists and psychologists of the time, were interested in theorizing these experiences as part of a normal continuum or spectrum of experience. Thus, in this context, Solomons and Stein's experiment was based on drawing parallels between the performance of secondary or double personality aligned to hysteria, with experiences of automatism which are often associated with particular habits of attention. Solomons and Stein (1896) argued that their experiments showed the limits of habit as it was conceived at the time and raised questions as to how to theorize more corporeal forms of knowing (see Blackman, 2008a).

The experiments took place in William James's psychological laboratory at Harvard, and have a significance for understanding the complex genealogy of psychic phenomena within psychology, as well as for creating a particular literary style that Stein famously went on to develop in her writing and particularly in her work titled 'Sacred Emily' (written in 1913 and published in 1922; see Meyer, 2001). As Andriopoulos (2008) has argued, the exchange between and across science, medicine, the legal system and literature, particularly in relation to the experience of automatism, was commonplace within the late nineteenth and early twentieth centuries. The idea of the double, experienced as a form of possession, was central to discussions of hypnotic crime, aligned to post-hypnotic suggestion, as well as to literary texts and their production based on techniques and experiments with automatic writing. One of the most famous phrases from Stein's 'Sacred Emily', 'A rose is a rose is a rose', transformed psychological and medical conceptions of automatism into an aesthetic style characteristic of Stein's avant-garde strategies. 'Sacred Emily' was produced using a technique of automatic writing, inventing a poetic literary style based on repetition of words and phrases and an inventive disconnection of thought.

Stein was not alone in her explorations of automatism within writing. Andriopoulos (2008) also discusses the aesthetics of the poet

Rainer Maria Rilke, and particularly *The Notebooks of Malte Laurids Brigge* (1910), which he argues were appropriations of Carl du Prel's (1891) conception of automatic writing. Automatism within this context was also characterized as a modality of communication with a spirit world, where the writer was positioned more as a medium or translator of the words of others, dead or alive. In a more contemporary context, the artist Susan Hiller has experimented with automatic writing in her 1972/1979 work, *Sisters of Menon*. Her experience of producing the work was one of automatism, where the words and phrases produced by her arm, which run to 20 pages, were experienced as having been produced 'extra-personally'. As she describes, 'the pencil seemed to have a mind of its own' (Heiser, 2011: 131). Automaton comes from the Greek word *automatos*, which captures the feeling of a secondary self acting, but where the 'self' producing the writing is devoid of consciousness (Heiser, 2011).

Solomons and Stein (1896) took the technique of automatic writing into the psychology laboratory in order to explore the experience of being governed by a foreign will or imperceptible force or agency. They used a particular artefact, known as a writing planchette, in order to create the experience of automatism within a scientific setting. A writing planchette consists of a glass plate which is mounted on metal balls with a metal arm attached to a pencil. The subject of the experiment holds the pencil in one arm and then engages in an activity, such as reading a novel, which is designed to hold their attention. The experiment is designed to create the experience of automatism, or secondary personality, through inducing a feeling of kinaesthetic movement. If the subject becomes sufficiently engrossed in the novel the arm attached to the pencil often moves and when the subject becomes aware of this movement (in the case of Stein) it is experienced as 'extra-personal', as being not-me. The experience of automatism in this setting happens through a form of kinaesthetic perception which registers the subject's barely perceptible experience of the sensation of movement. Based on this phenomenon Solomons and Stein developed the experiment to explore experiences which in contemporary psychology have come to be seen as skills of divided attention (Gerver, 1974; Spelke et al., 1976), where subjects can carry out tasks at the same time, but where one task is experienced as occurring automatically.

These experiments within contemporary psychology have an ambivalent status. For some, they are evidence of how behaviour can be facilitated by particular contingencies such that a person can be made to do things without conscious awareness. The experience of automatism within this setting is often aligned by contemporary psychologists to pseudo-science – that is, to artefacts which are seen to be produced by the experimental setting, rather than disclosing a capacity or threshold that might pre-exist the setting, such as a human's capacity for psychic action. This includes the famous arte-fact known as the experimental effect (Rosenthal, 1966), or the capacities of clever horses such as 'Hans the horse' (Despret, 2004a, 2004b) or Lady Wonder, a 'typing horse' (Christopher, 1970), or Lola the talking dog (Rhine and Rhine, 1929). These experiences are often discounted as biases that can be explained by behavioural cues or contingences (Jastrow, 1935), or as cognitive skills or processes that can be learnt or taught through training and practice (Spelke et al., 1976). These interpretations leave aside the more radical implications of exploring the performative basis of psychological experimentation and what it might reveal about the status of experi-ences designated as psychological or psychic.

Attention thus meets the criteria of threshold phenomena that I have developed throughout the book. Attention is intentional and non-intentional, cognitive and affective, material and immaterial, psychological and technical. In other words, attentional processes operate across such distinctions, and cannot be separated out accord-ing to such dichotomous thinking. Indeed, this paradox, as cogently evidenced in Crary's (1999) genealogy of attention, is apparent in the experiments on automatic writing carried out by Solomons and Stein (1896). Although Solomons and Stein use the criteria of invol-untariness or automaticity to describe the kinaesthetic experience of automatic writing, the production of such experiences does not operate according to such clear distinctions and designations. Even 'spontaneous automatic writing' is an invention that entangles the intentional with the non-intentional, the conscious with the non-conscious, the self with the other, and the material with the immate-rial. Automaticity is thus related to transitional processes of 'becoming unconscious' that require certain thresholds of sound, effort, repetition and sensation in order to take form. They are thor-oughly entangled processes that require particular kinds of technical framing in order to materialize. Despite my arguments regarding attention as a threshold phenomenon, attempts within cognitive psychology have continually been made to find, image, measure and map the information processing system(s) that might relate to auto-maticity (Moors and Houwer, 2006). It is assumed within this litera-ture that automaticity must be related to a different cognitive system that possibly corresponds to a particular part of the brain that might be revealed by brain-imaging studies. It is often assumed that automaticity is unintentional, uncontrolled, unconscious and autonomous (Moors and Houwer, 2006). It is these kinds of separations that assume that cognition (often seen or made to correspond to conscious, willed, volition) is separate from a parallel system that is often aligned to affect. The question then becomes related to how these two separate systems might interact or even interfere with each other.

However, if we return to Solomons and Stein's (1896) experiments, prior to the rise of contemporary cognitive psychology, these kinds of dichotomies and separations were not in evidence. The language of separation and interaction is not in play; what we see rather is a more processual approach to attentional processes, which rely upon practices and techniques of cultivation and inculcation. Attention is not a fixed capacity or fixed property of a central processing system, but rather assumed to be an *orientation* (Ahmed, 2006). This orientation is not simply about switching or focusing attention, where attention is assumed to be a capacity of a distinctly human sensory apparatus, but rather involves the co-mingling and co-enaction of the kinaesthetic, cognitive, and technical. What is important are the 'associated milieu' (Venn, 2010) and the generative potentialities which attention as a threshold phenomenon affords. Attention is never separate from technicity (Stiegler, 1998), which, as we have seen in the case of Solomons and Stein's experiments, involved human and non-human actors and agencies.

This more performative approach to phenomena designated psychological, and which come under the purview of the psychological and neurosciences, allows us to make sense of some of the contradictions and vagaries within the psychological literature. These oscillate between the acknowledgement that 'divided attention' or automacity can be produced within particular practices of training and discipline, including sports performance (Tenenbaum and Ekland, 2007), alongside a promissory desire to image the parts of the brain where 'automaticity' might be located. The conceptual underpinnings of such a promissory desire are explored in a meta-analysis of automaticity, presented by two contemporary psychologists who note the lack of coherent meaning or understanding of what automaticity as a concept is (Moors and Houwer, 2006). And perhaps this is the problem. Automaticity is perhaps not an 'it', an entity that can be aligned to a particular information processing system or part of the brain. Rather, automaticity is a phenomenon that can be produced, and its production discloses the more processual nature of psychological entities. It is the centrality of dichotomous thinking within contemporary psychology that prevents the insights of this statement from being adequately explored.

## The Paradox of Voice Hearing

As we have seen throughout the book so far, Henri Bergson, William James, Gabriel Tarde and others were all interested in marginal states as a way of theorizing the processual nature of perception, memory, consciousness and attention. Bergson (1946) developed his method of intuition, for example, which was based on techniques that would actualize the creativity that was viewed as an inherent part of this simultaneous, co-existing continuum of perception. James used the image of a 'stream of consciousness' to capture the transitive nature of perception which was not visual, but could be felt and sensed through particular kinds of bodily awareness. However, as I have argued throughout this book, the problem for James, which was articulated as the 'problem of personality', was how one lived singularity in the face of multiplicity. In other words, how could one 'hang together' in the face of process and multiplicity? Although this might seem to take us back to a politics of individual subjectivity, the problem of attention cast in this way might also direct us towards the way in which different registers and the movement between different registers of experience is technically mediated.

The paradox of attention that Crary (1999) cogently illustrates in his genealogical study is that attention is a threshold experience; it can be both binding and unbinding. Like voice hearing and suggestion, these experiences operate on thresholds, revealing above all the body's potential for mediation. They are not fixed psychological capacities, but rather potentialities that allow mediation to take form. The focus in this way on threshold experiences produces perhaps a minimal theory of subjectivity or the subject where affect is neither pre-individual nor a capacity existing independently of relationality. Affect crosses both and requires mattering processes in order to take form. These experiences then direct us towards what Bernard Steigler has termed 'psychotechniques', the technical ways in which attention is produced, augmented and modulated, such that the psychological or the psyche is always distributed across a range of actors and agencies, human and non-human.

This post-psychological approach to affect makes more sense of why psychology and psychiatry ultimately differentiate so-called normal modes of attention from those considered pathological in relation to *norms* of social performance. There is nothing inherent within individuals to make such a judgement, because, as we have seen in the example of Solomons and Stein (1896), attention and distraction can exist simultaneously and can be produced within very specific modes of experimentation. Thus, within contemporary psychiatric practice, although it is recognized that we are all capable of hearing voices, in that they are common following bereavement, during conditions of sensory deprivation, and even before falling asleep or awakening, ultimately the designation of voice hearing as pathological is made in relation to criteria based on the performance of social norms within the workplace and within family and intimate relationships (see Blackman, 2001). This is in sharp contrast to the findings of the Hearing Voices Network, which reveal the further paradoxes of voice hearing. At times voices may be comforting or reassuring, at others they might be experienced as threatening or persecuting. Indeed, a person may hear more than one voice and have experiences of voices as containing and unbinding at different times. Some people may wish to hear some voices, describing them as being like a good or trusted friend, and not hear others (see Blackman, 2007a).

The voice in this context cannot be characterized or differentiated according to social norms of performance, and indeed, I would argue, reveals the paradox at the heart of being both 'one yet many'. The voice cannot simply be spatialized or located within the head or mind. Voices are not contained by the boundaries of the skin and the conceptions of interiority that the skin-as-envelope engenders (see Anzieu, 1989; La France, 2009). Voices also can exist between subjects, not just in terms of intersubjectivity, but within distributed forms of perception and attention characterized more by a notion of kinship based on diaspora (Cho, 2008). Voices disclose the complex co-constitution of coherence with dissolution, or feelings of not having a clear separation between the inside and outside, self and other, material and sensual. Indeed, one of the successes of the Hearing Voices Network has been in helping voice hearers to live with voices, to be both 'one yet many', rather than to re-establish a sense of boundary and interiority through suppressing or actively denying the voices (see Blackman, 2001, 2007a). Indeed, Roland Littlewood (1996), a medical anthropologist who has written extensively on psychiatry and ethnicity, argues that ideas of dissociation and multiplicity were there at the very beginnings of psychology and psychiatry. Rather than presume voice hearing is evidence that distinctions between self and other have broken down, he rather argues that the subject is always already a 'split-self' or multiple self. To this extent the voice might disclose a 'non-unitary vision of the subject' (Braidotti, 2001: 5), rather than simply be taken as a sign of pathology or irrationality.

The paradox of voice hearing is therefore one that parallels work on the skin ego. Work on the skin ego, from the French psychoanalyst Didier Anzieu through to work within the Anglo-American tradition of object relations exemplified by Ester Bick and Thomas Ogden (see La France, 2009), reveals how early experiences are characterized by paradoxical relations, a feeling of coherence and separateness alongside the experience of incoherence and having no clear separation between self and other (which they posit is experienced by the infant as terrifying). What is important for these analysts are the practices which enable the infant to accomplish a sense of 'holding together'. This holding together is not achieved by a singular cognitive psychological subject, but rather achieved relationally and felt through bodily sensations. In other words, this work recognizes that we extend into our environments and yet paradoxically are required to live this extension as 'interiority'. Thus a sense of interiority is produced through our relations with others (human and non-human), which is experienced primarily as kinaesthetic and haptic, that is the relations are felt and sensed. Anzieu suggests, the skin ego is derived from bodily sensations and is not just a mental projection – it is not primarily visual. In order for the skin to acquire a containing function it needs a containing object and this can involve human and non-human others and also involve complex psychic defences (what Bick calls 'second skins').

These processes are not simply developmental but continually structure our encounters with what is taken to be the outside, and for me disclose the psychic complexity of being both 'one yet many'. As we will see in the next chapter, if neither being open nor closed is an adequate characterization of the ontology of subjectivity, then we need methods that enable us to examine the complex brain–body–world entanglements that mediate these processes in complex ways. We need to pay closer attention to the milieu (see Venn, 2010), and perhaps to work that explores experiences such as suggestion and voice hearing as threshold experiences which reveal the body's potential for mediation. These experiences act on the boundary or threshold between the corporeal and incorporeal, material and immaterial, self and other, psychological and social, past and present, inside and outside, and open our theorizations of affect to the complex forms of mediation which necessarily distribute the psyche beyond a closed, singular, psychological subject.

## Conclusion: The Problem of Ventriloquism

As we have seen throughout this chapter, the experience of automaticity or ventriloquism is one that is often aligned to the experience of voice hearing. Indeed, the apparent automaticity of voices plays on cultural fears and anxieties that voices might command the voice hearer to commit an act, aligning the voice to criminality and even homicide (Blackman, 2008b). As with hypnotic crimes in the nineteenth and early twentieth centuries, where legal responsibility for crime and particularly homicide was linked to post-hypnotic suggestion (Andriopoulos, 2008), voice hearing arguably appears as a contemporary form of possession. Indeed, many voice hearers I have met during my collaborations with the Hearing Voices Network attest to this view, and even with how their own experiences of possession are remade through their participation in the practices cultivated by the Network. Thus, voices that command can be lessened, or even changed, such that the person can begin the labour of experiencing their voices less as irrational perceptions and more as modalities of remembering. For many, this experience is one that does not shore up a clearly bounded, individual psychological subject. Rather it is an experience of the self as more divided and distributed, of the 'other' as part of me, and of living with automaticity as part of the spectrum of experience. Of course, this does not negate that at times the experience of automacity can become persecutory or overwhelming, and that the capacity to live with voices is one that extends beyond the individual capacities of a singular, psychological subject.

The focus in this chapter on 'voices', as modes of (divided) attention or remembering, allows us to develop our understandings of affectivity beyond an individual psychological body. The focus on embodiment allows us to approach bodies as 'assemblaged' in ways that allow psychological processes to be taken out of a closed psychological subject. I would argue that the terms 'psychological' and 'psyche' are still important in our understandings of affect, but that they must be understood as processes rather than fixed capacities or entities. To this end we might follow those such as marketers and advertisers, business consultants, politicians and media practitioners who know that capacities such as attention can be augmented and modulated in ways that assume psychological processes are transitive and processual. In the next chapter we will engage with work on the double brain and bicameral consciousness which will further help us reconfigure the importance of the psychological and the psyche to our understandings of affect. The double brain and bicameral consciousness are important sites genealogically for engaging debates about automaticity. This work shows how automaticity has travelled and taken form in ways which connect up work in subliminal psychology in the nineteenth and early twentieth centuries with contemporary work on affect across the humanities and sciences. This work provides one possible research agenda for further exploring the value of investigating threshold phenomena in developing our understanding of affective processes. It is also an area which importantly invites collaboration across science, arts and the humanities.

# Neuroscience: The Bicameral Mind and the Double Brain

This chapter will take the concept of the double brain as its focus. Of specific interest are the ways in which this concept was enacted in the work of Julian Jaynes (1976) with his concept of bicameral consciousness, and the revitalization of both the double brain and bicameral consciousness in the contemporary writings of the psychiatrist Iain McGilchrist (2009). I will argue that this work is of interest to body and affect studies as it engenders brainhood as distributed and embodied, in contrast to some neuroscientific approaches which attempt to house the brain within a bounded, unified individual. The historical antecedents of this work will be situated within nineteenth-century subliminal psychology whose debates (as I have argued throughout this book) provide a lineage to work within the humanities on the subject of affect. The particular approach I will take to the double brain and bicameral consciousness is genealogical, looking particularly at the continuities and discontinuities that exist between articulations of the double brain within nineteenth-century subliminal psychology and more contemporary work. The chapter is indebted to the work of the historian of science Anne Harrington, who in her book, *Medicine, Mind and the Double Brain* (1987), situates the shaping and emergence of the concept of the double brain within medical, psychological, literary and scientific attempts throughout the nineteenth and early twentieth centuries to explain phenomena such as hypnosis, psychopathology, hysteria, somnambulism, possession and the importance of the *double* to such imaginings.

This chapter has links to work within social and critical neuroscience which are challenging the cognitivist, localizationist thesis that has tended to dominate neuro-imaging studies of the brain – that is, that the brain can be thought of as an entity, situated within the boundaries of the singular, unified subject that can be mapped in terms of brain regions and areas. Work on the social brain, the emotional brain and the affective brain points towards a topology of brainhood which extends beyond and even connects individuals in ways which are little understood. In this way brain function might be said in some cases to be shared, or at least to point towards the fundamental connectedness of the self to the other. This chapter will link work on neuroscience and anomalous psychology, with work across the humanities which has begun to develop a paradigm of entanglement or co-production and co-constitution for exploring brain–body–world couplings. This paradigm extends work on affect considered in Chapter 1. It also provides a link to work in the previous chapter where the phenomenon of voice hearing was reconfigured through the concepts of diasporic vision and mediated perception developed in the context of work on haunting and the intergenerational transmission of memory.

The chapter opens up the parameters of a project for exploring affect that links neuroscience, narrative and discourse analysis, performance and cultural studies with work on the body and embodiment originating within body studies (see Blackman, 2008a). The chapter will begin by introducing Julian Jaynes's (1976) book, *The Origin of Consciousness in the Breakdown of the Bicameral Mind*, and consider why some of the issues and questions that Jaynes raises have refused to go away. This is evident in the contemporary problems and questions studied by many humanities and scientific scholars interested in affect theory, process, body studies and the vexed problem of subjectivity. The chapter will discuss nineteenth-century debates surrounding the 'double brain', the re-articulation and re-enactment of the 'double brain' within contemporary brain-imaging studies of voice hearing (auditory hallucinations), and how the paradigm of the double may be a fruitful way of reflecting upon the genealogical question at the heart of this book: how we can be 'one yet many', or, to use William James's framing, how we can understand the 'problem of personality'. I will argue that this problem cannot be contained by contemporary neuroscience nor affect theory unless we can adequately account for the problem of 'the one and the many'; how we live singularity in the face of multiplicity. The chapter will prioritize the importance and relevance of engaging with phenomena that in different ways challenge clear and bounded distinctions between self and other, inside and outside, affect and cognition, material and immaterial, past and present, and human and technology. This will include a focus on rhythm, voice hearing, suggestion, attention, affect, emotion and feeling, gesture and imitation. The question of how we can rethink 'interiority' in the context of this work will be a central focus of the chapter.

## The Origin of Consciousness in the Breakdown of the Bicameral Mind

It is true to say that Jaynes's book has become something of a cult classic, containing a controversial set of claims about the nature of consciousness which have produced a large volume of both critique and inspiration for philosophers, writers and scientists. From the American writer William Burroughs (1990) to the evolutionary biologist Richard Dawkins (2006), many have cited Jaynes's thesis as having informed their own writing and theories. To this day there exists a journal published by the Julian Jaynes Society, *The Jaynesian*, which publishes work that develops his writings within a contemporary context (see Masanori and Fujisawa, 2007). Jaynes worked as a psychologist, eventually teaching at Princeton, during which time he undertook the research for and writing of the book. He has been described as a maverick (see Keen, 1977), one who sought to provide an overarching thesis for explaining phenomena that continue to present a puzzling challenge to the psychological, psychiatric and neurosciences. Before writing this book I had been aware of how important Julian Jaynes's work on bicameral consciousness had been to many of the voice hearers I met whilst doing my research with the Hearing Voices Network (see Blackman, 2001). Many voice hearers attested to how important and useful the book had been to them in the profound changes they had gone through in experiencing their own voices differently. The link between both voice hearing and suggestion has been explored by many, and a growing archive of work in this area is available via the Julian Jaynes Society (www.julianjaynes.org). Contemporary experimental work on the bicameral mind links the practice and phenomenon of hypnotic suggestion with the phenomenon of voice hearing. This work fundamentally challenges the assumption that suggestion is simply evidence of a lack of will, and voice hearing a sign of disease and illness.

This work is also the subject of a recent book by the psychiatrist Iain McGilchrist (2009), who has taken it forward within the contemporary context of neuroscience, philosophy and psychiatry. I will start by outlining some of the arguments made in Jaynes's book. I will give an overview of his ideas, showing how some of the controversial concepts he introduced have refused to go away, and why they might be of interest to the transdisciplinary fields of body and affect studies. This work will be discussed within some of the reinventions of the phenomenon of voice hearing made within cultural theory discussed in Chapter 6. As we saw in that chapter, the concept of voice hearing as a modality of knowing cannot be reduced to irrationality or disease. Rather, such a modality of communication discloses our fundamental connectedness to each other, to our pasts, and even to past histories that cannot be known (see Cho, 2008). With this in mind, I will turn to Jaynes's concept of the bicameral mind and its links to the nineteenth-century concept of the 'double brain' as a way of further illuminating this presumption.

Jaynes was a highly eclectic figure, weaving throughout his book examples from literature, poetry, music, archaeology, evolutionary biology, metaphysics, psychology and psychiatry, to name some of his key areas of interest. There are parallels with contemporary work on affect, as he draws attention to registers of experience which are difficult to understand if you uphold singularity and separation as the key defining features of subjectivity (rather than connectivity and permeability which are closer to understandings mobilized across affect theory, for example). He cites examples of what we might call 'corporeal thinking' or kinaesthetic forms of intelligent learning, which are more about entrainment or attunement of sensitivities rather than the development and training of conscious will – aligned to the concept of sympathy. These forms of kinaesthetic intelligence could be captured by Bourdieu's concept of bodily hexis or practical intelligence – the idea of second nature or developing a feel for the game – but seem to be about a 'something else', an excess, that would be more aligned to an affective realm than to cognitive learning. There are similarities with contemporary reflections, such as those made by the Australian sociologist Ann Game (2001) on helping her horse KP to learn to walk and canter following paralysis. She argued that she had to 'let go' of what we might call self-consciousness or will, and forget that she was separate from the animal. She describes this as a form of attunement or entraining, concepts which are more derived from spiritual traditions such as Buddhism. What is important is not separateness, but *rhythm* and the flow of rhythms from those you are in connection with, human and non-human (see Blackman, 2008a).

Similarly, Jaynes was interested in *rhythms* and in experiences that undermined the cogito as the seat of reason and the foundation of the singular 'I' enacted through the capacity of will. What we might call the capacity for 'self-consciousness' for Jaynes could impede learning and was not necessary for what we might call intelligent forms of knowing. He was interested, for example, in forms of creative knowing which just seem to arise (possibly after a period of preparation, immersion and incubation) where we might experience a 'sudden insight' or illumination. As he recounts (Jaynes, 1976: 44): 'Indeed, it is sometimes almost as if the problem had to be forgotten to be solved'. This has rather interesting parallels with William James's (1902) aligning of synthesis with the experience of conversion, where change and transformation are not incremental, linear processes but seem to happen often in a flash (see Chapter 3). Jaynes was interested in the role of metaphor in how we account for subjectivity. The way, for example, that mental space is often equated with physical space, seen to be located somewhere – usually within our heads further reduced to the individual brain. In this sense, somewhat less controversially, self-consciousness, the ability to imagine an 'I' behaving in a world, is an enfolding of metaphoric language. As he says, 'it is an operation rather than a thing, a repository, or a function' (Jaynes, 1976: 65). This mentality of self-consciousness, as he calls it, is rather different to what he calls more bicameral forms of consciousness that we might find in Homer's *Iliad*, for example. He uses the fictional world of the *Iliad* to raise questions about subjectivity. As he asks: 'What is mind in the Iliad?' (p. 69). He concludes that in the *Iliad* there is no sense of subjective consciousness, no mind, no will or volition, no individual voluntarism. Rather people acted on the basis of the voices of gods through which they were able to act and follow commands and direct action. They were not heard as 'mental voices', as inner speech for example, but as voices that had the experiential quality of externally produced sounds.

Importantly, for Jaynes, these experiences of what he calls bicamerality have not simply gone away or been superseded by the rise of mentalities associated with autonomous selfhood. Rather, what he terms the vestiges of hearing without a sense of individual boundary or ego remain with us, and might suggest arguably different forms of healing than those prescribed by biomedical and allopathic approaches to voice hearing. He was keen to stress that bicamerality should not be aligned to a disease process. It should not be viewed as an abnormal process that ideally should be brought under the control of will. In order to illustrate his conceptual arguments about the bicameral mind he turned to evidence that might suggest that experience of hallucinations or voice hearing is fairly common within the general population and therefore should not be approached as merely a sign of disease or illness. This included linking evidence from a survey, the Census of Hallucinations, carried out by Henry Sidgwick in 1894, which was published in the *Proceedings of the Society for Psychical Research*. This is aligned to West's mass-observation questionnaire on hallucinations in 1948, through to many anecdotes told to him by voice hearers who had never been in contact with the psychiatric services. In the book he draws on accounts given by so-called normal people who have attended his lectures, and afterwards disclosed their own experiences of voice hearing that they have kept to themselves. As he recounts, 'one young biologist's wife said that almost every morning as she made the beds and did the housework, she had long, informative, and pleasant conversations with the voice of her dead grandmother in which the grandmother's voice was actually heard' (Jaynes, 1976: 86). From this evidence he suggests that hallucinations are evidence of forms of relatedness that disclose our fundamental connectedness to the other, dead or alive, rather than signs of disease or illness to be located within the head and mapped primarily through brain-imaging scans, for example.

## Voices and Brain Imaging

If we turn to contemporary brain-imaging studies of voice hearing we will see why Jaynes's views might be considered controversial or even preposterous by many. Arguably the implications of Jaynes's theories for the theory and practice of brain imaging has not been fully realized. Harrington (1987: 273) suggests that although previous literature on the double brain has failed to 'retain a place in neurology's collective memory', there is still ongoing debate about the nature and functioning of the two brain hemispheres. In the case of voice hearing, the right hemisphere is often seen to play a key role in the production of the voice hearing experience. As we saw in the previous chapter, right hemisphere involvement is usually considered a pathological deficit aligned to aberrant activation of the right middle temporal gyrus. The conclusions drawn from such studies are that this brain region is responsible for the self-monitoring of inner speech and that this ability allows one to distinguish between speech that is internally and externally generated. It is the capacity for self-monitoring that is viewed as defective in the brains of those who hear voices, who are seen to mistake inner speech for externally generated speech. In this framing of the 'double brain', the right hemisphere is viewed as capable of speech, but what is lacking is a particular property of mind – a cognitive capacity of self-monitoring – which would allow the subject to discern the inner from the outer and the internal from the external. This cognitive deficit is tied to what is taken to be the aberrant activation of certain regions in the right hemisphere, the right middle temporal gyrus, which give inner speech the experiential quality of externally generated sound. So in short, dysfunctions in the brain are seen to underlie the pathophysiology of the phenomenon of voice hearing, which generates a cognitive deficit, taken to be a property of mind. It is this property of mind which is taken to enable the distinction between inner and outer, self and other, and real and imagined central to the fiction of autonomous selfhood.

This engagement with the bi-hemispheric production of voice hearing is very different from the constitution of voice hearing within Jaynes's writing. Jaynes is not interested in the pathophysiology of the brain anatomy nor in what might have gone wrong or awry, in terms of cognitive deficits, to lead to inner speech being misrecognized as externally generated speech. Jaynes seeks to normalize the experience of voice hearing in order to highlight the potential of voice hearing to disclose something about consciousness that is disavowed by reducing mind to brain, and brain to anatomy and function. It is not surprising, Jaynes argues, that we tend to hear about the voices that those experiencing psychotic episodes might hear, rather than those who do not find themselves the subject of psychiatric diagnosis and intervention. As we saw in the previous chapter, this has also been the subject of the work of two contemporary Dutch psychiatrists, Marius Romme and Sandra Escher, who have been associated with the founding of the Hearing Voices Network (see Blackman, 2001, 2007a).

Jaynes links the phenomenon of voice hearing to a range of experiences which remain as anomalies, particularly if we presume that the foundational ontology of subjectivity is based on the autonomous self. These anomalous experiences are precisely those that are the subject of this book: hypnotic suggestibility, automatism and voice hearing, for example, what Jaynes (1976: 379) refers to as the 'family of problems which constitute psychology'. Jaynes draws from the neurological understandings current at the time of his writing which theorize the brain's involvement and participation in voice hearing. Although not wishing to see bicamerality as pathological, he was interested in the role certain forms of biochemistry associated with 'stress' might play in reactivating bicamerality. This reactivation is precisely a re-enactment of experiences that cannot be contained by the positing of the subject as singular, bounded and unified, and that reveal the openness of the subject to the other, human and non-human. There might be more fruitful theories for modelling the materiality of such processes, including epigenetics, for example (see epilogue).

The experiential dimensions of bicamerality for Jaynes were acutely disclosed in experiences of psychosis, which he aligned to the experience of voice hearing and the loss or dissolution of the self. Interestingly, he also posited a link between a suggestive realm and voice hearing by citing studies which seem to show the role of expectation and anticipation in the frequency of voices. For example, he cites a study where particular groups of voice hearers were told over a two-week period that they could expect their voices to lessen in frequency. Of course they did. Though I might add to this that, as Anne Harrington (2006), Elizabeth Wilson (2006), Monika Greco (1998) and others have cogently shown us, saying that a behaviour or experience can be influenced by belief, expectation, suggestion, or 'positive thinking' does not mean that we understand the processes through which 'expectation' is enacted. Harrington (2006) makes this important point in her study of the 'placebo effect', where she argues that, although seen as a legitimate object of scientific inquiry (even if ideally the effect should be eliminated), the conclusion that it is all down to suggestion actually tells us nothing because of course it assumes there is a timeless object, suggestion, and that we know how suggestive processes work. Leaving aside these puzzling and fascinating problems, I want to turn instead to ask what we are to make of Jaynes's notion of bicamerality and why we should be interested. In order to understand the historical antecedents of the concept of bicamerality we need to turn to the vast literature and discussion of the double brain which was dominant until the 1920s and then disappeared from neurology, making a return in the 1960s (see Harrington, 1987).

## The Double Brain

In this section I want to turn to a discussion of the 'double brain', the concept which Jayne saw as unifying a range of experiences, including creativity, the role of rhythm in poetry and music, hypnotic suggestibility and voice hearing, and which tied his research to a tradition of neurological thinking which dates back to the mid-nineteenth century. The double brain, in short, is a concept which suggests that the brain has two functional hemispheres connected by fibres called the corpus callosum, and that, rather than simply one hemisphere being dominant (usually the left), there is more of a duality and even a parallelism in terms of our functioning. During the nineteenth century the concept of the double and the double brain was a central organizing trope for understanding a range of phenomena, practices and experiences, including secondary personality, hysteria, hypnosis, mediumship, telepathy and madness. As we have seen throughout this book, these experiences were all seen to be linked through their dissolution of clear and distinct boundaries between the self and other, such that the person could be governed by imperceptible forces (see Andriopoulos, 2008). If the self could be divided against itself, then the brain was also imagined as 'an organ divided-against-itself' (Harrington, 1987: 103).

Throughout its history the double brain has offered up a contested space or process for thinking about duality. The terms of debate have hinged around the potential of duality for refiguring subjectivity, the threats it was seen to pose to civilization, and a set of colonial and gendered debates about the nature of what it means to be human. These are summed up in Harrington's (1987) book, where for many writing at the time, the left hemisphere was aligned to humanness, located within the frontal lobe, and linked to motor activity, volition, intelligence, consciousness and reason, and was fundamentally male and white. In contrast, the right hemisphere was more often aligned to animality, located within the occipital lobe and linked to sensory activity, instinct, passion/emotion, organic life, unconsciousness and madness, and was fundamentally female and non-white. These debates about duality and the double brain were particularly played out within studies of madness where questions were posed about the nature of sanity in relation to duality – for example, if we have two brains do we have two minds? For others the double brain adds neurological weight to why psychopathology might take the form it does in industrialized societies; that although we might have a double brain, what is important is how this is unified, and this unifying principle is down to the will – a property of mind, not brain.

In this view, normative mental life enables the co-operation of the two hemispheres rather than a more profound rethinking of subjectivity as intersubjectivity or intercorporeality, for example. We saw earlier how this distinction is clearly enacted within contemporary brain-imaging studies of voice hearing. What is seen to be important is the experience of unity and singularity and how this is co-ordinated. To sum up, for some the debate was framed through a distinction between the double brain and the importance of specifying the unity of mind. For others, the double brain introduces an ontology of subjectivity that enacts bodies as more porous and permeable to others, human and non-human. This view undermines the assumption that there are strict borders and boundaries between mind and body, self and not-self, and the material and ephemeral. These debates are complex and ongoing within the contemporary neurosciences (see McGilchrist, 2009), but instructive for this chapter. Ann Harrington's (1987) book is one of the few that introduces the significance of these debates, and to an area which has largely been neglected by humanities scholars, despite the interest of many contemporary cultural scholars in the biological and neurosciences.

In nineteenth-century discussions of the double brain one of the key aims was to localize brain function, and particularly language. One of the most famous proponents of the localization thesis was Paul Broca (1824–1880); the area of the brain (the left brain in those who are right-handed) seen to be aligned to speech is now known as Broca's area. Broca importantly also suggested that the hemispheres both had the potential for speech and language but are educated differently, leading to asymmetry in terms of function. For many writing at this time, asymmetry was superior and an expression of the civilizing process, with Gustave Le Bon, the French Royalist known in sociology and media studies for his treatise on crowd psychology, arguing that women, so-called savages and children were more prone to symmetry and ambidexterity (see also Chapter 2). Of course, as Harrington (ibid.) highlights, the conclusion of Le Bon's arguments were that women would not benefit from higher education and should stay at home! This evaluation of the possible duality of brain function was echoed in work which increasingly located the will within the left hemisphere, providing a neurological home for what was to become viewed as a normative capacity of personhood. As Harrington (1987: 80) suggests, commenting upon the denigration of the right hemisphere/brain: even if

> it was permitted to remain in an uneducated, half-savage state, the reputation of that side of the brain would doubtless have suffered from its association with occipital lobe functioning. Thus, it began to be argued that the right hemisphere played a predominant role in passive sensibility, emotion, activities serving trophic instinctual life, sleep, unconscious thought processes, criminality, and madness, in this sense neatly complementing the assertive, civilized, intellectual capacities of the left hemisphere.

The right hemisphere was the site of affectivity, cross-cut by racial, classed and gendered distinctions. The dualist epistemology that was to refigure the potential multiplicity of subjectivity was framed through a hierarchy between the higher and the lower, the superior and the inferior and the voluntary and the involuntary. This was an attempt to contain the possible openness of the subject to itself and others (divided self) positing a mental operation (the will) that would account for how subjects might live singularity in the face of multiplicity. Accounts of madness within this dualist epistemology posed the problem of how the brain hemispheres could both co-exist in unity, and then operate incongruously producing psychopathology (see Harrington, 1987, for an extended discussion). Although the discussion mainly concentrated on the idea of the divided self, one of the more controversial aspects of duality was the subject's possible openness to others, human and non-human, living and dead. This is illustrated by the work of Frederic Myers on the subliminal self developed from his study of psychical phenomena. Myers's work on the survival of the 'personality' beyond death in his 1903 book *Human Personality and Its Survival of Bodily Death* (see Myers, 1903) influenced the work of Boris Sidis (1898) and William James (1890; see Chapter 4), and also paradoxically was one of the conditions which led to the rejection of a hypnotic paradigm within the psychological sciences (see Blackman, 2010a; Luckhurst, 2002).

Myers was interested in the question of whether there was anything that was located within an individual's personality 'which can survive bodily death' (1934: 1). The concept of personality enacted within Myers's work was oriented to the problem of 'the one and the many'. Myers's concept of personality drew parallels with James's framing of the 'problem of personality' as a central problem for psychology and philosophy. As we have seen, James framed this problem as a problem of how the subject could achieve unity or 'hang together' when the self was divided from or discordant with itself due to a register of non-conscious experience. James attested to the affectivity of this register through his fascination with anomalous experiences, such as experiences of conversion, depression, psychotic hallucinations and delusions, multiple personality, drug-induced states of altered consciousness, hypnosis, automatic writing and mediumship. His interest in these experiences is made most explicitly in *Varieties of Religious Experience: A Study in Human Nature* (James, 1902), but also forms the backdrop to his seminal work in psychology published in the two volumes of *The Principles of Psychology* (James, 1890; see Chapter 3).

Personality was organized through a relational ontology which was based on connection of selves and non-selves rather than separation and unity of selfhood. The unity of self was an achievement that was continually usurped or undermined by the possibility of communications emanating from subliminal and supraliminal consciousness. Psychic unity was always 'federative and unstable' (Myers, 1903: 16) and there was a constant travel and transfer of communication between attendant and parallel forms of consciousness which were not under the control of will. The concept of will was to become an important nodal point within such discussions, referring within a dualist epistemology, to both the mind's control over the body, and later the brain's control over the nervous system (see Smith, 1992). However, as we will see, telepathy was seen to undermine such ordered regulations of self and other. The subliminal self provided a vehicle for transmission of communications that were registered through an infra-language that was primarily neurophysiological. This infra-language recorded the effects of a suggestive realm on personality through the action of the central nervous system: the senses, the vasomotor system, and the imagination. The imagination was another imputed agency of transmission that could also be developed, trained and focused in order to induce healing and change.

Myers had staged his notion of imagination as an expression of 'man's own self-suggestive power' (1934: 202) through the use of a measuring device known as the spectroscope. This device refracted light waves emitted from matter through a prism, materializing what was taken to be immaterial through a specific experimental apparatus. Barad (2007: 73) suggests that diffractions do not simply reveal what is already there, but rather, 'bring the reality of entanglements to light'. Thus the apparatus, which included Myers and his particular theoretical concepts (that is, the subliminal and supraliminal self), allowed the interference of light waves producing light as a spectrum rather than as having determinate properties. This provided an analogy for Myers in his notion of a spectrum of consciousness which allowed him to align a range of anomalous experiences, such as trance, sleep, lethargy, auditory and visual hallucinations, crystal vision, pre-cognition, and psychical invasion to the action of suggestion.

This action or transfer was registered through the central nervous system (subliminal self) and through experiences (supraliminal) which were constituted as vibrational communications with 'a meta-etherial world' (Myers, 1903: 223). Thus imagination was an agency of communication that opened links with a spirit world and thus for Myers opened up the possibility of communication with the dead. Telepathy, hypnoticism, spirit-healing, dreams and prayer, for example, were all considered manifestations of this supraliminal realm. The subliminal and supraliminal self were not considered separate entities, but rather as existing in continuous movement or transport, thus undermining the notion of a bounded, unified self. Myers's notion of a subliminal secondary self was also indebted to work on the double brain, and equated the so-called automatic writing of psychics with the kinds of writing produced by asphasic subjects. In Myers's reversal of the prevailing dualist epistemology he refigured the right hemisphere as the site of creativity and genius and as being a 'neurophysiological pipe-line to the spirit world' (Harrington, 1987: 139). The analogy that was made, largely derived from nineteenth-century energy physics, was that consciousness was not a property of brain (considered topographically and spatially), but was 'all around' in the 'ether', much like the invisible, flowing forces of electricity, the wireless, radiation and so forth (see Asendorf, 1993; Benthall, 1976; see also Chapter 3).

Myers's work was very important for William James, who argued that Myers's formulations of the subliminal and supraliminal selves were 'the first attempt in any language to consider the phenomena of hallucination, hypnoticism, automatism, double personality, and mediumship as connected parts of the whole subject' (Murphy and Ballou, 1960: 39). Luckhurst (2002) suggests that the interest in the after-life and the possible transport of communication between the material and the ephemeral was one of the main conditions which would shift such interest to the margins. As he argues:

> Ironically, as orthodox psychiatric opinion was beginning to accept hypnosis in England, Mrs Piper was the occasion for many of the most respected psychical researchers to concede that telepathy was insufficient to explain her powers; she had to be in contact with the dead. What had led psychical research into orthodoxy was what would edge it to the margin. (Luckhurst, 2002: 106)

Luckhurst concludes his genealogy of telepathy by claiming that subliminal psychology was pushed to the periphery, taking up residency within the psychological sciences as a marginalized subdiscipline, parapsychology (see Chapter 3), rationalized under a newly emerging concept of extra-sensory perception. Despite these endings, Luckhurst also suggests that there are other histories to write: particularly those that might consider 'the halo of "occult phenomena" in psychology' (2002: 277; see also Blackman, 2010a).

### Affect and the Bicameral Mind

What does this work suggest for humanities scholars interested in engaging with the neurosciences? One contemporary strategy for engaging with neuroscience, illustrated in the seminal work of Massumi, is to perform what is likened to a practice of 'creative contagion'. Massumi (2002a) reconfigures the usual language of the higher and the lower found within experimental psychology, in order to enact the central nervous system as a site of a non-conscious corporeality that registers the flow and intensity of affect, prior to any engagement or recognition of the action of cognition. This is authorized through engaging with particular stagings or enactments of image reception within experimental psychology, which suggest that there are certain responses (to television, for example) that occur 'automatically', have an immediacy of felt intensity, guide action and yet are not easily available for conscious deliberation or articulation (see Leys, 2011a, for an important critique of this strategy). They are wordless, and thus for Massumi suggest the primacy of affect in our communications. This is what Massumi likens to a secondary non-conscious 'self' that enables the movement of intensive flows. Similar to Myers's refiguration of the prevailing dualist epistemology structuring discussions of the double brain, the central nervous system is figured as an unruly affective process that divides self-consciousness against itself.

This strategy mirrors debates about the double brain, which although disappearing from neuroscience from the 1920s to the 1960s make a comeback in the 1960s and 1970s when, as Harrington (1987) suggests, work on the double brain is seen to be pushing new frontiers. This work echoes previous nineteenth-century debates that, as we have seen, were divided between those who were interested in the mental operations that allowed unity to emerge from multiplicity, and those who were more interested in what were seen to be the more poetic, creative and artistic processes that were seen to originate within the right hemisphere. Within the counterculture of the 1970s, the right hemisphere was upheld as the site which was underdeveloped within Western cultures associated with technological rationalism. Its development would enable the emergence of all kinds of processes more aligned to intuition, the psychic, and the spiritual allowing forms of communication which were associated with Eastern psycho-spiritual traditions. The right hemisphere again was to re-emerge as a psychophysiological pipeline to the other, human and non-human.

This contestation which reveals the anomalies in discussions of the double brain is interesting as it suggests that, aside from assumptions made about the significance of the right and left hemisphere, and their apparent asymmetry of function, the fundamental challenge of this work has not been realized. I want to stress that what I do *not* want to do in this book is simply to authorize a particular approach to brainhood and my own particular take on affect and embodiment. This would simply be reproducing many of the problems that have been identified with the way in which humanities scholars have engaged with the neurosciences, particularly in relation to the subject of affect (see Chapter 1). I am more interested in exploring how a focus on experimentation, mediation and technicity might refigure the value of concepts of duality and the double brain for developing research programmes to explore the subject of affect. I do, however, think that there is something interesting in work on the double brain and bicameral consciousness which has not been fully explored, either in the humanities or the neurosciences.

This view is echoed by Iain McGilchrist (2009) in his re-evaluation of this area of study in the seminal book, *The Master and his Emissary: The Divided Brain and the Making of the Western World*. He argues that although not considered a respectable area of neuro-scientific study, often pushed to the margins within areas such as anomalous psychology, there is a mass of experimental evidence which suggests that 'there is something profound here that requires explanation' (McGilchrist, 2009: 2). Like Jaynes, and work within contemporary affect theory, McGilchrist argues that this evidence will only be understood through interdisciplinary projects that can combine understandings from areas such as neurology, psychology, philosophy, literature, the arts, anthropology and even archaeology. What I want to take from both Jaynes's thesis and McGilchrist's re-evaluation of this within a contemporary context, is what McGilchrist (2009: 9) characterizes as the 'importance of being two'. This moves beyond Jaynes's thesis which documents the existence of what are seen as *vestiges* of bicamerality within the present (in poetry, music, hypnotic suggestion, voice hearing and psychosis, for example), to rather approach bicamerality as a threshold experience which takes form within particular milieux and settings. I seek to understand and develop this through the concept of mediation. In other words, we can be both 'one yet many', and the question of how this is enacted requires a different kind of language than that which tends either to dichotomize experience, or to talk in terms of interaction.

## A Stroke of Insight

A moving example of what I think McGilchrist (2009) is pointing towards can be found in a recent lecture given by the American neuroscientist Jill Bolte Taylor, who herself suffered a stroke (see Bolte Taylor, 2006). On the basis of the experiential dimensions of this neurological event she came to some surprising and startling conclusions. Her interest in the brain derives from her brother's experiences of psychotic delusions, and his subsequent diagnosis with schizophrenia. Her engagement with her brother's experiences had been made, prior to her experience of a stroke, through working as an advocate for the National Alliance for Mental Illness. She also had worked as a research scientist examining the micro-circuitry of brains of those diagnosed with mental health difficulties. However, on the morning of 10 December 1996, she found herself in the unique position of being able to examine some of her own brain processes as she was having a left hemisphere stroke. She recounts in the lecture and book how she experienced this stroke, and what conclusions she draws about the double brain on the basis of this.

We have explored arguments about the double brain and bicameral mind throughout this chapter. What is interesting about Taylor's account are the experiential dimensions that link the right brain to an experience of expansion, to the present moment and to more corporeal forms of consciousness – that is, to thinking kinaesthetically. We might also link this to an experience of the 'somatically felt body' (Blackman, 2008a) – that is, to an experience of the body where the borders and boundaries between the inside and outside, the self and other are dissolved. This dissolution is primarily experienced synaesthetically; through smelling, feeling, tasting and hearing connectedness and permeability. Taylor contrasts this with left hemisphere difference, literally equated to a different personality, which is the experience she lost or experienced only fleetingly and momentarily. This is described by Taylor as one of separateness – of experiencing oneself as a separate, solid individual; what she terms the 'I am'. The right brain experience is aligned to flow, to an oceanic experience of oneness and a sense of enormity which she experienced as profoundly peaceful.

We might contrast this profoundly peaceful and oceanic experience of oneness with a more distressing account of doubleness or dividedness. The American fiction writer, Siri Hustvedt (2010), has written a neurological memoir, *The Shaking Woman or A History of My Nerves*, reflecting upon her own experiences of intense and uncontrollable shaking during a public speech. On the basis of this experience, which she describes as one of extreme and visceral dividedness, she undertakes an informed and incisive analysis of the sciences, and how they might speak to the phenomena she has repeatedly felt. This excursion through the sciences also takes in nineteenth-century subliminal psychology, as well as the contemporary neurosciences. She concludes that the contemporary neurosciences seem to have dismissed earlier work on some of the phenomena that we have explored throughout this book so far, including automatic writing. Hustvedt argues that these phenomena are now largely seen as taboo. She suggests that there must be a relationship between work on dissociative phenomena, including automatic writing, and contemporary neurological cases published in the journal *Brain*. This includes cases such as 'Neil' who, following radiation treatment for a brain tumour, 'lost' his memory. More precisely, he had no memory that he could *talk* about, but he could remember when he *wrote* it down. However, he was unable to read it back, or recall what he had written. According to Hustvedt (2010: 65), 'his memory appeared to exist solely in a mind-hand motor connection'. As she argues:

> The *Brain* authors do not know what to make of Neil's case. They do say his 'performance' resembles 'automatic writing, a dissociative phenomenon that was once the subject of intense study in both experimental and clinical psychology'. ... The authors also mention a 1986 study of two 'neuropsychiatric patients' with temporal lobe epilepsy and an affective disorder who produced pages of text without knowing it. Surely these phenomena are related. The question is, How? And why do the researchers, who seem aware of the earlier medical history, resist discussing it? (Hustvedt, 2010: 65)

Hustvedt (2010: 79) concludes that science, and particularly contemporary neuroscience, is trapped 'in preordained frames that allow little air in or out, imaginative science is smothered'. Hustvedt's focus, like that of Jaynes, and those working within subliminal psychology during the nineteenth and twentieth centuries, was on those experiences which derange the 'feeling of subjective ownership of parts of the body' (2010: 86). If we compare Hustvedt's account with Jill Bolte Taylor's we do not need to subscribe entirely to Taylor's evaluation of this experience. This is ultimately couched within both a New Age spiritual reading and a neoliberal injunction to 'choose'; as she says, 'to step to the right hemisphere and find this peace'. Following these accounts and the puzzling experiences they articulate, I am interested in pursuing the idea of the bicameral mind as a potentiality or threshold experience that cannot be isolated from practices of extension and mediation. This is how I have been exploring rhythm, suggestion and voice hearing throughout this book thus far. Before I turn to these debates and the ontological arguments they suggest in the concluding epilogue, I want to consider Iain McGilchrist's (2009) recent evaluation of Jaynes's thesis on the bicameral mind, and Daniel Dennett's work on software archaeology inspired by Jaynes's thesis. Issues that both of these scientists identify converge with the approach to affect and corporeality that I wish to develop.

### Affect, Milieu and Mattering

Iain McGilchrist (2009) is one scientist along with Daniel Dennett (1986) who although critical of much of the neuroscientific research and commentary on the double brain (which Dennett at times describes as preposterous), also finds that the challenges that this research poses present much that should be taken very seriously by science and humanities scholars. Dennett, along with other scientists interested in the problem of consciousness (see Kuijsten, 2006), has identified Jaynes's thesis as providing a bridge between matter and inwardness, or what I would prefer to term the material and immaterial. Dennett equates this to the difference between a brick and a bricklayer, where agency and sentience are only accorded to the bricklayer and never to the brick. For Dennett, under certain conditions we might have some sense of what it means to be a bricklayer, but it is doubtful, within the specificities of consciousness as we currently know and understand it, that we could ever know what it might mean to be a brick. This argument might be more usefully extended within the humanities by considering the difference between understanding the body as an entity and as a process. The concept of the body as having a 'thing-like' quality, where the body is reconceived as a form of property, is one that has taken on a truth status since at least its incorporation into the Habeas Corpus Act of 1679 (see Cohen, 2009). As Cohen (2009: 81) suggests, 'determining the body as the legal location of the person radically reimagines both the ontological and political basis of personhood'. This act conceives the body as an object possessed or owned by individuals, what Cohen (2009) terms a form of 'biopolitical individualization'. Within this normative conception of corporeality bodies are primarily material objects that can be studied in terms of their physicochemical processes, and are objects owned by individuals who can maintain and work upon them in order to increase the individual's physical and cultural capital.

This conception of embodiment and personhood, Cohen argues, reconfigured allopathic medicine in the mid to late nineteenth century, and disavowed and excluded other vitalist approaches to healing which conceived bodies more processually (see Blackman, 2010b). Importantly, Dennett's focus, which exemplifies his concerns with the nature of consciousness, is on the extent to which one might have an experience of such distinctions in the first place. In other words, as human subjects we can have an experience of our bodies as both being property and process, but, for Dennett, we can never know a brick's experience because we cannot impute consciousness to a brick in the way that we can to a human subject. I do not want to enter into a vexed discussion about the nature of consciousness, but rather to consider why Dennett suggests that Jaynes's thesis might have something important to add to these debates.

Dennett explores why Jaynes does not impute the capacity to experience what we might term consciousness or self-consciousness to the brain, reified as an information-processing organ. He argues that we can only ever know this by situating the brain within its brain–body–world milieu, what Venn (2010: 130) terms an 'integrative milieu' (see also Connolly, 2002). This is where Jaynes's focus on archaeology and history is integral to the assumptions he makes about bicamerality as a form of consciousness. In a breathless set of inferences made from his analyses of archaeology and artefacts from historical periods, particularly 1400 BC, he argues that the different literary forms and architectural designs which appear in this period, and which stand in a radical discontinuity with the present, can tell us something important about the nature of bicameral consciousness and its emergence, development and transformation (notwithstanding the obvious critiques and historical inaccuracies that can be levied at this work). In short, the brain is not a thing, but should be understood more processually as a set of potentialities which are co-produced and co-constituted according to the milieu and setting. This paradigm of entanglement or co-production is very different from a language of interaction and influence. Interaction implies two (or more) objects or entities which pre-exist the encounter or setting. The kind of approach that is more attentive to the coupling between milieu and body starts from the position that all we can ever document and analyse are *entanglements*, and in that sense the question of what is biology, what is culture, what is economy, politics, the social and so forth is impossible to determine (see also Blackman, 2008a, 2010b; Latour, 2005). The language of entangled processes is one that is being explored in different ways across body studies and related disciplines, and opens up interesting ways of reconceiving the relationship between affect and the im/material, as we saw in Chapter 1.

Couze Venn (2010) approaches this issue through the writings of the French philosopher Gilbert Simondon to provide a way of theorizing the interconnectedness of affect and im/material processes. The affective, as we saw in Chapter 1, refers to all the mechanisms and processes 'that involve nonconscious, visceral, propriocentric, affective processes connecting bodies' (Venn, 2010: 130). In other words, not just emotions or feelings housed and experienced within singular bodies, but those trans-subjective processes that connect bodies, that collapse common distinctions between space and time, and even the human and non-human. This work, as we have already explored, radically reconfigures how we might approach phenomena such as memory, voice hearing and suggestion, for example. Coupled with this is the importance of the milieu, or what we might also call 'mattering processes' (Kavka, 2008).

Venn (2010) makes links to ecological psychology and particularly the work of J.J. Gibson (1979). Gibson wrote in opposition to perceptual psychology and argued that the environment and organism co-implicate each other (see also Henriques, 2010, 2011). Gibson's concept of 'affordance' relates to those features in the environment that allow or afford certain kinds of response, which in turn reflect back on how environments are perceived and shaped. This is a dynamic process which includes conscious and non-conscious processes which are shared and transmitted between human and non-human actors. Perception in this sense is likened to a kind of non-conscious attunement, what Venn (2010: 136) also terms 'an immersion in a milieu', which is rather different from the view of perception that was dominant within perceptual psychology, at least at the time of Gibson's writing (see also Crary, 1990). This was one which Gibson equates to perception modelled on the fixed aperture of a camera, rendering motion static, and reifying perception as a primarily visual experience.

Venn extends this work by situating it within Simondon's philosophy of relationality. Venn (2010: 139) describes Simondon's philosophy as one that involves the 'coming of an individual into an already constituted field that alters both itself and the other active elements of the field'. It is what he calls an allagmatic relation or one of 'reciprocal constitutive interaction' (p. 139). The milieu or setting within this modelling operates as 'the technical actualization of a potentiality' (p. 139). Thus if we take the example of the brick, to relate back to Dennett's previous arguments about bicameral consciousness and the difference between a brick and a bricklayer, the brick as a 'thing' is only a thing by virtue of the active dynamics and processes that allow it to take a particular form. Quoting from Simondon (2005: 42), Venn (2010: 139) suggests that there is a 'process of becoming in which a potential in the system made up of "mould-hand-clay" is actualised according to a "positivity" of the taking form (*prise de forme*) in which none of the components is privileged as determining'. This focus on the setting or associated milieu within this approach is equally important for understanding affective processes within this dynamic constellation.

Affect is not just an amorphous intensity or set of intensities, a formless process that flows through bodies, captured through emotion (Massumi, 2002a). Rather, affect is part of the process through which adjustments to the milieu take place, including adjustments that involve the participation of human subjects, but which cannot be understood as singular human adjustments. Simondon importantly retains a focus on the psychic or psychical dimensions of becoming, which is often lost within work on affect (see Chapter 1). This has similarities with William James's focus on the 'problem of personality', of how we live singularity in the face of multiplicity. Simondon expressly uses the concept of personality to explore such processes, and, rather than reifying these processes as cognitive, conscious adjustments, this process of individuation is primarily seen to occur through the registers of affect, emotion and feeling. These are shared, dynamic processes of attunement which cannot be reduced to the psychological in the traditional sense. In this sense affect is a process that links human and non-human actors; it requires mediation and 'is a potentiality inherent in living beings' (Venn, 2010: 149).

The important focus on the milieu and mediation in Venn's development of Simondon's work (see also Simondon, 1992), in the context of rethinking concepts such as affect, embodiment and cognition for example, has resonances with work on televisual affect that we explored in Chapter 3. Kavka combines Massumi's more processual account of affect with a more psychoanalytic approach that explores how affects can be channelled or materialized such that television becomes a social conduit for the circulation, transmission and embodiment of affective intensities. The television screen is viewed as a technology of mediation that is generative of affect, providing an interface for affect to take form. Kavka (2008: 30) suggests that affect has 'object-potential, as opposed to [being] object-less or independent of the social world'. In other words, affect requires mediation in order to be felt and in this sense strict separations between cognition and affect are harder or impossible to sustain. Thus, affective intensities or resonances can be produced without there necessarily being an ideological/discursive channelling or structuring of meaning capturing such intensities. It represents what Kavka terms a 'different way of knowing' that is felt but perhaps difficult to articulate (see also Blackman, 2011b, for a development of these ideas in relation to reality TV).

The concept of mattering also has similarities to Karen Barad's concept of 'intra-action'. Barad (2007) develops the concept of intra-action, as opposed to interaction, to suggest that we should not talk of pre-existing entities interacting, but employ a more relational ontology that explores how entities emerge from intra-actions consisting of human and non-human agencies. These relational couplings are seen to produce, through their specific entanglements, what we take entities or phenomena to be. Thus, we are always studying 'entangled phenomena' and not the interaction or interpenetration of separate entities. This work has a relationship to what both Dennett (1986) and McGilchrist (2009) identify as being one of the important insights of Jaynes's (1976) work on the bicameral mind. I will develop Dennett's (1986) concept of 'software archaeology' and McGilchrist's (2009) concept of the milieu in the next two sections to draw out the significance of work on bicameral consciousness and the double brain for rethinking affect and embodiment within the present. I will also consider what work across the humanities can contribute further to these debates in relation to the paradigm of co-consitution of contiguous processes that I am beginning to develop.

## The Master and His Emissary

Dennett has published a position statement about his approach to artificial intelligence and software archaeology on the website devoted to celebrating and developing Julian Jaynes's approach to the bicameral mind. As discussed previously, the Julian Jaynes Society (see www.julianjaynes.org) publishes articles and work of contemporary authors inspired by Jaynes's work. Dennett identifies the importance of Jaynes's focus on the brain–body–world coupling which conditioned the shift from the bicameral mind to one more associated with atomized, individualized subjects. That is a view of human subjectivity based on 'affective self-containment' (Brennan, 2004) where subjects view their own actions as emanating from decisions undertaken through their capacity for self-conscious, rational action. He draws parallels with Jaynes's history of consciousness derived from archaeological fragments and traces of the past in the present, with the actions of artificial intelligence engineers attempting to design intelligent machines. In this sense, like Jaynes, Dennett suggests that the brain has remained the same for thousands of years (what he likens to the hardware), 'but what had to happen was that the environment had to be such as to encourage the development, the emergence, of certain concepts, certain software, which then set in motion some sort of chain reaction' (p. 7). He equates this potentiality to 'unconscious concepts', that is, they remain as potentialities that have yet to be realized. Thus the software design or archaeology provides the processes of mediation or mattering that enable something new or novel to emerge. It would seem that there is much within humanities and social science research which would help Dennett develop this view. Indeed, if we turn to work on artificial intelligence within the humanities, Elizabeth Wilson's (2010) recent book on *Affect and Artificial Intelligence* provides an important way forward in this respect.

Iain McGilchrist (2009) also identifies the importance of attending to the milieu to understand Jaynes's concept of bicameral consciousness. McGilchrist reverses the importance that Dennett gives to the brain, preferring instead to ask what the structure of the brain (as consisting of two asymmetrical hemispheres) brings forth in terms of particular brain–body–world couplings. As he suggests:

> My thesis is that for us as human beings there are two fundamentally opposed realities, two different modes of experience; that each is of ultimate importance in bringing about the recognisably human world; and that their difference is rooted in the bihemispheric structure of the brain. It follows that the hemispheres need to co-operate, but I believe they are in fact involved in a sort of power struggle, and that this explains many aspects of contemporary western culture. (McGilchrist, 2009: 2)

He equates the bi-hemispheric structure of the brain to two different modalities of attention. These sensory modalities of communication do not exist simply as dichotomized structures. Rather they are modalities of attending which co-exist, but depending on the milieu will be co-enacted differently producing rather different worlds. The left and right hemispheres therefore involve different ways of attending to the world, reminiscent of Jill Bolte Taylor's experience of a stroke, where the right hemisphere (if left-handed) brings forth a more relational world, governed by immediacy, flow, intensity and interconnection as opposed to a left hemisphere modality which produces a more static, separate, bounded way of imagining oneself and others. Interestingly, McGilchrist also distributes these modes of attending throughout the body, rather than seeing the brain as a separate anatomical structure. In this sense McGilchrist's way of approaching the brain is closer to work on embodied cognition and affect, which distributes neurological processes throughout the body, such that the body can be seen to be psychologically attuned via the enteric nervous system, for example (see Wilson, 2006). It also has similarities with work on the 'extended mind' which extends cognition beyond the mind, understood as an 'organismic skin-bag' (Clark, 2008: xxviii). Indeed, the idea of the body being made up of 'body-parts' and having a static, thing-like structure – what Massumi (2002a) equates to 'mirror-vision' – is itself aligned to a left hemisphere modality of attention. The idea of 'movement-vision' (Massumi, 2002a) or body-without-an-image (Featherstone, 2010) which, as we saw in Chapter 1, produces the body as more affective, defined by its capacities to affect and be affected, is much closer to the way in which McGilchrist describes right hemisphere modalities of attending.

Right hemisphere modalities of attention are open to interconnectedness and are linked by McGilchrist to a more emotional or social brain. Thus McGilchrist argues that the fundamental differences in attention across the right and left hemispheres are distributed and embodied neuropsychologically, anatomically, physiologically and chemically, for example. This might include the location of the capacities of empathy, attunement, suggestion, imitation and so forth within right hemisphere modalities of attention which are enacted through neuropsychological concepts such as mirror neurons, or in detecting facial expressivity in emotion, prosody (detecting vocal intonation), gesture and body posture. Indeed, in of those capacities which Featherstone (2010: 195) equates to a body-without-an-image. The body-without-an-image relates to a more 'non-visual sense of the body; the haptic and proprioceptive feelings', which are transmitted between bodies, disclosing perhaps our fundamental interconnectedness and openness to the other. This is a more processual view of embodiment, which is largely non-conscious, difficult to articulate and yet profoundly moves us.

Featherstone equates this to affect, where, he argues, 'other bodies and the images of other bodies in the media and consumer culture may literally move us, make us feel moved, by affecting our bodies in inchoate ways that cannot easily be articulated or assimilated to conceptual thought' (Featherstone, 2010: 195). The affective body therefore is not a mental image of the body (mirror vision – see Chapter 1), but is co-enacted through a greater proprioceptive awareness which is largely un- or non-conscious, operating at levels beneath conscious awareness. McGilchrist draws on neurological studies that suggest that our capacity for reading facial expression occurs in the right hemisphere (the fusiform gyrus), where 'emotional shifts that are expressed in minute facial changes are mirrored and synchronously matched by the observer's right hemisphere within 300–400 milliseconds, at levels beneath conscious awareness' (McGilchrist, 2009: 71). In the humanities and social sciences this has been described by Nigel Thrift (2004) as the 'half-second delay'. McGilchrist extends his evidential base for linking right hemisphere modalities of attending to a more affective, social or emotional brain, by aligning such modalities to the perception of music (to rhythm, harmony, tone, timbre, pitch and so forth). This extends Jaynes's thesis within the context of contemporary neuroscience, albeit recognizing that the experimental literature is constantly shifting, is contested and is enormously diverse when considering just how to understand the significance of the bi-hemispheric structure of the brain (see also Callard and Papoulias, 2010, for the potential problems for humanities scholars of engaging with neuroscience).

One of McGilchrist's main aims is to challenge the machinic-like metaphors for imagining the body, which hamper our understanding of such significances. Rather than localize brain function, McGilchrist is more interested in approaching these differences as different *dispositions* which align the right hemisphere to 'meaning beyond words' – that is, to the registers of affect, feeling and emotion. McGilchrist uses the term 'immaterial' to describe such dispositions, which are about the *feel* of something or someone and are intersubjective rather than atomistic and clearly bounded in terms of a singular or even distinctly human subject. McGilchrist uses the examples of bodily movement in performance (see Purser, 2011), or counter-transference within the analytic encounter (see Campbell and Pile, 2010), or singing (see Blackman, 2011b), where what is emphasized are forms of communication which are affective; where thought and thinking occur other than through signification, which are transmitted between bodies, and which carry meaning through a more kinaesthetic, corporeal consciousness (see Maxine Sheets-Johnstone, 2009). McGilchrist, like Dennett, is also interested in the milieu or setting which affords certain modes of attention rather than others. Thus, the social or affective brain always has to be considered within its context, where 'there are certain modes of attention which are naturally called forth by certain kinds of object' (McGilchrist, 2009: 133). Thus, mattering processes or affordances are also part of dispositional activities, thus locating the potentiality of bi-hemispheric modalities of attending, to distinct brain–body–world couplings. I will spend a little time in the next section considering how McGilchrist specifically approaches the co-production and co-enaction of disposition (with milieu) before concluding the chapter.

### Disposition, Milieu, Mattering

McGilchrist's (2009) approach to disposition and milieu is close to work being developed across the humanities from a paradigm of co-evolution, co-production and co-enactment focusing upon entanglements, rather than interactions. McGilchrist's approach to attention draws from Heideggerian philosophy, recognizing that approaches to apprehending the world produce the world in particular ways, stressing the importance of both technological extension and mediation. He is particularly interested in how these arguments about embodiment, which we might recognize as operating at a more cultural level, become enacted at a neurological, chemical and anatomical level. The concept of the threshold, in terms of neuronal activity or the action of the nervous system, moves the firing of neurons away from a linear model of cause and effect to one which recognizes that the receptivity and generative nature of neuronal activity depends on certain conditions. As McGilchrist (2009: 194) suggests, 'they behave in a reciprocal, reverberative fashion'.

The concept of reverberation is one useful to McGilchrist who extends this model of neuronal activity to explore gene transmission in areas such as epigenetics. Epigenetics is an area of genetic science which focuses on the cultural factors which influence gene expression. In other words, this is an area of genetic science which recognizes that there are modes of transmission which cannot be contained by the phenomenon of natural selection. Epigenetics identifies different scales of transmission across generations, where what is transmitted and how this transmission is enacted and embodied raise interesting questions about brain–body–world couplings. The challenges that epigenetics makes to genetic science is similar to other phenomena, such as microchimerism, which challenge the idea of the fortress, defended self. That is the idea that immunity describes the capacity of the body to defend against the other, to enact immunologically a self–other distinction.

Aryn Martin (2010) cogently shows the challenges that the phenomenon of microchimerism makes to immunology and, particularly, transplant medicine. Microchimerism is an identified phenomenon where cell traffic between mothers and their foetuses has been found materializing in organs, such that cells from the foetus have become part of the mother's organs and vice versa. That is, two distinct populations of cells, with different DNA, have been found in organs, reflecting bidirectional cell traffic and transfer between mothers and foetuses. As Martin (2010: 25) argues in her consideration of this little understood phenomenon, the 'entanglements of language, practice and ontology in this case have important consequences for debates about the biological and social relationship of self and other'. Scholars such as Karen Barad (2007) and the philosopher Moira Howes (2008) have argued that our conceptions of nature or biology are often challenged by 'the liveliness of (biological) being' (Martin, 2010: 40). What is interesting about this work, in the context of both McGilchrist's re-evaluation of the double brain and my own re-evaluation of phenomena such as suggestion and voice hearing, is precisely that they resist some of the foundational conceptions of the body and embodiment that have been used to describe, produce and contain them. This is no more so than in the foundational conception of autonomous selfhood that is enacted by forms of biopolitical individualization (see Cohen, 2009), which underpin biomedicine as both discourse and practice.

The ubiquity and challenges of such phenomena are not lost on McGilchrist (2009). He is also interested in what such processes disclose about the limits of current biomedical understandings. In the context of epigenetics McGilchrist turns to work on mimesis that has been undertaken by anthropologists such as Mick Taussig (1993). The capacity for mimesis or imitation is one that many have argued perhaps characterizes human subjectivity more than the concept of rational, autonomous subjectivity (Borch, 2006; Campbell and Pile, 2010; Orr, 2006). Equating work on the meme with work on mimesis, he argues that contagion is perhaps a better and more productive way of approaching transmission than the gene reduced to DNA. Contagion in the form of imitation, he argues, works faster than natural selection and challenges the atomistic view of subjectivity founded on separation and unification. The kind of mimetic paradigm that McGilchrist is developing foregrounds the concept of *reverberation* as being at the heart of becoming and places the body/brain back within its milieu. Epigenetics, microchimerism and the double brain might be more aptly described as enacting human bodies as the very paradoxical beings that we are; rather than existing as bounded, autonomous subjects, we exist in shared ecologies. We are perhaps characterized more by the paradox of being both one yet many, of being thoroughly singular-plural beings (see also Blackman, 2008a).

## Conclusion

The focus of this chapter has been on the as yet unmet challenges that work on the double brain and bicameral mind makes to both neuroscience and work on affect within the humanities. Work on the double brain, although receding until Jaynes's thesis was published in 1976, has never quite gone away. Indeed, as we have seen in this chapter, the double brain allows for the resurfacing of debates about

suggestion, contagion, imitation and other forms of 'affective transfer' that were central to debates within subliminal psychology in the
nineteenth and early twentieth centuries, as we have explored
throughout this book. Although these debates are not acknowledged
by McGilchrist, the mimetic paradigm he is developing takes us back
to the writings of Tarde on suggestion, William James on the problem of personality, and Frederic Myers and Boris Sidis on suggestion
and telepathy. As we have seen throughout the book, they were all
interested in forms of communication which happened at a distance
and which challenged separation and unification of selves, human
and non-human, and even dead and alive.

What I think is under-explored in contemporary revitalizations of
this area, and opens up debate within the context of a genealogy of
non-intentionalism, is precisely one of the conclusions to emerge
from work on the double brain that has not been developed in this
chapter. That is that the distinction between affect and cognition is
very difficult to uphold if one approaches the bi-hemispheric structure of the brain as disclosing interdependency and parallelism,
rather than separation and hierarchy of function and structure. As
we saw, the imposition of hierarchy and asymmetry of structure on
duality emerged in a very particular historical context, one which is
tied to colonialist and patriarchal thinking at the turn of the twentieth
century, and then to responses to this framing within the counter-
cultural discourses of the 1960s and 1970s. These responses, as we
have seen, were aligned to technological rationalism and the training
and overvaluation of the left hemisphere in contrast to the right. The
turn to the right enabled the splitting between the will and affect to
be enacted in a new way, which prioritized all that was seen to be
excluded from scientific and technological rationalism. It is within
this context of experimentation and its sedimentation throughout
the psychological sciences that Massumi's creative engagements
with the psychological and neurological sciences arguably can be
historically located.

As Harrington (1987) illustrates, neurology's rediscovery of duality in the 1960s and 1970s was led by the anomalies that certain
brain injuries presented to the localization thesis. In short, when
recovering from brain damage or brain lesions, the brain was afforded
a certain plasticity in that 'all parts of the brain are in a state of
dynamic interdependence' (p. 263). What is needed arguably is a
more democratic view of the brain which does not impute cerebral
dominance at the cost of finding non-dichotomous ways of thinking,
practicing and experimenting in relation to brainhood. Harrington's

genealogy of the double brain importantly discloses how many working with concepts of duality throughout the nineteenth and early twentieth centuries were not working with what she argues was a 'rather static, bipolar imagery' (p. 256). This version of duality is 'clearly inappropriate' (p. 256) when we consider the complexity of ways in which the double brain was imagined throughout this period, which do not fit with this popularized version of the double or divided self, nor with the contemporary obsession with imaging areas or functions of the brain. In the concluding epilogue of this book I will return to some of these debates, in light of contemporary neuroscience, within the context of the subject of affect. This will allow me to sketch out some of my preliminary suggestions for how we might take this work forward in order to extend our conceptions of affect, the body and embodiment across both the humanities and science in our understanding of what it means to be human.

# Epilogue

As I finish this book, work on affect is further intensifying, characterized by a volume of critique and counter-critique exploring the status of affect in the biocultural organization of perception (see Connolly, 2011a, 2011b; Leys, 2011c; Wetherell, 2012). My own contributions are largely to be qualified by what emerges from these debates. I hope that the genealogy written in this book can open the ambivalent duality that affect affords to further genealogical and critical inquiry. One direction is suggested by a recent commentary on the significance of the writings of the nineteenth-century sociologist Gabriel Tarde (see Candea, 2010). Andrew Barry extends Tarde's interest in hypnosis by refocusing attention on the importance of mediation in his writing. As we have seen throughout this book, Tarde, along with his contemporaries, such as James and Bergson, was interested in hypnotic suggestion as a possible ontology of the social. However, as Barry (2010) argues, Tarde's interest in hypnosis was also methodological. As well as using a model of hypnosis to understand processes of subjectification, he also saw in hypnosis a set of experimental procedures and practices for producing suggestion. As well as a possible ontology of the social, his interest in hypnosis was also *technical*. As Barry (2010: 182) argues: 'Hypnosis did not merely *record* a process of suggestion and imitation; it *produced* the forms of inter-psychological relationship which Tarde wished to observe'.

This echoes the approach I have been developing throughout the book to what I have termed 'threshold phenomena'. That is, our understanding of what comes to matter cannot be separated from the fundamental technicity of affectivity. Although one definition of bodies to come out of affect studies is the capacity of bodies to affect and be affected (see Chapter 1), the invocation of concepts such as flow to understand such processes is problematic. Flow implies some kind of continuous passage or movement which in some perspectives is equated to the realm of the virtual – that which is seen to exceed and exist as a pre-autonomic intensive remainder (see Chapters 1 and 3). Although this breaks down distinctions between the human and the non-human, there are problems with the status of subjectivity within these accounts. It is assumed that affect does not require a subject, whilst at the same time minimal theories of subjectivity are assumed, implicitly and explicitly, which require examination. One of these is the distinction made between affect and cognition, where affect is aligned to non-intentionality (see also Leys, 2011a).

As we saw in Chapter 1, there is a tension in accounts which wish to displace the centrality of the human, but rely on often unexamined assumptions about the place of the brain, nervous system and endocrine system, in the production and conduction of affective processes. The non-intentionality of affect is therefore seen to bypass cognition, and is located within forms of bodily affectivity, requiring rather materialist conceptions of affectivity in order to displace the subject; this might include mirror neurons and so forth (Thrift, 2010). Neuroscience becomes a privileged knowledge practice within such accounts in order to explain such processes. These unexamined assumptions point towards the importance of reinventing our concept of experimentation and not simply deploying positivist experiments from the neurosciences or the cognitive or psychological sciences in order to authorize affect (see also Callard and Papoulias, 2010). These problems will be examined in the next section where I want to engage with recent debates within critical neuroscience in order to frame my own engagement with brainhood. This will situate my discussion of the double brain and the concept of bicameral consciousness and my reasons for resurrecting this neglected archive. My focus will be on what questions, issues and research programmes a re-engagement with this archive opens up for the sciences and humanities.

### Neuroscience

With the rise in the popularity and standing of neuroscience, reflected by the increase in public engagement and funding, the interest in the brain and brainhood among scholars from the arts, social sciences and humanities is also increasing. The status of the neurosciences as having a unique purchase on the question of what it means to be human is also accompanied by the development of critique, particularly in the form of what has come to be known as 'critical neuroscience' (Choudhury et al., 2009). The prefix 'critical' in front of a scientific knowledge practice has a long history. One form of engagement is reflected by those within and sometimes outside the discipline of psychology, who align themselves with the project of 'critical psychology' (see Blackman et al., 2008). Critical psychology and neuroscience share a focus on developing critique of the methodologies used within both experimental psychology and the neurosciences for examining brainhood. I am using the term 'brainhood' following Fernando Vidal (2009), who draws parallels with the genealogical work on the psychological sciences carried out by the British sociologist Nikolas Rose. Rose (1999) developed the concept of the 'autonomous self' as a way of examining the normative image of personhood that became embedded and produced within psychology, which became central to strategies of governance and regulation such as neoliberalism (see also Henriques et al., 1984). Rose (2007) has more recently extended his genealogical analyses to the neurosciences, with his figurations of neurochemical and somatic selfhood. Similarly, Vidal uses the concept of the 'cerebral self' as an 'anthropological figure' (2009: 5) to emphasize the historical formation of the concepts and explanatory structures which are enacted within knowledge practices such as the neurosciences.

The impact of the 'psychology' of neoliberalism is one that has equally shaped the formation of the neurosciences. As Vidal (2009: 7) argues:

> The individualism characteristic of western and westernized societies, the supreme value given to the individual as autonomous agent of choice and initiative, and the corresponding emphasis on interiority at the expense of social bonds and contexts, are sustained by the brainhood ideology and reproduced by neurocultural discourses.

He argues that practices such as brain imaging which have become integral to most neuroscientific practice, evidence and experimentation, enact such an anthropological figure. What is important, he argues, is to challenge how neuroscience has taken form in the present. This requires a focus on the historical conditions of possibility which have led to the brain being considered an entity which can be mapped, isolated, measured and observed. That is, as a substance that can be separated from mind, body and world and primarily explained through neuronal or physicochemical processes. Despite the attachment of brain-imaging studies to mapping areas of the brain in terms of location and function, one of the emergent concepts of the brain to challenge such a rigid topography of the brain-as-entity has come from studies of brain imaging itself. As Vidal (2009: 19) cogently argues:

> At the same time, these techniques confirm the anatomical, functional and developmental evidence that the brain is neither a mosaic of punctuate sites, nor a hard-wired collection of neuronal circuits, but an array of interconnected and parallel networks, highly plastic and capable of repairing itself.

The concept of brain plasticity is one that has taken form from the recognition of the influence of *context* on brain imaging. As Catherine Malabou (2008) has argued, localization of brain function, which has driven brain-imaging studies, is no longer considered a 'rigid topography' (see also Chapter 7). This has led to a delocalization of function with the acknowledgement that brain imaging also maps temporarily activated networks of neuronal connections. However, one of the problems with the confrontation of neuroscience by the plasticity of the brain itself is precisely how to incorporate this insight into experimental design and interpretation of findings. I will argue that this work foregrounds mind–matter relations, although the 'neuronal' is largely figured as a system separate from the 'mental', and to that extent reproduces many of the problems with the split between intentionality and non-intentionality that has characerized contemporary neuroscience (see also Leys, 2011b). The brain has largely been refigured as malleable potential rather than fixed entity, although the implications of this for brain–body–world relations have not yet been realized. Although brain plasticity is increasingly becoming one of the dominant concepts of the neurosciences, Malabou argues that this in itself has led to something of an impasse when considering just how to enact, understand and extend such a concept. In the next section I want to consider some of Malabou's arguments in more detail, particularly as they connect with some of the questions, issues and problems my own engagement with the double brain and bicameral consciousness has brought to the foreground.

## Another Plasticity

Catherine Malabou is primarily a philosopher, influenced by Derrida, Deleuze, Heidegger and also contemporary neuroscience. Her more recent work has engaged with the significance of the concept of brain plasticity for contemporary politics (2008, 2010). Her book, *What Should We Do With Our Brain?*, repeats a refrain that, she argues, carries the ambivalence at the heart of contemporary neuroscientific engagement with brain plasticity. The refrain, 'the brain is a work, and we do not know it' is returned to throughout the book. The repetition of this phrase, she argues, captures the failure of current neuroscientific conceptions of brain plasticity to animate the potential of this concept. She argues that this is because the neuroscientific community is tied to what she terms a specific 'neuronal ideology' (2008: 11). This ideology is one which she associates with neoliberal forms of capitalism which align plasticity to *flexibility*. Neuroplasticity challenges the understanding that the brain should be equated to a machine in terms of function and processing. The notion that the brain is a kind of command control centre is displaced by a number of concepts, including the concepts of network and flow, which refigure the brain as more adaptable and mobile, refigured as flexible process. However, Malabou argues that the concept of flexibility is governed by a number of presuppositions that need examining if plasticity is to do justice to the historicity of brainhood itself. She invites the reader to consider the question 'What should we do so that consciousness of the brain does not purely and simply coincide with the spirit of capitalism?' (2008: 12). It is this question that I would like to comment on in light of arguments made throughout my book. I want to argue that the continuities between the subliminal archive of the nineteenth and early twentieth centuries, and the rearticulation of similar problems, issues and questions within debates on the double brain and bicameral consciousness explored in the previous chapter, are important to displace the centrality of a particular version of plasticity-as-flexibility. This archive is part of neurology's forgotten history and enacts changing conceptions of brainhood which cannot be contained by the translation of plasticity into flexibility.

The 'economy of flexibility' (Malabou, 2008: 46) that governs neuroscientific discourse is one that circulates and appears across a range of sites and practices. Malabou specifically ties this to a discourse of management, aligning the model of the brain enacted within neuroscience to the 'entrepreneur of flexible labour' (p. 49). The shift in organizational development and management is captured by practices such as 'change management', which position the manager as a facilitator, enhancing or more commonly *coaching* employees to develop their capacities for adaptability and flexibility. The flexible employee is required to be lean, agile, constantly on the move and able to respond anew to changing organizational conditions. This is mimicked by a flatter organizational structure characterized as supple rather than as a fixed, centralized, hierarchical system. Malabou argues that the brain is modelled on such a formulation, equating plasticity to flexible adaptation naturalizing a logic which has become a neurological hegemony. In previous work I have explored how the logic underpinning the concept of brain plasticity is one also produced through the explanatory structures of computational neuroscience (see Blackman, 2005; see also Chapters 4 and 5). This includes the computational modelling and simulation of a variety of cognitive processes, including thinking and remembering by computer networks. These networks have been considered self-emergent and autonomous such that a concept of flexibility is an *a priori* structure built into the systems. These systems are seen to mimic brain activity reconceived as non-linear and polysemic. The brain is seen to be characterized by 'dialogicity' and enacts new forms of exclusion reproducing what Malabou (2008: 53) terms 'an extremely normalizing vision of democracy'.

## The Dialogical Self

Malabou (2008) explores the forms of social exclusion which are enacted in relation to the imparting of dialogicity to the brain. Following Manuel Castel's (2002) book, *From Manual Workers to Wage Laborers: Transformation of the Social Question*, she explores how particular social groups, such as the long-term unemployed, are aligned to immobility, seen as lacking the (dialogical) skills to enact their own flexible adaptation. As many cultural theorists have shown, habit or avoidance of fixation has become the shadowy 'other' to the injunction of flexibility within neoliberal forms of governmentality (Bauman, 2000; Sennett and Cobb, 1988). The inability to enact the capacity to be 'one yet many' becomes a problem of information processing or dialogicity aligned to the mind viewed as an expression of brain. Malabou asks what ontology of selfhood underpins this conception of brain plasticity-as-flexibility. She argues that despite synaptic plasticity, what is integral to many neuroscientific theories which work with plasticity is the invocation of some kind of proto-self which is seen to orchestrate coherence. Thus approaches such as those of Damasio (see Chapter 4) impute a non-conscious self which permits 'a synthesis of all the plastic processes at work in the brain' (Malabou, 2008: 58). Thus mentalist and cognitivist conceptions of selfhood are at play in addressing the problem of personality, of how one can achieve coherence or unity in the face of multiplicity, for example. Malabou rightly argues that the mentalist conceptions of selfhood which lie in the background orchestrating unity are based on interpretations and analyses which are insufficiently developed. She equates them, such as in the work of Damasio, to psychological forms of Darwinism (Malabou, 2008: 65). As we can see, flexibility is not without limits, but ultimately these limits are based on ascribing psychological capacities and characteristics to a singularly bounded individual. The problem of the psychic or psychological lies in the background, haunting analyses which for many affect theorists have been offered as a possible model for explaining affective communication (see Chapters 1 and 4).

## The Future of Affect Studies

As I finish this book I do not want to argue that we should simply replace one ontology with another – relational with quantum, or neuronal with subliminal, for example (see Chapter 1). Georgie Born (2010), in her recent commentary on my engagement with Tarde (Blackman, 2007b), has rightly argued that we should be cautious in importing ontologies of personhood or life that claim to 'know' in some way *who* and *what* we are. She equates this to a form of 'ontological projection' (Born, 2010: 233), and argues for the importance of ethnographies which can access the 'cosmologies of others' (p. 232). I am not arguing that we replace rationality with suggestion, or anti-mimesis with mimesis. I want to be more circumspect in relation to the view that affect can be simply aligned with the non-cognitive. This split between affect and cognition has its own genealogies, to which I hope this book has partially contributed. I do, however, think that the challenges of concepts of the double brain and bicameral consciousness have not been fully realized within either the neurosciences or the humanities' engagement with brainhood. I want to return to one of Mike Featherstone's (2010) questions explored in Chapter 1 about the distinction between mirror vision and movement vision. What is important to adequately theorize is how precisely subjects move between these different registers. This requires a different conception of embodiment which is neither fully open nor closed. One of the implications of the genealogy constituted within this book is the importance of refiguring bodily potentialities as thresholds which require mattering processes to take form. Thresholds introduce leaps, gaps, tensions, ruptures and conflicts to conceptions of change and transformation, avoiding the dangers of aligning plasticity to flexibility (see also Malabou, 2008). Thresholds also direct our attention to mediation, but, as I have argued throughout this book, mediation requires extension by the development of more creative and inventive approaches to *experimentation*. This is in contrast to simply authorizing approaches to the brain, mind, body and world which originate within positivist forms of experimentation characteristic of the psychological and neurosciences.

   This is more than simply saying that any collaborative inquiry between the neurosciences and the humanities will be hampered by the problem of method (Cromby, 2007). Choudhury et al. (2009) have argued for the importance of reflexivity with a call to neuroscientists to critically examine their own scientific practices, forms of experimental design and the social contexts within which they work. They argue for the importance of historical contextualization in order to reflect on the paradigms, concepts and explanatory structures which have become imported into neuroscientific practice. As well as recognizing the importance of developing creative and critical forms of experimentation what becomes central to such research programmes and projects is collaboration across the sciences, arts and humanities. As these areas are separated out due to the funding of teaching and research across the university sector in the UK and elsewhere, the need for distributed forms of alliance which can model affect, embodiment and mediation in innovative ways is all the more urgent. As we have seen throughout this epilogue, the modelling of plasticity within the neurosciences and its import as a concept into affect studies is often tied to neoliberal conceptions of personhood (see also Blackman, 2010a). As many such as Claire Hemmings (2005) have argued, the current interest in affect is one which promises to emancipate the subject from social constraint, and thus to sideline theories and (paranoid) theorists who might wish to explore affect as an enduring mechanism of social reproduction. This oscillation between affect as openness and affect as regulation is reproduced in the ambivalent duality which characterizes what I have termed 'threshold phenomena'.

As we have seen throughout this book, suggestion, voice hearing and other phenomena that might be characterized in this way enact both a subject's openness to the other, and a set of cultural fears and fantasies about possession or being governed by another's gaze. Andriopoulos (2008) has made a cogent argument as to why possession must be inserted into cultural histories of modernity. This is particularly so if we are to fully realize the importance of phenomena such as suggestion to modelling possible ontologies of the self and social. One interesting historical trajectory that work on the double has taken is in the work of Du Bois (1903), writing in the same context as William James and his contemporaries (see Chapter 6). As Paul Gilroy (1993) has argued, Du Bois developed the concepts of double consciousness to theorize the condition of being a colonial subject within modernity. As Gilroy (1993: 120) argues, black music became a 'cipher for the ineffable, sublime, pre-discursive and anti-discursive elements in black expressive culture'. Thus black expressive culture was seen to transmit those elements which were produced out of the ambivalence and conflicts surrounding the colonial stereotype (see Bhabha, 2004). These include the ties and connections that bind intergenerationally and point towards the continuities that circulate across space and time. These are attachments that might not necessarily be spoken or easily articulated and yet are embodied in complex ways. Gilroy's (1993) illuminating work on diaspora re-establishes in this context the importance of exploring how this background of felt dispositions is commemorated and routed. As Vikki Bell (2007: 32) has argued, these are 'those relations that are neither simply of identification nor of alterity, that is, those of genealogical connection' (see also Blackman, 2011a, in relation to theorizing affect and performance).

As an alternative model of plasticity, concepts of the double brain and bicameral consciousness reintroduce 'dialectical tension' (Malabou, 2008: 82) into the politics of affect, and recognize the ambivalences at the heart of modernity. Rather than affect not needing a subject, my conclusion is that the turn to affect invites us to develop models of the psychic, psychological and subjectivity which extend our conceptions of mind, brain, body and world across space *and* time. This model must adequately deal with the enduring problem of how to theorize the relationships between mind and matter. The problem of personality is not over, neither has it been fully resolved in the current turn to affect. There is much work in body studies, on situated cognition (Suchman, 2007), the extended mind (Clark and Chalmers, 2008), and related perspectives, which have done much to distribute cognition across space. Cognition within such approaches is distributed between human and non-human agencies and actors and therefore taken out of a singularly bounded psychological subject. One question which might be asked of this work is how to think about affective relations which might be transmitted across *time*, and which are not so easy to map or model (see Manzotti, 2011). This for me is one of the important legacies of the subliminal archive that forms the central focus of this genealogy. The problem of 'the one and the many' and how to think this ambivalent duality is central to thinking about processes of subjectification within contemporary neoliberal forms of governmentality. This is the subject that affect requires. It is one of the unacknowledged conditions of possibility for some of the current work on affect and embodiment that promises to transform our conceptions of life, the body, the human and politics. This genealogy as yet cannot be written.

# Bibliography

Abbas, A. and Erni, J.N. (2005) *Internationalizing Cultural Studies: An Anthology.* Oxford: Blackwell Publishing.

Abraham, N. and Torok, M. (1994) *The Shell and the Kernel: Renewals of Psychoanalysis*, Volume 1. Chicago: University of Chicago Press.

Ahmed, S. (2004) *The Cultural Politics of Emotion.* London and New York: Routledge.

Ahmed, S. (2006) *Queer Phenomenology: Orientations, Objects, Others.* Durham, NC: Duke University Press.

Ahmed, S. (2010) *The Promise of Happiness.* Durham, NC: Duke University Press.

Alliez, E. (2001) 'Tarde intempestif', *Multitudes*, 7(December): 171–176. Translated as 'The difference and repetition of Gabriel Tarde', http://www.goldsmiths.ac.uk/csisp/papers/tarde/alliez.pdf (accessed October 2007).

Allport, F.H. (1924) *Social Psychology.* Boston: Houghton Mifflin.

Andriopoulos, S. (2005) 'Psychic television', *Critical Inquiry*, 31(3): 618–637.

Andriopoulos, S. (2008) *Possessed: Hypnotic Crimes, Corporate Fiction and the Invention of Cinema.* Chicago: University of Chicago Press.

Ansell-Pearson, K. (1999) *Germinal Life: The Difference and Repetition of Deleuze.* London and New York: Psychology Press.

Ansell-Pearson, K. (2001) 'Pure reserve: Deleuze, philosophy and immanence', in M. Bryden (ed.), *Deleuze and Religion.* London and New York: Routledge.

Anzieu, D. (1989) *The Skin Ego.* New Haven, CT: Yale University Press.

Apfelbaum, E. and McGuires, G.R. (1986) 'Models of suggestive influence and the disqualification of the social crowd', in C.F. Graumann and S. Moscovici (eds), *Changing Conceptions of Crowd Mind and Behaviour.* New York: Springer-Verlag.

Artaud, A. (1958) *The Theatre and Its Double.* New York: Grove Weidenfeld.

Asendorf, C. (1993) *Batteries of Life: On the History of Things and their Perception in Modernity.* Berkeley, CA: University of California Press.

Bachelard, G. (1971) *The Poetics of Reverie.* Boston: Beacon Press.

Barad, K. (2007) *Meeting the Universe Halfway: Quantum Physics and the Entanglement of Matter and Meaning.* Durham, NC: Duke University Press.

Barrows, S. (1981) *Distorting Mirrors: Visions of the Crowd in Late Nineteenth Century France.* New Haven, CT: Yale University Press.

Barry, A. (2005) 'Pharmaceutical matters. The invention of informed materials', *Theory, Culture & Society*, 22(1): 51–69.

Barry, A. (2010) 'Tarde's method: Between statistics and experimentation', in M. Candea (ed.), *The Social after Gabriel Tarde: Debates and Assessments.* London and New York: Routledge.

Baudrillard, J. (1983) *In the Shadow of the Silent Majorities: Or, the End of the Social and Other Essays.* New York: Semiotext(e).

Bauman, Z. (2000) *Liquid Modernity.* Cambridge: Polity Press.

Becker, R.O. and Shelden, G. (1985) *The Body Electric.* New York: William Morrow and Co.

Bell, P. (2010) *Confronting Theory: The Psychology of Cultural Studies.* Chicago: Intellect, The University of Chicago Press.

Bell, V. (2007) *Culture and Performance. The Challenge of Ethics, Politics and Feminist Theory.* Oxford: Berg.

Bentaleb, L.A., Beauregard, M., Liddle, P. and Stip, E. (2002) 'Cerebral activity associated with auditory verbal hallucinations: A functional magnetic resonance imaging study', *Journal of Psychiatry and Neuroscience*, 27(2): 110–115.

Benthall, J. (1976) *The Body Electric: Patterns of Western Individual Culture.* London: Thames and Hudson.

Bergson, H. (1889) *Essai Sur Les Donnés Immédiates de la Conscience.* Paris: Felix Alcan.

Bergson, H. (1911) *Creative Evolution.* London: Henry Holt and Co.

Bergson, H. (1920) *Mind-Energy. Lectures and Essays.* New York: H. Holt.

Bergson, H. (1935/1977) *The Two Sources of Moral and Religion.* London: Macmillan.

Bergson, H. (1946) *The Creative Mind: An Introduction to Metaphysics.* New York: Kensington Publishing Group.

Berlant, L. (2010) 'Cruel optimism', in M. Gregg and G.J. Seigworth (eds), *The Affect Theory Reader.* Durham. NC: Duke University Press.

Bhabha, H. (2004) *The Location of Culture.* London and New York: Routledge.

Blackman, L. (2001) *Hearing Voices: Embodiment and Experience.* London: Free Association Books.

Blackman, L. (2004) 'Self-help, media cultures and the problem of female psychopathology', *European Journal of Cultural Studies*, 7(2): 241–258.

Blackman, L. (2005) 'The dialogical self, flexibility and the cultural production of psychopathology', *Theory and Psychology*, 15(2): 183–206.

Blackman, L. (2006) 'Inventing the psychological: Lifestyle magazines and the fiction of autonomous selfhood', in J. Curran and D. Morley (eds), *Media and Cultural Theory.* London and New York: Routledge.

Blackman, L. (2007a) 'Psychiatric cultures and bodies of resistance', *Body & Society*, 13(2): 1–24.

Blackman, L. (2007b) 'Reinventing psychological matters: The importance of the suggestive realm of Tarde's ontology', *Economy and Society*, 36(4): 574–596.

Blackman, L. (2008a) *The Body: The Key Concepts.* London and New York: Berg.

Blackman, L. (2008b) 'Affect, relationality and the problem of personality', *Theory, Culture & Society*, 25(1): 27–51.

Blackman, L. (2008c) 'Is happiness contagious?', *New Formations* 63: 15–22.

Blackman, L. (2009) 'The re-making of sexual kinds: Queer subjects and the limits of representation', *Journal of Lesbian Studies*, 13(2): 122–135.

Blackman, L. (2010a) 'Embodying affect: Voice-hearing, telepathy, suggestion and modelling the non-conscious', *Body & Society*, 16(1): 163–192.

Blackman, L. (2010b) 'Introduction: Bodily integrity', *Body & Society*, 16(3): 1–10.

Blackman, L. (2011a) 'Affect, performance and queer subjectivities', *Cultural Studies*, 25(2): 183–199.

Blackman, L. (2011b) 'This is a matter of pride: The choir: Unsung town and community transformation', in H. Wood and B. Skeggs (eds), *Reality TV and Class.* Basingstoke: BFI and Palgrave.

Blackman, L. (forthcoming) 'Habit and affect: A forgotten history'. *Body & Society*, special issue on habit (in press).

Blackman, L. and Harbord, J. (2010) 'Technologies of mediation and the affective: A case study of the mediated environment of MediacityUK', in D. Hauptmann and W. Neidich (eds), *Cognitive Architecture: From Biopolitics to Noopolitics. Architecture and Mind in the Age of Communication and Information.* Amsterdam: 010 Publishers.

Blackman, L. and Venn, C. (2010) 'Affect', *Body & Society*, 16(1): 1–6.

Blackman, L. and Walkerdine, V. (2001) *Mass Hysteria: Critical Psychology and Media Studies*. Basingstoke: Palgrave.

Blackman, L., Cromby, J., Hook, D., Papadopoulos, D. and Walkerdine, V. (2008) 'Creating subjectivities', *Subjectivity*, 22: 1–27.

Bleuler, E. (1923) *Textbook of Psychiatry*. London: Alien.

Bohr, N. (1963) *Essays 1958–1962 on Atomic Physics and Human Knowledge*. London: Ox Bow Press.

Bolte Taylor, J. (2006) *My Stroke of Insight: A Brain Scientist's Personal Journey*. Lulu.com.

Boothroyd, D. (2009) 'Touch, time and technics: Levinas and the ethics of haptic communication', *Theory, Culture & Society*, 26(2–3): 333–345.

Borch, C. (2005) 'Urban imitations: Tarde's sociology revisited', *Theory, Culture & Society*, 22(3): 81–100.

Borch, C. (2006) 'The exclusion of the crowd. The destiny of a sociological figure of the irrational', *European Journal of Social Theory*, 9(1): 83–102.

Born, G. (2010) 'On Tardean relations: Temporality and ethnography', in M. Candea (ed.), *The Social after Gabriel Tarde*. London and New York: Routledge.

Bourdieu, P. (1984) *Distinction: A Social Critique of the Judgement of Taste*. London: Routledge.

Boyle, M. (1990) *Schizophrenia: A Scientific Delusion*. London: Routledge.

Braidotti, R. (2001) *Metamorphoses: Towards a Materialist Theory of Becoming*. Cambridge: Polity Press.

Braidotti, R. (2006) *Transpositions: On Nomadic Ethics*. Cambridge: Polity Press.

Brennan, T. (2004) *The Transmission of Affect*. Ithaca, NY: Cornell University Press.

Brown, S. and Stenner, P. (2009) *Psychology without Foundations: History, Philosophy and Psychosocial Theory*. London: Sage.

Bryden, M. (2001) 'Introduction', in M. Bryden (ed.), *Deleuze and Religion*. London and New York: Routledge.

Burchill, C., Gordon, C. and Miller, P. (1991) *The Foucault Effect: Studies in Governmentality: With Two Lectures and an Interview with Michel Foucault*. London: Harvester Wheatsheaf.

Burroughs, W.S. (1990) 'Sects and death', in I. Stang (ed.), *Three Fisted Tales of 'Bob'*. Ladylake, FL: Fireside.

Butler, J. (1993) *Bodies That Matter: On the Discursive Limits of 'Sex'*. London: Routledge.

Callard, F. and Papoulias, C. (2010) 'Biology's gift: Interrogating the turn to affect', *Body & Society*, 16(1): 29–56.

Camic, C. (1986) 'The matter of habit', *American Journal of Sociology*, 91(5): 1039–1087.

Campbell, J. (2009) 'Rhythms of the suggestive unconscious', *Subjectivity*, 26: 29–50.

Campbell, J. and Pile, S. (2010) 'Telepathy and its vicissitudes: Freud, thought transference and the hidden lives of (the repressed and non-repressed) unconscious', *Subjectivity*, 3: 402–435.

Candea, M. (ed.) (2010) *The Social after Gabriel Tarde*. London and New York: Routledge.

Carter, P. (2004) 'Ambiguous Traces, Mishearing and Auditory Space', in V. Erlmann (ed.) *Hearing Cultures. Essays on Sound, Listening and Modernity*. Oxford, New York: Berg.

Castel, M. (2002) *From Manual Workers to Wage Laborers: Transformation of the Social Question*. New Brunswick, NJ: Transaction.

Chertok, L. and Stengers, I. (1992) *A Critique of Psychoanalytic Reason: Hypnosis as a Scientific Problem from Lavoisier to Lacan.* Stanford, CA: Stanford University Press.

Cho, G. (2008) *Haunting the Korean Diaspora: Shame, Secrecy, Silence and the Forgotten War.* Minneapolis: University of Minnesota Press.

Choudhury, S., Nagel, S.K. and Slaby, S. (2009) 'Critical neuroscience: Linking neuroscience and society through critical practice', *Biosocieties*, 4: 61–77.

Christopher, M. (1970) *ESP, Seer and Psychics: What the Occult Really Is.* New York: Crowell.

Clark, A. (2008) *Supersizing the Mind: Embodiment, Action and Cognitive Extension.* Oxford: Oxford University Press.

Clark, A. and Chalmers, D. (2008) 'The extended mind', in A. Clark, *Supersizing the Mind: Embodiment, Action and Cognitive Extension.* Oxford: Oxford University Press.

Clement, M. (1994) *Syncope: The Philosophy of Rapture.* Minneapolis: University of Minnesota Press.

Clough, P. with Halley, J. (2007) *The Affective Turn: Theorizing the Social.* Durham, NC: Duke University Press.

Clough, P. (2008) 'The affective turn: Political economy and the biomediated body', *Theory, Culture & Society*, 25(1): 1–24.

Clough, P. (2010a) 'The affective turn: Political economy, biomedia and bodies', in M. Gregg and G.J. Seigworth (eds), *The Affect Theory Reader.* Durham, NC: Duke University Press.

Clough, P. (2010b) 'Afterword: The future of affect studies', *Body & Society*, 16(1): 222–230.

Clough, P. and Wilse, C. (eds) (2011) *Beyond Biopolitics: Essays on the Governance of Life and Death.* Durham, NC: Duke University Press.

Cohen, E. (2009) *A Body Worth Defending: Immunity, Biopolitics and the Apotheosis of the Modern Body.* Durham, NC: Duke University Press.

Coleman, R. (2008) 'The becoming of bodies. Girls, media effects, and body image', *Feminist Media Studies*, 8(2): 163–179.

Connerton, P. (1989) *How Societies Remember.* Cambridge: Cambridge University Press.

Connolly, W. (2002) *Neuropolitics: Thinking, Culture, Speed (Theory Out Of Bounds).* Minneapolis: University of Minnesota Press.

Connolly, W. (2011a) *A World of Becoming.* Durham, NC: Duke University Press.

Connolly, W. (2011b) 'The complexity of intention', *Critical Inquiry*, 37(4): 791–798.

Connor, S. (2003) *The Book of Skin.* Ithaca, NY: Cornell University Press.

Connor, S. (2004) 'Edison's teeth: Touching hearing', in V. Ehlmann (ed.), *Hearing Cultures: Essays on Sound, Listening and Modernity.* New York: Berg.

Cottom, D. (1988) 'On the dignity of tables', *Critical Inquiry*, 14(4): 765–783.

Crary, J. (1999) *Suspensions of Perception: Attention, Spectacle and Modern Culture.* Cambridge, MA: MIT Press.

Cromby, J. (2007) 'Integrating social science with neuroscience: Potentials and problems', *Biosocieties*, 2: 149–169.

Cromby, J., Newton, T. and Williams, S.J. (2011) 'Editorial: Neuroscience and subjectivity', *Subjectivity*, 4(3): 215–226.

Cronin, A. (2000) *Advertising and Consumer Citizenship: Gender, Images and Rights.* London and New York: Routledge.

Crossley, N. (2001) *The Social Body: Habit, Identity, Desire.* London: Sage.

Csordas, T. (1994) 'Words from the Holy People: A Case Study in Cultural Phenomenology', in T. Csordas (ed.) *Embodiment and Experience. The Existential Ground of Culture and Self.* Cambridge: Cambridge University Press.

Csordas, T. (2008) 'Intersubjectivity and intercorporeality', *Subjectivity*, 22: 110–121.

Dale, C. (2001) 'Knowing one's enemy: Deleuze, Artaud, and the problem of judgement', in M. Bryden (ed.), *Deleuze and Religion*. London and New York: Routledge.

Damasio, A. (1994) *Descartes' Error: Emotion, Reason and the Human Brain.* London: Putnam.

Damasio, A. (2000) *The Feeling of What Happens: Body, Emotion and the Making of Consciousness.* London: Vintage.

Darwin, C. (1909) *On the Origin of Species.* Harmondsworth: Penguin.

Davoine, F. and Guadilliere, J.M. (2004) *History Beyond Trauma*. New York: Other Press.

Dawkins, R. (2006) *The God Delusion.* Boston: Houghton Mifflin Co.

Deleuze, G. (1987) *A Thousand Plateaus: Capitalism and Schizophrenia*. Minneapolis: University of Minnesota Press.

Deleuze, G. (1990) *Logic of Sense.* New York: Columbia University Press.

Deleuze, G. (1994) *Difference and Repetition.* New York: Columbia University Press.

Deleuze, G. and Guattari, F. (1983) *Anti-Oedipus: Capitalism and Schizophrenia.* Minneapolis: University of Minnesota Press.

Dennett, D. (1986) 'Julian Jaynes's software archaeology', http://www.julianjaynes.org/pdf/dennett_jaynes-software-archeology.pdf.

Despret, V. (2004a) 'The body we care for: Figures of anthropo-zoo-genesis', *Body & Society*, 10(2–3): 111–134.

Despret, V. (2004b) *Our Emotional Make-up: Ethnopsychology and Selfhood.* New York: Other Press.

Dierks, T., Linden, D., Jandl, M., Formisano, E., Goebel, R. and Lanformann, H. (1999) 'Activation of Heschl's Gynos during auditory hallucinations'. *Neuron*, 22(3): 615–621.

Doherty, R.W. (1998) 'Emotional contagion and social judgement', *Journal of Motivation and Emotion*, 22(3): 187–209.

Dolar, M. (2006) *A Voice and Nothing More.* Cambridge, MA: MIT Press.

Donnolley, M. (1983) *Managing the Mind.* London: Tavistock.

Du Bois, W.E.B. (1903) *The Souls of Black Folk.* Chicago: A.C. McClurg and Co.

Du Prel, C. (1891) 'Das automatische Schreiben'. *Sphinx.* 6, 11: 65–70, 152–160, 201–207.

Ehlmann, V. (2004) *Hearing Cultures: Essays on Sound, Listening and Modernity.* New York: Berg.

Ekman, P. (2006) *Darwin and Facial Expression: A Century of Research in Review.* Los Altos, CA: Malor Books.

Ellenberger, H.F. (1970) *The Discovery of the Unconscious.* New York: Basic Books.

Ettinger, B. (2006) *The Matrixial Borderspace. Theory out of Bounds, Volume 28.* Minneapolis: University of Minnesota Press.

Evans, D. (1995) 'Psychical violence: Suggestion and the ethics of psychoanalysis', unpublished MA dissertation, Kent University.

Faculty of Political Science of Columbia University (1909) (eds), *Studies in History, Economics and Public Law*. Volume 33. New York: Columbia University Press.

Falk, P. (2004) *The Consuming Body.* London: Sage.

Featherstone, M. (1990/2007) *Consumer Culture and Postmodernism.* London: Sage.

Featherstone, M. (2010) 'Body, image and affect in consumer culture', *Body & Society*, 16(1): 193–221.

Ferguson, H. (1997) 'Me and my shadows: On the accumulation of body images in Western society: Part 1', *Body & Society*, 3(3): 1–31.

Foucault, M. (2003) *Abnormal: Lectures at the College de France, 1974–1975*. New York: Picador Press.

Frank, A.W. (1990) 'Bringing Bodies Back in: A Decade Review' *Theory, Culture and Society*, 7(1): 131–162.

Frank, A.W. (2010) *Letting Stories Breathe: A Socio-Narratology*. Chicago: University of Chicago Press.

Fraser, M., Kember, S. and Lury, C. (2005) *Inventive Life: Approaches to the New Vitalism*. London: Sage.

Freud, S. (1922) *Group Psychology and the Analysis of the Ego*. New York: Boni and Liveright.

Gallagher, S. (2005) *How the Body Shapes the Mind*. Oxford: Oxford University Press.

Game, A. (2001) 'Riding: Embodying the centaur', *Body & Society*, 70(4): 1–12.

Gerver, D. (1974) 'The effects of noise on the performance of simultaneous interpreters: Accuracy of performance', *Acta Psychologica*, 38: 159–167.

Gibbs, A. (2008) 'Panic! Affect Contagion, Mimesis and Suggestion in the Social Field'. *Cultural Studies Review*, 14(2): 130–145.

Gibbs, A. (2010) 'After affect: Sympathy, synchrony, and mimetic communication', in M. Gregg and G.J. Seigworth (eds), *The Affect Theory Reader*. Durham, NC: Duke University Press.

Gibson, J.J. (1979) *The Ecological Approach to Visual Perception*. Boston: Houghton Mifflin.

Gilroy, P. (1993) *The Black Atlantic. Modernity and Double Consciousness*. Cambridge, MA: Harvard University Press.

Gitre, E.J.K. (2006) 'William James on divine intimacy: Psychical research, cosmological realism and a circumscribed re-reading of *The Varieties of Religious Experience*', *History of the Human Science*, 19(2): 1–21.

Goddard, L. (2007) *Staging Black Feminisms: Identity, Politics, Performance*. Basingstoke: Palgrave Macmillan.

Goddard, M. (2001) 'The scattering of time crystals: Deleuze, mysticism and cinema', in M. Bryden (ed.), *Deleuze and Religion*. London and New York: Routledge.

Goffman, E. (1959) *Presentation of Self in Everyday Life*. New York: Doubleday Anchor Books.

Gordon, A. (2008) *Ghostly Matters: Haunting the Sociological Imagination*. Minneapolis: University of Minnesota Press.

Gorton, K. (2009) *Media Audiences: Television, Meaning, Emotion*. Edinburgh: Edinburgh University Press.

Gough, B. and McFadden, M. (2001) *Critical Social Psychology: An Introduction*. Basingstoke: Palgrave Macmillan.

Gowan, J.C. (1975) *Trance, Art and Creativity*. Buffalo, NY: Creative Education Foundation, State University College.

Greco, M. (1998) *Illness as a Work of Thought: Foucauldian Perspective on Psychosomatics*. London: Routledge.

Greeley, A. M. (1974) *Ecstasy: A Way of Knowing*. Englewood Cliffs, NJ: Prentice Hall.

Gregg, M. and Seigworth, G.J. (eds) (2010) *The Affect Theory Reader*. Durham, NC: Duke University Press.

Guattari, F. (1984) *Molecular Revolution: Psychiatry and Politics.* Harmondsworth: Penguin.

Guattari, F. (1995) *Chaosmosis: An Ethico-aesthetic Paradigm.* Bloomington: Indiana University Press.

Hacking, I. (1998) *Mad Travellers: Reflections on the Reality of Transient Mental Illness.* Cambridge, MA: Harvard University Press.

Hatfield, E., Cacioppo, J.T. and Rapson, R.L. (1994) *Emotional Contagion.* Cambridge: Cambridge University Press.

Hamera, J. (2005) 'The answerability of memory: "Saving" Khmer classical dance', in A. Abbas and J.N. Erni (eds), *Internationalizing Cultural Studies: An Anthology.* Oxford: Blackwell Publishing.

Hansen, M. (2006) *Bodies in Code: Interfaces with Digital Media.* London and New York: Routledge.

Haraway, D. (1991) *Simians, Cyborgs and Women: The Reinvention of Nature.* London and New York: Routledge.

Haraway, D. (2007) *When Species Meet: Posthumanities.* Minneapolis: University of Minnesota Press.

Harrington, A. (1987) *Medicine, Mind and the Double Brain: A Study in Nineteenth Century Thought.* Princeton, NJ: Princeton University Press.

Harrington, A. (2006) 'The many meanings of the placebo effect: Where they came from, why they matter', *Biosocieties*, 1: 181–193.

Hauptmann, D. and Neidich, W. (eds) (2010) *Cognitive Architecture: From Biopolitics to Noopolitics. Architecture and Mind in the Age of Communication and Information.* Amsterdam: 010 Publishers.

Hayles, K. (1999) *How We Became Posthuman: Virtual Bodies in Cybernetics, Literature and Informatics.* Chicago: University of Chicago Press.

Heiser, J. (2011) 'Messages suppressed by culture do not cease to exist', in A. Gallagher (ed.), *Susan Hiller.* London: Tate Publishing.

Hemmings, C. (2005) 'Invoking affect: Cultural theory and the ontological turn', *Cultural Studies*, 19(5): 548–567.

Henriques, J. (2010) 'The vibrations of affect and their propagation on a night out on Kingston's dancehall scene', *Body & Society*, 16(1): 57–89.

Henriques, J. (2011) *Sonic Bodies: Reggae Sound Systems, Performance Techniques and Ways of Knowing.* London and New York: Continuum.

Henriques, J., Hollway, W., Urwin, C., Venn, C. and Walkerdine, V. (1984) *Changing the Subject: Psychology, Social Regulation and Subjectivity.* London: Methuen.

Heyes, C.J. (2007) *Self-Transformations: Foucault, Ethics and Normalized Bodies.* Oxford: Oxford University Press.

Hird, M.J. (2010) 'Meeting with the microcosmos', *Environment and Planning D: Space and Society*, 28: 36–39.

Holyoake, G.J. (1906) *Self-Help. A Hundred Years Ago.* London: Swan Sonnenschein.

Howes, D. (ed.) (2009) *The Sixth Sense Reader.* Oxford and New York: Berg.

Howes, M. (2008) 'Conceptualising the maternal-fetal relationship in reproductive immunology', in K. Kroker, P.M.H. Mazumdar and J. F. Keelan (eds), *Crafting Immunity: Working Histories of Clinical Immunology.* Aldershot: Ashgate.

Hoy, D.C. (1986) *Foucault: A Critical Reader.* Oxford: Blackwell.

Hughes, E.C. (1961) 'Tarde's Psychologie Economique: An unknown classic by a forgotten sociologist', *American Journal of Sociology*, LXVI(6): 553–559.

Huitt, W. (1999) 'Conation as an important factor of mind'. *Educational Psychology Interactive*. Valdosta, GA: Valdosta State University. http://www.edpsycinteractive. org/topics/conation/conation.html (accessed 12 December 2011).

Hustvedt, S. (2010) *The Shaking Woman or A History of My Nerves*. New York: Henry Holt.

Huxley, A. (1961) *The Doors of Perception and Heaven and Hell*. Penguin: London.

Illingworth, S. (2011) *The Watch Man*. Balnakiel. London: Film and Video Umbrella.

James, W. (1890) *The Principles of Psychology*. New York: Henry Holt and Co.

James, W. (1902) *Varieties of Religious Experience: A Study in Human Nature*. London and Bombay: Longmans, Green and Co.

Jameson, F. (1991) *Postmodernism, or The Cultural Logic of Late Capitalism*. Durham, NC: Duke University Press.

Jastrow, J. (1935) *Wish and Wisdom: Episodes in the Vagaries of Belief*. New York: D. Appleton-Century.

Jaynes, J. (1976) *The Origin of Consciousness in the Breakdown of the Bicameral Mind*. Boston: Houghton Mifflin.

Johnston, J. (1999) 'Machinic vision', *Critical Inquiry*, 26: 27–48.

Jones, E.E. and Gerard, H.B. (1967) *Foundations of Social Psychology*. New York: Wiley.

Josephs, I.E. (2002) 'The Hopi in me: The construction of a voice in the dialogical self from a cultural psychological perspective', *Theory and Psychology*, 12: 161–173.

Kane, S. (2001) *Sarah Kane: Complete Plays*. London: Methuen.

Kavka, M. (2008) *Reality TV, Affect and Intimacy: Reality Matters*. Basingstoke: Palgrave.

Keen, S. (1977) 'Julian Jaynes: Portrait of the psychologist as a maverick theorizer'. *Psychology Today*, 11.

Kittler, F. (1990) *Discourse Networks 1800/1900*. Stanford, CA: Stanford University Press.

Kraepelin, E. (1919) *Dementia Praecox and Paraphrenia*. Edinburgh: E. and S. Livingstone.

Kristeva, J. (1989) 'Gesture: Practice or communication?', in T. Polhemus (ed.), *Social Aspects of the Human Body*. Harmondsworth: Penguin.

Kuhn, A. (1985) *The Power of the Image: Essays on Representation and Sexuality*. London: Routledge & Kegan Paul.

Kuijsten, M. (ed.) (2006) *Reflections on the Dawn of Consciousness: Julian Jaynes' Bicameral Mind Theory Revisited*. Henderson, NV: Julian Jaynes Society.

La France, M. (2009) 'Skin and self: Cultural theory and Anglo-American psycho-analysis', *Body & Society*, 15(3): 3–24.

Laing, R.D. (1970) *Knots*. New York: Pantheon Books.

Laing, R.D. (1985) *Wisdom, Madness and Folly: The Making of a Psychiatrist 1927–1957*. London: Macmillan.

Lamont, P. (2004) 'Spiritualism and a mid-Victorian crisis of evidence', *Historical Journal*, 47(4): 897–920.

Lasch, C. (1979) *The Culture of Narcissism: American Life in an Age of Diminishing Expectations*. New York: Norton.

Laski, M. (1961) *Ecstasy*. London: Cresset Press.

Latour, B. (2002) 'Gabriel Tarde and the end of the social', in P. Joyce (ed.), *The Social in Question: New Bearings in History and the Social Sciences*. London and New York: Routledge.

Latour, B. (2004) 'How to talk about the body? The normative dimensions of science studies', *Body & Society*, 10(2–3): 205–230.

Latour, B. (2005) *Reassembling the Social: An Introduction to Actor Network Theory.* Oxford: Oxford University Press.

Leary, T. (1968) *High Priest.* London: World Publishing.

Leary, T. (1973) *The Politics of Ecstasy.* London: Granada Publishing.

Lewis, M.D. (2002) 'The dialogical brain: Contributions of emotional neurobiology to understand the dialogical self', *Theory & Psychology*, 12: 175–190.

Le Bon, G. (1896) *The Crowd: A Study of the Popular Mind.* London: T. Fisher Unwin.

Leys, R. (1993) 'Mead's voices: Imitation as foundation, or, the struggle against mimesis', *Critical Inquiry*, 19(2): 277–307.

Leys, R. (2000) *Trauma: A Genealogy.* Chicago: University of Chicago Press.

Leys, R. (2007) *From Guilt to Shame: Auschwitz and After.* Princeton, NJ: Princeton University Press.

Leys, R. (2010a) 'How did fear become a scientific object and what kind of object is it?', *Representations*, 110(1): 66–104.

Leys, R. (2010b) 'Navigating the Genealogies of Trauma, Guilt and Affect: An Interview with Ruth Leys', *University of Toronto Quarterly*, 79(2): 656–679.

Leys, R. (2011a) 'The turn to affect: A critique', *Critical Inquiry*, 37(3): 434–472.

Leys, R. (2011b) 'On Catherine Malabou's "What Should We Do with Our Brain?"', June, nonsite.org.

Leys, R. (2011c) 'Affect and intention: A reply to William E. Connolly', *Critical Inquiry*, 37: 799–805.

Lindesmith, A. and Strauss, A. (1956) *Social Psychology.* New York: Holt, Rinehart and Winston.

Littlewood, R. (1996) 'Reason and necessity in the specification of the multiple self'. Occasional Paper No. 43, Royal Anthropological Institute of Great Britain and Ireland.

Luckhurst, R. (2002) *The Invention of Telepathy, 1870–1901.* Oxford: Oxford University Press.

Lury, C. (1995) *Prosthetic Culture: Photography, Memory and Identity.* London and New York: Routledge.

Lysaker, P.H. and Lysaker, J.T. (2002) 'Narrative structure in psychosis: Schizophrenia and disruptions in the dialogical self', *Theory & Psychology*, 12: 207–220.

Malabou, C. (2008) *What Should We Do With Our Brain?* New York: Fordham University Press.

Malabou, C. (2010) *Plasticity at the Dusk of Writing: Dialectic, Destruction, Deconstruction.* New York: Columbia University Press.

Manning, E. (2007) *Politics of Touch: Sense, Movement, Sovereignty.* Minneapolis: University of Minnesota Press.

Manning, E. (2010) 'Always more than one', *Body & Society*, 16(1): 117–127.

Manzotti, R. (2011) 'The spread mind: Seven steps to situated consciousness', *Journal of Cosmology*, 14: 4526–4535.

Margulis, L. and Sagan, D. (1986) *Origins of Sex: Three Billion Years of Genetic Recombination.* New Haven, CT: Yale University Press.

Marks-Tarlow, T. (1999) 'The self as a dynamical system', *Non-linear Dynamics, Psychology, and Life Sciences*, 3(4): 311–345.

Martin, A. (2010) 'Microchimerism in the Mother(land): Blurring the borders of body and nation', *Body & Society*, 16(3): 23–50.

Martin, E. (2007) *Bipolar Expeditions: Mania and Depression in American Culture.* Princeton, NJ: Princeton University Press.

Masanori, I. and Fujisawa, T. (2007) 'Chinese pictograms and the bicameral mind', *The Jaynesian,* 1(1): 8–10.

Maslow, A.H. (1954) *Motivation and Personality.* New York: Harper & Row.

Massumi, B. (2002a) *Parables for the Virtual: Movement, Affect, Sensation.* Durham, NC: Duke University Press.

Massumi, B. (ed.) (2002b) *A Shock to Thought: Expression after Deleuze and Guattari.* London and New York: Routledge.

Massumi, B. (2010) 'The future birth of the affective fact: The political ontology of threat', in M. Gregg and G.J. Seigworth (eds), *The Affect Theory Reader.* Durham, NC: Duke University Press.

Maudsley, H. (1879) *Pathology of the Mind.* London: Macmillan and Co.

McCarthy, A. (2009) 'Stanley Milgram, Allan Funt and me: Post-war social science and the "first wave" of reality TV', in S. Murray and L. Ouellette (eds), *Reality TV: Remaking Television Culture.* New York: New York University Press.

McDougall, E. (1910) *An Introduction to Social Psychology.* London: Methuen.

McGilchrist, I. (2009) *The Master and His Emissary: The Divided Brain and the Making of the Western World.* New Haven, CT: Yale University Press.

McNay, L. (1992) *Foucault and Feminism.* Cambridge: Polity Press.

Meyer, S. (2001) *Irresistible Dictation: Gertrude Stein and the Correlations of Writing and Science.* Stanford, CA: Stanford University Press.

Moors, A. and De Houwer, J. (2006) 'Automaticity: A conceptual and theoretical analysis', *Psychological Bulletin,* 132: 297–326.

Moscovici, S. (1985) *The Age of the Crowd: A Historical Treatise on Mass Psychology.* Cambridge: Cambridge University Press.

Murphy, G. and Ballou, R.O. (eds) (1960) *William James on Psychical Research.* New York: Viking Press.

Myers, F. (1903) *Human Personality and Its Survival of Bodily Death, Volume 1.* New York, London and Bombay: Longmans, Green and Co.

Nancy, J.L. (2000) *Being Singular Plural.* Stanford, CA: Stanford University Press.

Nancy, J.L. (2007) *Listening.* New York: Fordham University Press.

Newland, C. Bingham (1916) *What is Instinct? Some Thoughts on Telepathy and Subconsciousness in Animals.* London: John Murray.

Nye, D.E. (1990) *Electrifying America: Social Meanings of a New Technology.* 1800–1940. Cambridge, MA: The MIT Press.

Orr, J. (2006) *Panic Diaries: A Genealogy of Panic Disorder.* Durham, NC: Duke University Press.

Ouspensky, P.D. (1968) *The Psychology of Man's Possible Evolution.* New York: Bantam.

Overholser, L.C. (1985) *Ericksonian Hypnosis: A Handbook of Clinical Practice.* New York: Irvington Publishers.

Parisi, L. (2004) *Abstract Sex: Philosophy, Bio-technology and the Mutations of Desire.* London: Continuum.

Pels, P. (2003) 'Spirits of Modernity: Alfred Wallace, Edward Taylor and the Visual Politics of Facts', in B. Meyer and P. Pels (eds), *Magic and Modernity: Interfaces of Revelation and Concealment.* Stanford: Stanford University Press.

Peters, J.D. (1999) *Speaking into the Air: A History of the Idea of Communication.* Chicago: Chicago University Press.

Pollack, D. (2005) 'Introduction', in A. Abbas and J.N. Erni (eds), *Internationalizing Cultural Studies: An Anthology*. Oxford: Blackwell Publishing.

Porter, R. (1987) *Mind-Forg'd Manacles: A History of Madness in England from the Restoration to the Regency*. London: Athlone Press.

Porter, J.E. (2005) 'The spirit(s) of science: Paradoxical positivism as religious discourse among spiritualists', *Science as Culture*, 14(1): 1–21.

Potter, J. and Wetherell, M. (1986) *Discourse and Social Psychology: Beyond Attitudes and Behaviour*. London: Sage.

Purser, A. (2011) 'The dancing body-subject: Merleau-Ponty's mirror stage in the dance studio', *Subjectivity*, 4: 183–283.

Radin, D. (2006) *Entangled Minds: Extrasensory Experiences in a Quantum Reality*. New York: Pocket Books.

Rhine, J.B. and Rhine, L.E. (1929) 'An investigation of a mind-reading horse'. *Journal of Abnormal and Social Psychology*, 23: 449–466.

Riley, D. (1983) *War in the Nursery*. London: Virago.

Riskin, J. (2009) 'The Mesmerism investigation and the crisis of sensationist science', in D. Howes (ed.), *The Sixth Sense Reader*. Oxford and New York: Berg.

Rogers, C. (1961) *On Becoming a Person*. Boston: Houghton Mifflin.

Romme, M. and Escher, S. (eds) (1993) *Accepting Voices*. London: Mind.

Romme, M., Escher, S., Dillon, J., Corstens, D. and Morris, M. (2009) *Living with Voices: 50 Stories of Recovery*. Ross-on-Wye: PCCS Books, in association with Birmingham City University.

Rose, N. (1985) *The Psychological Complex: Psychology, Politics and Society in England, 1869–1939*. London: Routledge & Kegan Paul.

Rose, N. (1990) *Governing the Soul: The Shaping of the Private Self*. London: Routledge.

Rose, N. (1996) *Inventing Ourselves: Psychology, Power and Personhood*. Cambridge: Cambridge University Press.

Rose, N. (1999) *Governing the Soul: The Shaping of the Private Self*, 2nd edition. London: Free Association Books.

Rose, N. (2007) *The Politics of Life Itself: Biomedicine, Power and Subjectivity in the 21st Century*. Princeton, NJ: Princeton University Press.

Rosenthal, R. (1966) *Experimenter Effects in Behavioral Research*. New York: Appleton-Century-Crofts.

Ross, E.A. (1909) *Social Psychology: An Outline and Source Book*. New York: Macmillan.

Roustang, F. (1980) *Psychoanalysis Never Lets Go*. Baltimore, MD: Johns Hopkins University Press.

Schlichter, A. (2011) 'Do voices matter? Vocality, materiality, gender performativity', *Body & Society*, 17(1): 31–52.

Schuman, S. (2009) *The Sartorialist*. London: Penguin.

Schwarz, B. (2006) 'The poetics of communication', in J. Curran and D. Morley (eds), *Media and Cultural Theory*. London and New York: Routledge.

Sconce, J. (1998) 'The Voice from the Void. Wireless Modernity and the Distant Dead', *International Journal of Cultural Studies*, 1(2): 211–232.

Sconce, J. (2000) *Haunted Media: Electronic Presence from Telegraphy to Television*. Durham, NC: Duke University Press.

Sedgwick, E.K. (1994) *Tendencies*. London and New York: Routledge.

Sedgwick, E.K. and Frank, A. (1995) *Shame and its Sisters: A Silvan Tomkins Reader*. Durham, NC: Duke University Press.

Sedgwick, E. Kosofsky (2003) *Touching Feeling: Affect, Pedagogy, Performativity*. Durham, NC: Duke University Press.

Seigworth, G.J. and Gregg, M. (2010) 'An inventory of shimmers', in M. Gregg and G.J. Seigworth (eds), *The Affect Theory Reader*. Durham, NC: Duke University Press.

Sennett, R. and Cobb, J. (1988) *The Hidden Injuries of Class*. New York: Random House Press.

Serres, M. (2008) *The Five Senses: A Philosophy of Mingled Bodies*. London: Continuum.

Sheets-Johnstone, M. (2009) *The Corporeal Turn: An Interdisciplinary Reader*. Exeter: Imprint Academic.

Sheets-Johnstone, M. (2011) 'Embodied minds or mindful bodies: A question of fundamental, inherently inter-related aspects of animation', *Subjectivity*, 4(4): 451–466.

Shilling, C. (2003) *The Body and Social Theory*, 2nd edition. London: Sage.

Sidis, B. (1898) *The Psychology of Suggestion: A Research into the Subconscious Nature of Man and Society*. New York: D. Appleton and Co.

Siertz, A. (2006) *In Yer Face Theatre: British Drama Today*. London: Faber and Faber.

Simondon, G. (1992) 'The genesis of the individual', in J. Crary and S. Kwinter (eds), *Incorporations*. New York: Zone Books.

Simondon, G. (2005) *L'Individuation à la lumière des notions de forme et d'information*. Grenoble: Millon.

Skeggs, B., Thurmin, M. and Wood, H. (2008) 'Oh goodness I am watching reality TV: How methods make class in audience research', *European Journal of Cultural Studies*, 11(1): 5–24.

Slatman, J. and Widdershoven, G. (2010) 'Hand transplants and bodily integrity', *Body & Society*, 16(3): 69–92.

Smiles, S. (1864) *Self Help, With Illustrations of Character and Conduct*. London: John Murray.

Smith, R. (1992) *Inhibition: History and Meaning in the Sciences of Mind and Brain*. Berkeley: University of California Press.

Sobchack, V. (2010) 'Living a phantom limb: On the phenomenology of bodily integrity', *Body & Society*, 16(3): 51–68.

Sokal, A.D. and Bricmont, J. (1998) *Fashionable Nonsense: Postmodern Intellectuals' Abuse of Science*. New York: Picador.

Solomons, L. and Stein, G. (1896) 'Normal motor automatism', *Psychological Review*, 3: 492–512.

Spelke, E., Hirst, E., Neisser, U. (1976) 'Skills of divided attention', *Cognition*. 4: 215–230.

Stacey, J. and Suchman, H. (2012) Special Issue on 'Animation and Automation – The Liveliness and Labours of Bodies and Machines, *Body & Society*, 18(1) March.

Stengers, I. (1997) *Power and Invention: Situating Science*. Minneapolis and London: University of Minnesota Press.

Stengers, I. (2008) 'Experimenting with refrains: Subjectivity and the challenge of escaping modern dualism', *Subjectivity*, 22: 38–59.

Stenner, P. (2008) 'A.N. Whitehead and subjectivity', *Subjectivity*, 22: 90–109.

Stern, D. (1985) *The Interpersonal World of the Infant*. New York: Basic Books.

Sterne, J. (2003) *The Audible Past: Cultural Origins of Sound Reproduction*. Durham, NC: Duke University Press.

Stiegler, B. (1998) *Techniques and Time: The Fault of Epimetheus No. 1*. Stanford, CA: Stanford University Press.

Suchman, L. (2007) *Human Machine Reconfigurations*. Cambridge: Cambridge University Press.

Susman, W. (1979) '"Personality" and the making of twentieth-century culture', in J. Higham and P. Conkin (eds), *New Directions in American Intellectual History.* Baltimore, MD: Johns Hopkins University Press.

Susman, W. (1985) *Culture as History: The Transformation of American Society in the Twentieth Century.* London: Pantheon.

Swanson, G. (2007) 'Shattered into a multiplicity of warring functions: Synthesis, disintegration and distractibility', *Intellectual History Review,* 17(3): 305–326.

Tarde, G. (1902) *Psychologie Économique.* Paris: Felix Alcan.

Tarde, G. (1962) *The Laws of Imitation,* trans. R. Howell. Gloucester, MA: Peter Smith.

Tarde, G. (1969) *On Communication and Social Influence.* Chicago: Chicago University Press.

Taussig, M. (1993) *Mimesis and Alterity: A Particular History of the Senses.* London and New York: Routledge.

Taylor, E. (2002) 'Introduction', in W. James, *Varieties of Religious Experience: A Study in Human Nature.* London and New York: Routledge.

Tenenbaum, G. and Ekland, R.C. (eds) (2007) *Handbook of Sport Psychology.* Oxford: R. C. Wiley.

Thacker, E. (2004) *Biomedia.* Minneapolis: University of Minnesota Press.

Thacker, E. (2005) *The Global Genome: Biotechnology, Politics and Culture.* Cambridge, MA: MIT Press.

Thacker, E. (2010) *After Life.* Chicago: University of Chicago Press.

Thrift, N. (2004) 'Intensities of feeling: Towards a spatial politics of affect', *Geografiska Annaler,* 86B(1): 55–76.

Thrift, N. (2007) *Non-Representational Theory: Space, Politics, Affect.* London and New York: Routledge.

Thrift, N. (2008) 'I just don't know what got into me: Where is the subject?', *Subjectivity,* 22: 82–89.

Thrift, N. (2010) 'Understanding the material practices of glamour', in M. Gregg and G.J. Seigworth (eds), *The Affect Theory Reader.* Durham, NC: Duke University Press.

Thurschwell, P. (2009) 'The erotics of telepathy: The British SPR's experiments in intimacy', in D. Howes (ed.), *The Sixth Sense Reader.* Oxford and New York: Berg.

Toews, D. (2003) 'The new Tarde: Sociology after the end of the social', *Theory, Culture & Society,* 20(5): 81–98.

Tuke, D.H. (1872) *Illustrations of the Influence of the Mind upon the Body: In Health and Disease.* London: Churchill.

Tuke, D.H. (1892) *Dictionary of Psychological Medicine, Volumes 1 and 2, A–H.* London: Churchill.

Turner, B. (1996) *The Body and Society: Explorations in Social Theory,* 2nd edition. London: Sage.

Valiaho, P. (2010) *Mapping the Moving Image. Gesture, Thought and Cinema (circa 1900).* Amsterdam: Amsterdam University Press.

Van Kleef, G.A., de Dreu, C.K.W. and Manstead, A.S.R. (2010) 'An interpersonal approach to emotion in social decision making: The emotions as social information model', in M.P. Zanna (ed.), *Advances in Experimental Social Psychology,* Volume 42. San Diego, CA: Academic Press.

Venn, C. (2010) 'Individuation, relationality, affect: Rethinking the human in relation to the living', *Body & Society,* 16(1): 129–162.

Vidal, F. (2009) 'Brainhood, anthropological figure of modernity', *History of the Human Sciences*, 22(1): 5–36.

Wake Cook, E. and Podmore, F. (1903) *Spiritualism. Is Communication with the Spirit World an Established Fact?* London: Isbister and Co. Ltd.

Walkerdine, V. (1990) *Schoolgirl Fictions*. London: Verso.

Walkerdine, V. (2010) 'Communal beingness and affect: An exploration of trauma in an ex-industrial community', *Body & Society*, 16(1): 91–116.

Walkerdine, V., Lucey, H. and Melody, J. (2001) *Growing Up Girl: Psychosocial Explanations of Gender and Class*. Basingstoke: Palgrave.

Waters, S. (1997) 'Ghosting the interface: Cyberspace and spiritualism', *Science as Culture*, 6(3)8: 414–443.

Wegenstein, B. and Ruck, N. (2011) 'Physiognomy, reality television and the cosmetic gaze', *Body & Society*, 17(4): 27–56.

Weil, A. (1973) *The Natural Mind*. London: Jonathan Cape.

Weiner, N. (1989) *Cybernetics: or, The Control and Communication in the Animal and the Machine*. Cambridge, MA: MIT Press.

Weiss, G. (1999) *Body Images: Embodiment as Intercorporeality*. London: Routledge.

Wetherell, M. (2012) *Affect and Emotion: A New Social Science Understanding*. London: Sage.

Whitehead, A.N. (1938) *Modes of Thought*. Free Press.

Whitehead, A.N. (1979) Process and Reality: An Essay in Cosmology. Free Press.

Williams, C. (2010) 'Affective processes without a subject: Rethinking the relation between subjectivity and affect with Spinoza', *Subjectivity*, 3(3), 245–262.

Williams, R. (1977) *Marxism and Literature*. Oxford: Oxford University Press.

Wilson, E. (2004) *Psychosomatic: Feminism and the Neurological Body*. Durham, NC: Duke University Press.

Wilson, E. (2006) 'The work of anti-depressants: Preliminary notes on how to build an alliance between feminism and psychopharmacology', *Biosocieties*, 1: 125–131.

Wilson, E. (2010) *Affect and Artificial Intelligence*. Seattle: University of Washington Press.

Wilson, E. (2011) 'Neurological Entanglements: SSRI's and Suicidal Ideation', *Subjectivity*, 14(3): 277–297.

Wood, H. and Skeggs, B. (2008) 'Notes on ethical scenarios of self on British "reality" TV', *Feminist Media Studies*, 4(2): 205–208.

Wood, H. and Skeggs, B. (eds) (2011) *Reality TV and Class*. Basingstoke: BFI and Palgrave.

Woodward, W.R. and Tower, J.F. (2006) 'Julian Jaynes: Introducing his life and thought', in M. Kuijsten (ed.), *Reflections on the Dawn of Consciousness: Julian Jaynes' Bicameral Mind Theory Revisited*. Henderson, NV: Julian Jaynes Society, pp. 13–68.

# Index